MURALI !

Thank you!

Trading by Numbers

Trading by Numbers

Scoring Strategies for Every Market

RICK SWOPE

W. SHAWN HOWELL

WILEY

John Wiley & Sons, Inc.

Published by John Wiley & Sons, Inc., Hoboken, New Jersey.
Published simultaneously in Canada.

For general information on our other products and services or for technical support, please contact our Customer Care Department within the United States at (800) 762-2974, outside the United States at (317) 572-3993, or fax (317) 572-4002.

Wiley also publishes its books in a variety of electronic formats. Some content that appears in print may not be available in electronic books. For more information about Wiley products, visit our web site at www.wiley.com.

Library of Congress Cataloging-in-Publication Data:

Swope, Rick, 1964–
    Trading by numbers : scoring strategies for every market / Rick Swope and W. Shawn Howell.
        p. cm. – (Wiley trading series)
    Includes index.
    ISBN 978-1-118-11507-7 (cloth); ISBN 978-1-118-22438-0 (ebk);
    ISBN 978-1-118-23753-3 (ebk); ISBN 978-1-118-26245-0 (ebk)
    1. Electronic trading of securities.   2. Stocks.   3. Risk management.
I. Howell, W. Shawn, 1968–   II. Title.
    HG4515.95.S96   2012
    332.63'2042–dc23

                                                                2011042684

Printed in the United States of America

10   9   8   7   6   5   4   3   2   1

I have learned that a true teacher is characterized by who they are rather than what they do. This book is dedicated to teachers and mentors. My parents—having invested their lives in teaching generations. My professional mentors—Dr. Richard M. Wyskida and R. Wayne Penrod are among the best. Those who serve with passion—Lisa Phelan, Lisa Colson, and more. Mentors for eternity—Mike Schmid and Joe Donohue come to mind. Teachers from the ages—C. S. Lewis and G. K. Chesterton.
—Rick Swope

This book is dedicated to my family. To my parents: Thank you for the double dose of the "teacher gene" and for your enduring and unfaltering confidence that my abilities are limitless. The life lessons you taught me are woven throughout this book and hopefully will enrich many others' lives as they've enriched my own. To my wonderful children Katie and Will: You both have brought me immeasurable joy. You have incredible adventures ahead, lives to live, stories to tell, and gifts to share with the world. Remember, follow your passion, trust your inner voice, and stay a child at heart. To my wife Shelly: You've been my unswerving advocate, cheerleader, advisor, partner, friend, and copilot on our amazing journey thus far. In a life filled with countless blessing, the gift that is you, our bond, our children, and our life is without equal.
—W. Shawn Howell

Contents

Acknowledgments

When a book manuscript is finally completed, nobody feels more like a turtle on a fencepost than the author. You realize that you didn't get there through your own efforts alone. We'd like to acknowledge some important people who have helped us to the top of our fencepost.

We're grateful to our professional colleagues who invested their time and energy into reviewing the manuscript for technical accuracy. These include Jim Bittman, Marty Kearney, Peter Lusk, and Russell Rhoads from the Chicago Board Options Exchange (CBOE) Options Institute. We also appreciate the review from our friend and colleague, Dan Gramza, of Gramza Capital Management.

Our sincere thanks go to our business partners, through whom we're able to teach multitudes of traders and investors. These include the Options Industry Council and E*TRADE. A big thanks to Kat and Diana, the best event gurus we could work with. Thanks also to Chris Young and Chris Larkin, who have supported us through a terrific partnership. And a special thanks to the "Frank" behind our model trader throughout the text—Frank Tirado. Without the outstanding team of partners surrounding us, we would still be looking up at the top of the fencepost.

Writing a book is a long and tedious process. When you begin, you're staring at several hundred blank pages that are waiting to be filled. The team at Wiley makes that process manageable and even enjoyable. Laura Walsh was the one who first spotted our potential as authors—we're indebted to her for taking that chance. Judy Howarth has been an encouragement along the way as we've fed her a chapter at a time and welcomed her feedback.

No acknowledgment is complete without a special thanks to our families and friends. The long hours on the laptop, missed schedules, impatience, and distracted attention are not borne by the authors alone. Dani Swope and Shelly Howell have continued to run quarterback for all the plays that Rick and Shawn have neglected this year. They are truly our support. Caleb Swope and Will Howell are the best sons a couple of guys could ask for—they will be fine young men, indeed. Katie Howell and Tori Swope are two peas in a pod. They may very well rule the world one day.

Finally, thanks to you, the reader, for trusting us to present you with the best trading and investing education. We don't take that trust lightly and we hope you find the information contained in these pages worthy of your time.

Rick Swope
W. Shawn Howell

Introduction

The genesis of this book came from a very simple concept. We wanted to write a book that we wished was available when we started our trading careers. As hard as it may be to believe now, it wasn't too long ago that a new trader pretty much had two choices for learning the markets: (1) Find an experienced trader who would let you shadow his every move or (2) open an account and hope you had equity left over after you learned all the painful and expensive lessons. Sure, there have always been the in-depth books that cover various trading topics in excellent detail, but most never seemed to have that practical edge—the kind of edge that takes the material from the realm of the academic to the realm of being real-life applicable.

Trading by Numbers is our attempt to provide the necessary depth for understanding the markets and strategies while still maintaining a level of practicality that allows you to try these strategies on your own tomorrow. We wanted to provide you with a user's manual, rather than a reference book.

The material is presented in two main sections. The first four chapters lay out an approach to adding structure to your analysis. The two key market dimensions that every trader must understand are trend and volatility. Chapter 1 sets the stage for analyzing trend and volatility by examining the role of technical analysis. Chapter 2 discusses trends and how to quantify them for your trading decisions. We want to be clear that we're not ascribing a level of precision that doesn't exist in the markets. Rather, the goal of scoring is to help you remove emotion and opinion from the process so that you can take an honest look at what the market is trying to tell you. Chapter 3 follows with a structured, quantified approach to market and trade candidate volatility. The result of both chapters will be a two-dimensional score that will help you choose the appropriate strategy.

Chapter 4 is a stand-alone chapter discussing risk and how to manage it in an uncertain market. In our view, managing risk is perhaps the most important discipline you can master in the markets. For many traders, we recommend starting with Chapter 4 if you are not inclined to read a book through in sequence.

The second major grouping of the book begins with Chapter 5 and continues through to Chapter 16. Each of these chapters deals with a different strategy. We start with some of the simpler strategies such as covered calls in Chapter 6 and move on to more complex strategies like the iron condor in Chapter 16. While we generally have sequenced these according to complexity and the order in which many traders naturally learn them, you can start anywhere and jump around at will. If you already understand basic directional strategies, feel free to start with straddles and strangles in Chapter 8. The point is that each strategy mostly stands alone, so there's no requirement to take them in the order presented. On the few occasions where we do reference other material, we include the chapter reference for you to easily review.

You'll notice that we liberally apply stories to the strategies, especially in the introductions. Our style of teaching is to establish a common understanding of concepts from other life experiences and then draw the parallels to the trading strategy. While not perfect, we hope it better accomplishes our goal of making this text more usable. Finally, we want to thank our model (albeit fictitious) trader, Frank, for serving as the example of the strategies in action. By seeing examples of the strategy played out, we trust you'll gain a better appreciation of when to use or forgo the various options available to you.

CHAPTER 1

Market Scoring

It is not enough to do your best; you must know what to do, and then do your best.

—W. Edwards Deming

Many sports enthusiasts consider October 25, 1964 the date of one of the most embarrassing moments in sports. During a game against the San Francisco 49ers, Minnesota Vikings defensive end Jim Marshall had the good fortune to scoop up a fumble. He then ran 66 yards for the end zone and threw the ball away in celebration. Unfortunately, he had crossed into the wrong end zone and scored a safety for the opposing 49ers.

"My first inkling that something was wrong was when a 49er player gave me a hug in the end zone," commented Marshall after the game.

Best efforts, in sports as well as in trading the markets, are noble but not always fruitful. Jim Marshall had the necessary skills and certainly put forth his best effort, but he lost sight of his position and ended up on the losing side of the play.

A trader who "does his best" will memorize 50 candle patterns, run fundamental and technical screens at the start of every trading day, and hold his own in any discussion about the merits of Fibonacci retracements versus Elliott waves. To be sure, there are prerequisite skills that a trader should master before entering the markets, but knowing which skills to master and how to use those skills to manage your position can mean the difference between winning and losing.

INTUITION CAN BE HIGH TUITION

Let's begin with the obvious question: Why do we need a market-scoring system? Of course, we'll describe and develop the system in the following chapters, but we should start with a purpose. Is it really important to set a structure to our analysis of the markets rather than follow our instinct and intuition? Following only intuition can be costly in the markets because our intuition isn't always reliable in the face of a multitude of market data.

Let's look at a simple question. The following question is not complex, so read it and answer as quickly as you can.

A bat plus a ball costs $1.10.
The bat is $1.00 more than the ball.
How much does the ball cost?

If you're like many people, your first response—your intuition—will lead you to respond with 10¢ as the cost of the ball. However, if the ball is 10¢ and the bat is $1.00 more, then the sum of the two is $1.20, not $1.10. Therefore, the ball must cost 5¢ and the bat is $1.05 for the correct total of $1.10.

In their bestselling book, *Nudge: Improving Decisions About Health, Wealth, and Happiness*, Richard Thaler and Cass Sunstein refer to two distinct ways of processing information: the automatic system and the reflective system.

The automatic system is rapid and feels instinctive, and it does not involve what we associate with the word *thinking*. When you duck because a ball is thrown at you unexpectedly, get nervous when your airplane hits turbulence, or smile when you see a cute puppy, you are using your automatic system.

The reflective system is more deliberate and self-conscious. You use the reflective system when you are asked, "How much is 411 times 37?"

People speak their native language using their automatic system and tend to struggle to speak another language using their reflective system.

Many readers will doubtless relate to having a teen driver in the household. Consider the myriad decisions that a new driver has to process: foot on the brake, hand on the wheel, turn the ignition key, release when the engine engages, shift into drive, check rear and side mirrors—and the list goes on. Each of these decisions is a discrete point of thought and decision for a new driver. On the other hand, an experienced driver will perform all the same steps but without a conscious thought assigned to any of them. In fact, the experienced driver may go through all of these steps while loading the dog into the car and taking a phone call. The teen driver is operating entirely within the reflective system mode, whereas the experienced driver operates within the automatic system.

Now consider what might happen if the teen driver chooses to go with her intuition rather than thinking through each step. She may do her very best with all good intentions, but without rules, guidelines, and experience, she'll very likely meet trouble in short order. As a new driver, she needs structure and rules. As she applies those guidelines, her experience will grow and she'll develop an automatic system that she can rely on for most of her driving activities. Of course, new situations will arise, such as icy roads, which will require new rules and some period of reflective system decisions. But these, too, will eventually lead to a new level of experience and a return to the automatic system of driving.

New traders are not at all unlike our new driver. Good intentions and underdeveloped intuition are not enough to navigate today's markets. Consider just a few of the many decisions that a trader needs to process:

- Which product to trade? Stock, ETF, option?
- Which chart style to use? Line, candlestick, bar?
- What time horizon on the chart? Intraday, daily, weekly?
- Which technical indicators to include?
- How much fundamental analysis to add?
- What risk management parameters to use?
- How to execute the opening and closing trades?

Failing on any one of these decision points may result in a losing trade. Imagine how the failure rate increases when a trader fails on multiple levels. Although having a structured approach to the markets doesn't guarantee success, it does help to ensure that the appropriate level of reflective system is applied where the automatic system isn't sufficient.

A flawed approach that many traders take is to overload the analysis. This is the "best-effort" strategy that is based on the belief that if a little is good, more must be better. If you find value in the 50-day and 200-day simple moving averages, then you assume you'll make better decisions by adding the 100-day exponential moving average along with stochastics. Besides, you really feel like you're making progress and putting forth your best effort when you grind through studying various technical trading strategies. It's better to think of your analysis like lawn fertilizer: The proper amount with the correct application can do wonders. Too much will leave you with a burnt mess.

THE ROLE OF TECHNICAL ANALYSIS

Because we're going with the premise that gut feeling and best intentions are inadequate for traders and investors, we have to recognize that additional tools of analysis are required. The primary set of tools that we'll use falls under the category of technical analysis. Technical analysis simply refers to the analysis of price, volume, and derivative patterns and indicators. This differs from fundamental analysis, which focuses on the health and performance of the underlying company. The balance between the two may be thought of in this way: Fundamental analysis helps you decide *what* to buy and sell; technical analysis helps you decide *when* to buy and sell.

Many people will argue that technical analysis is redundant to fundamental analysis because the two should be fairly well aligned. That may be true to a certain extent, but there are often great divergences between them. A company that is performing well from a fundamental standpoint may have a very weak stock price, and vice versa. The economist John Maynard Keynes is said to have warned investors that although markets do tend toward rational positions in the long run, "the market can stay irrational longer than you can stay solvent."

An example we often cite is Webvan (former ticker symbol: WBVN). Webvan had its initial public offering (IPO) in 1999. On the first day of trading, traders gave it a market capitalization (shares outstanding multiplied by the share price) of $11 billion. From a technical perspective, the stock had extraordinary strength coming out of the gate. However, the company lost $12 million on *zero* revenue during the year prior to its IPO. There is hardly a clearer example of a significant disconnect between stock price performance and company performance.

Five Benefits of Technical Analysis over Fundamental Analysis

1. Technical analysis is real-time.

One of the key sources of fundamental analysis information for most traders and investors is the quarterly earnings report. Of course, there are other reports and news releases that may be issued more frequently, but the quarterly news tends to be dominant. Based on events and performance of the previous quarter, the company compiles their results and that becomes the basis of the quarterly report. Now consider that by the time you read the report, several months or longer may have passed since the occurrence of those events. In other words, the key reports that you rely on for fundamental analysis are lagging the events that drive the reports by weeks or months.

Compare the time lag that is inherent to fundamental analysis with the real-time nature of technical analysis. Technical analysis starts with price and volume, which dynamically update with each trade. As a trade occurs, the price and volume instantly reflect the new information. For that reason, technical analysis is a much more responsive analysis for the trader. Price and volume (trading activity) are expected to reflect all that the market knows about a company's news, expectations, performance, and so on. Although an individual trader may not know about pending litigation, poor sales, geographic instability, or any of the other factors that may be influencing a company's fundamental position, the market as a whole will absorb and process this information and reflect the collective consensus through the price charts. In effect, the fundamental analysis of the market as a whole becomes distilled into real-time technical analysis for the individual trader.

2. Technical analysis can be simpler.

The bread and butter of technical analysis is price and volume. Price simply reflects the current price that a buyer and seller agree on for the trade. Volume is typically a cumulative number that resets after each trading session. When a buyer agrees to purchase 1,000 shares from a seller, the transaction is complete and the total volume for that day rises by 1,000 shares. These concepts are very simple and straightforward. Beyond price and volume there are a handful of relatively simple technical concepts such as price gaps, support, resistance, and trends. These help the trader determine price direction, momentum, and other key factors that make up the technical analysis. Beyond the relatively simple concepts, there is a seemingly endless supply of more advanced technical indicators and concepts. The key point we're making here is that the salient aspects of technical analysis aren't dependent on arcane and complex concepts; they rest on the basics.

With fundamental analysis, there are various financial and accounting metrics that feed into a complete analysis. Furthermore, it is incumbent upon the trader to calculate how these metrics will ultimately translate into price. After all, profit or loss from a trade is entirely a function of the difference between the purchase price and the sales price. So although it is often useful to understand the fundamental dynamics behind the company in question, the trader still must decide how that will influence the stock price. Let's suppose that you've looked at the price/earnings to growth (PEG) ratio, debt to total capital, and return on assets. What are the magnitude, direction, and timing of the influence on the stock price of these metrics? Compare that to a simple candlestick chart that shows green candles with rising volume. The candlestick chart gives a simpler and more immediate indication that the buyers are in control for a short-term uptrend.

3. Technical analysis is more responsive for short-term traders.

When a trader is choosing the correct balance between fundamental and technical analysis, she needs to consider her trading time horizon. As a general rule, the longer the time horizon for the trade, the more important fundamental analysis is. In contrast, the value of fundamental analysis diminishes as the time horizon shortens. Very-short-term day traders—the scalpers—rarely, if ever, use fundamental analysis. Earnings per share growth really has no influence on where the stock price will be in 15 minutes. Therefore, technical analysis is the primary tool for determining strategy and execution for very-short-term traders.

Please don't misunderstand that long-term traders and investors then should use fundamental analysis to the exclusion of technical analysis. Though day traders find little use for fundamental analysis, the other end of the time horizon is different. Long-term traders and investors can use technical analysis very effectively to complement their fundamental views. As we noted earlier, technicals can help with the question of timing: when to buy or sell a long-term position. After identifying a trade candidate through fundamental analysis, technical analysis can focus on the best timing for executing the trade.

4. **Technical analysis shows what traders are doing, not just what they're saying.**

The old saying, "Pay attention to what they do, not what they say," is never more true than in the markets. Words are cheap, but actions reveal the truth more accurately. Today's market is full of news programs, articles, web sites, and trading rooms that have no lack of opinions and analyses from all corners. A CEO will appear on a market interview program and give his top three reasons why his company's stock should outperform the market. Gurus abound who offer a bullish or bearish assessment of a stock price in rapid-fire succession. In short, everyone has something to say about XYZ's stock price.

The beauty of technical analysis is its dispassionate delivery of facts. Every program on TV may be talking about reasons why XYZ stock should be falling, but if the charts continue to show an uptrend with sustaining volume then the fact remains that buying pressure exceeds selling pressure. Never lose sight of an important tenet of mass media programming: Market shows are in business to make money through building their audience, which then commands greater ad revenue. Market programs are not successful because you become more successful as a trader. Therefore, your success in the markets is incidental to their success. That may be a harsh reality, but it is reality nevertheless. If the program can capture your attention, work your emotions, and connect with you as a trader, the information and analyses they offer are secondary. The best analysis for your trade is up to you.

5. **Technical analysis is essential for managing risk.**

There aren't too many soapboxes that we'll jump on, but this is one of them. We firmly believe that traders and investors cannot effectively manage risk without an understanding of the basics of technical analysis. This is partly due to the fact, mentioned earlier, that technical analysis is real-time, whereas fundamental analysis has a built-in time lag. Information flows too quickly these days for you to expect that you can respond to news or shifting fundamentals before the rest of the market. Technical analysis is a real-time monitoring system to alert you when it's time to exit the trade. A proper analysis of price will give you support and resistance levels that serve as your price targets for both profit and loss. If the trade moves against you, you have a precise point at which you've determined in advance that you'll exit the trade for a limited loss.

Risk management based on technicals then becomes a binary decision. If your analysis tells you that support is at $40 and your exit (stop order) is at $38, then anything above $38 keeps you in the trade. If the stock is trading at $38.01, you don't worry and fret over your next move; you stay in the trade. At $38, you don't start to rationalize why you should or shouldn't exit the trade. You have a plan based on an analysis of the charts and you execute without hesitation. Without technical analysis, that precise price at which you exit a trade to limit your losses is little more than a guess.

Technical Analysis Tells a Story

When you look at a price chart, your first goal should be to answer a simple question: Who is in control? The answer to that question will be (1) buyers, (2) sellers, or (3) nobody. If buyers are in control of the trading, we expect to see prices generally trending higher. Likewise, a downtrend indicates that sellers are in control. If neither is in control, prices trend sideways in a channel. The degree to which these trends are in place and the level of volatility within the trends is what we want to discern from our analysis. This is the key information that a market-scoring system will help you quantify.

Please recognize that pulling the story out of the charts doesn't allow you to predict the future. You'll be sorely disappointed if you have the expectation that the proper analysis in sufficient quantities will tell you where prices will be in a week, a month, or a year. The story tells you what has happened, how it happened, and what is happening right now. As traders, we all deal with the "hard right edge" of the chart—the uncertainty of tomorrow. Past and current activity help to serve as a guide for price direction and momentum, but risk management is always crucial to your success. Key strategies for managing risk are presented in later chapters.

So if the future can't be gleaned with certainty from technical analysis, does that invalidate its use? Absolutely not! The primary purpose of technical analysis is to protect, not predict. Technical analysis helps you identify key support and resistance levels, price gaps, trends, and trading patterns that serve as guides to signal your buying and selling points. Investors and traders who use fundamental analysis for decision making experience the same issue. A company that pays a high dividend or reports a high return on equity is not guaranteed a rising stock price. Nevertheless, you have a reasonable expectation that your analysis will lead to improved success over random stock picking.

The best way to think about your analysis—both technical and fundamental—is to liken it to a Lego set. Most readers are familiar with the small, plastic Lego pieces. Each piece contains a small, discrete bit of information: color, size, and shape. Taken alone, that information is of little benefit. The real value in the Lego piece is seen when many different pieces are assembled together and they take the shape of a dragon or castle. The best Lego shape is made when the right pieces come together to tell a story, even if all the pieces aren't used. Price candles, moving averages, volume, and other technical metrics are your Lego pieces. Deciding which pieces to use and how to fit them together is your challenge. Through market scoring, we're providing you with an assembly guide to help you choose the right pieces and fit them together. Once you see the shape that the market is building—the story—you'll be ready to execute the correct strategy for trading success.

CHAPTER 2

Trend Scoring

We always say: Ride to ride another day. We go out there with the attitude that we're going to do it in a way that we can do it again tomorrow.
— Laird Hamilton, world champion
big wave surfer

Trends are to the trader what waves are to the surfer. You never see a surfer jump on a board in flat water because he has a gut feeling that a wave will develop. He waits until the wave starts to develop and then positions himself to catch the best part of the wave for the longest ride. However, when the wave starts to crash, he jumps off to get ready for the next wave.

Take particular care to notice what the surfer does and doesn't do. First of all, a new surfer isn't going to ride the big waves of Hawaii's North Shore. He starts with the one- or two-foot waves and moves up as his skills and experience grow. He always waits for the wave to tell him when to start the ride. The wave begins to develop and the surfer's goal is to identify the wave as early as possible by reading the water. He doesn't anticipate where the wave will be at some future time or convince himself that a wave *should* be where it's not. Once he starts his ride, he stays on for as long as the wave will allow. Eventually, the wave breaks apart and the surfer moves on to the next wave. He doesn't pick a spot near the shore where he thinks the wave should crash and then only jump off at that predetermined location. During the ride, he's constantly watching and feeling the water and making adjustments as necessary. And every surfer knows that as good as you may be, there will be waves that take you under the swell. That's when you remember that you're riding to ride another day.

As a trader, you should approach the market very much as the surfer approaches the ocean. Start with small, easy trends. The ride might not be as exhilarating, but the wipeouts won't be as painful, either. It never ceases to amaze us how often new traders want to trade something like a far-out-of-the-money call in a highly volatile stock because they think they're going to win the market lottery. If you're patient and prudent, you'll get to the point where you can confidently take larger risks for greater potential profit. Along the way, learn to read the story of the market so you can identify the trends as they begin to develop. Then you'll be positioned to ride the trend for maximum gain and know when it's time to jump off and look for the next opportunity.

TREND-SCORING SYSTEM

A good scoring system should start by identifying key parameters to be scored. The system should include enough parameters to provide for a strong score but limit the number to ensure that the system is usable. More is not necessarily better and will only make the system too burdensome to use in practice. Second, an effective scoring system should attempt to reduce the influence of user bias. This is best accomplished by using binary scores when possible. A binary score yields a yes/no answer rather than a subjective answer. For example, consider the following two approaches to determining whether the price is in an uptrend or downtrend:

1. Rate the strength of the trend:
    a. Very weak
    b. Weak
    c. Neutral
    d. Strong
    e. Very strong

2. Rate the strength of the trend:
    a. Red candle, close lower than the moving average
    b. Green candle, close lower than the moving average
    c. Neutral candle (doji or spinning top)
    d. Red candle, close higher than the moving average
    e. Green candle, close higher than the moving average

You can easily see that the first approach could have widely varying answers, depending on who is making the assessment. Two traders may look at the same chart but arrive at different conclusions if the analysis and definitions aren't held to the same standard. The second approach, however, should yield the same answer regardless of how many different traders are asked to respond.

The trend-scoring system captures four separate parameters for scoring: market sentiment, stock sentiment, candle patterns, and volume. We'll combine the four individual scores to yield a composite trend score with a value between −10 (strong negative) and 10 (strong positive). For example, a value of −10 indicates that all four trend factors are at the greatest downtrend value, telling you that the sellers are firmly in control. You would then choose an appropriate bear market strategy for your trade. A composite score of 0 might be the result of an individual stock strength being offset by overall market weakness. In this instance, you would choose a strategy that fits a sideways trend, or channel. Remember that the goal of a scoring system is to provide structure to your reflective system decision making until you have the skill and experience to trust your automatic system decisions. Further, even after you reach the point where you can more confidently rely on your automatic system, a scoring system will help you maintain your market discipline.

Parameter	Min Value	Max Value
Market Sentiment	−3	+3
Stock Sentiment	−3	+3
Candle Pattern	−2	+2
Volume	−2	+2
Composite	**−10**	**+10**

Four Legs of Trend Scoring

1. Market Sentiment (−3 to +3)   We're going to start with an analysis of the overall market conditions. Although it is true that stocks may often move counter to the overall market, it is also true that market sentiment weighs on strong and weak stocks alike. The old adage, "A rising tide lifts all boats," may not be precisely true for every stock, but a very strong market does tend to buoy marginally strong or even weak stocks. Similarly, when the prevailing market mood is panic selling, many good companies will see their stock prices fall in the sell-off.

Representative Market Indexes   In order to analyze the overall market conditions, we have to start by defining what we mean by "the market." For most people, the Dow Jones Industrial Average (DJIA) represents the market. The DJIA consists of 30 stocks whose prices are aggregated to form a composite index price. Though this is the traditional market index, it is far from comprehensive. Looking only at the DJIA to understand the market conditions would be like looking only at retail space to understand local real estate conditions. Besides retail, there is single-family residential, multifamily housing, commercial, industrial, raw land, and so on. The point is if you want to understand what the real estate market is doing, you need to analyze a representative cross section of the overall market. The same is true with the stock market. For our purposes, we will look at five key indexes when determining the trend in the overall market:

1. **Dow Jones Industrial Average (ticker symbol: DJX)**

   As we stated, this is the go-to index for most people and the index most commonly reported by the mass media. The 30 stocks that make up this index are generally household names like Coca-Cola Company (ticker symbol: KO), McDonald's (ticker symbol: MCD) and Walt Disney Company (ticker symbol: DIS). Some traders argue that this old-guard index can't accurately portray economic conditions because it only contains 30 stocks. In spite of this, the two reasons to recommend including the DJIA are (1) it is widely reported and followed; and (2) it represents very large, ubiquitous companies whose businesses extend into all parts of the global economy.

2. **S&P 500 (ticker symbol: SPX)**

   The Standard & Poor's 500 list (S&P 500) was first published in 1957 and captures leading companies in leading industries. As the title implies, there are 500 large-cap companies included in the index. Stocks are chosen for market capitalization, liquidity, and industry representation. Think of the S&P 500 as the single-tenant, class A commercial real estate of the market.

3. **Nasdaq 100 (ticker symbol: NDX)**

   The 100 stocks in the Nasdaq 100 are designed to track the performance of the 100 largest and most actively traded nonfinancial domestic and international securities listed on the Nasdaq Stock Market, based on market capitalization. The NDX exchange-traded fund (ETF) trades under the symbol QQQ that earned it the nickname "Qs" or "Cubes."

4. **S&P MidCap 400 (ticker symbol: MID)**

   Generally, mid-cap stocks represent companies with a market capitalization between $2 billion and $10 billion. The S&P MidCap 400 captures about 7 percent of the total market value of all U.S. equities. Many traders follow the MidCap 400 because it provides a good balance between the confidence of a large company and the growth rate of a small company.

5. **Russell 2000 (ticker symbol: RUT)**

　　The Russell 2000 contains 2,000 of the smallest-capitalization stocks in the market. Because smaller dollar amounts influence market capitalization to a greater degree with small-cap stocks, the index is adjusted annually. As of July 2011, the largest company in the Russell 2000 had a market cap of just over $3 billion, whereas the index median market cap was only $519 million. Traders generally look to the small-cap stocks for growth over stability.

Scoring Metrics

1. **Closing price**

　　Very simply, the closing price is the last trade price for the index for the trading session. Although a trading session may be defined for any time horizon (week, day, or intraday), we recommend using the daily data for market scoring. That provides enough granularity of data to provide quick results while still smoothing out the volatility of intraday trading. We focus on the closing price because it represents the final consensus price after the buyers and sellers have moved the price throughout the day. Looking at it another way, buyers at the close have to be confident enough in their trade price to hold it for a night or weekend.

2. **Short-term moving average**

　　Most traders and investors intuitively understand a moving average, which makes it one of the most popular technical indicators. The concept of an average is one that is applied in everyday life. We talk about average salary, average height, and average fuel economy in a new vehicle. The moving average updates the average value each time a new data point appears on the chart. Moving averages often act as a support level when the price is above the average and as a resistance level when the price is trading below the average.

　　The simple moving average (SMA) is the arithmetic mean of the data set. The equation for the SMA is as follows:

$$SMA = (X1 + X2 + \cdots + Xn)/n$$

where Xi = closing price of period i
　　　　n = number of data points

　　Therefore, the 20-day SMA would have 20 data points consisting of the closing price of the most recent 20 days. The 20 points are totaled and divided by 20 to arrive at the average value. When a new trading day is complete, the new closing price is added into the total and the oldest is dropped. In this way, the average "moves" with the progression of time.

The period of choice for the short-term average depends on your time horizon as a trader. In order to keep the scoring system simple, we'll define two time horizons: (1) short-term is any trade under six months, and (2) long-term is any trade longer than six months. If you anticipate that your trade will move to your target in less than six months, you should apply the short-term strategy.

Short-term traders need to have a short-term moving average that isn't overly sensitive to day-to-day volatility but still provides a fast response to changing market conditions. Long-term traders and investors need to ensure that short market swings don't influence their long-term trade decisions. For the trend scoring system, the short-term moving average used is 20 days for short-term trades and 50 days for long-term trades.

3. **Long-term moving average**

The long-term moving average is also calculated as an SMA, but over a longer time period. The purpose of the long-term SMA is to provide additional smoothing so that short-term price swings have less influence on the consensus price. Only price moves of the greatest magnitude or longest duration will influence the long-term moving average.

The trend scoring system applies the 50-day SMA for short-term trades and the 200-day SMA for long-term trades. By combining the short-term moving average with the long-term moving average, you get to see how the short-term and long-term price trends are moving relative to each other. For example, if the stock price has been in a long downtrend, the short-term moving average will be below the long-term moving average and both will be trending lower. As the price starts to reverse and move higher, the short-term moving average will respond more quickly, eventually trending up through the long-term moving average.

Scoring Guide   In order to assign trend-scoring values to market sentiment, we will consider the following combinations:

- Short-term average above long-term average, price above both.
- Short-term average above long-term average, price between.
- Short-term average above long-term average, price below both.
- Long-term average above short-term average, price above both.
- Long-term average above short-term average, price between.
- Long-term average above short-term average, price below both.

The reader may ask why we're not accounting for the trend direction of the moving averages. These scoring combinations do not take into account the direction of the short-term and long-term moving averages for two reasons. First, the relative position of the averages will generally account for the trend direction. For example, the short-term moving average will be above the long-term moving average when (1) the trends have been positive over the period of calculation, (2) the short-term trend accelerates above the long-term trend due to a recent positive price reversal, or (3) the price is channeling and the averages are essentially moving sideways. All three of these scenarios represent more bullish markets than the scenarios represented by the short-term moving average below the long-term moving average. Second, if we required an assessment of trend direction, the reader would have to visually determine direction or calculate the difference between the current moving average value versus a previous value. Both of these could introduce error in assessment or calculation and would not add substantially to the utility of the score.

1. Short-term average above long-term average

When the short-term moving average is above the long-term moving average, the scoring ranges from −2 to +3 (maximum possible value). Even though there may be instances where the price is below both moving averages, the lowest score of −3 is not assigned because the relative positions of the moving averages indicate recent short-term strength. In general, the short-term moving average will be above the long-term moving average when the overall trend has been positive over the length of the long-term moving average (Figure 2.1) or when the trend has been flat to negative over the long-term period but positive for the most recent short-term period (Figure 2.2).

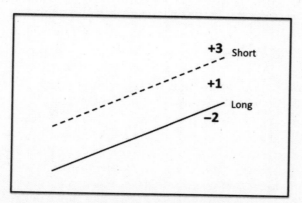

FIGURE 2.1 Short-Term Positive above Long-Term Positive

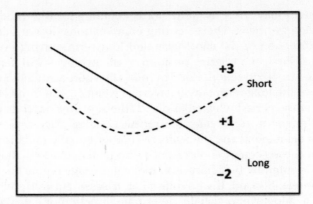

FIGURE 2.2   Short-Term Positive above Long-Term Negative

2. Long-term average above short-term average

The scenarios where the long-term moving average is below the short-term moving average will yield the most negative scores, indicating more bearish market conditions. The markets will be most bearish when the trend has been in a long-term sustained downtrend over the period of both moving averages. In general, the long-term moving average will be above the short-term moving average when the overall trend has been negative over the length of the long-term moving average (Figure 2.3) or when the trend has been flat to positive over the long-term period but negative for the most recent short-term period (Figure 2.4).

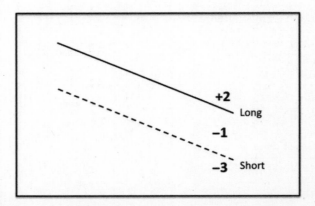

FIGURE 2.3   Long-Term Negative above Short-Term Negative

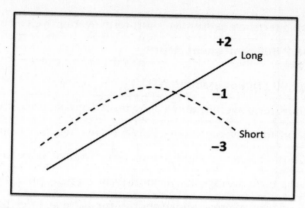

FIGURE 2.4 Long-Term Positive above Short-Term Negative

Scoring Template—Market Sentiment For each of the following five market indexes, select the current price and moving average position combination. Enter the corresponding score (−3 to +3) at the bottom of each table to score the individual index sentiment.

1. Dow Jones Industrial Average (ticker symbol: DJX)

+3	Short-term average above long-term average, price above both
+1	Short-term average above long-term average, price between
−2	Short-term average above long-term average, price below both
+2	Long-term average above short-term average, price above both
−1	Long-term average above short-term average, price between
−3	Long-term average above short-term average, price below both
	Dow Jones Industrial Average Sentiment Score

2. S&P 500 (ticker symbol: SPX)

+3	Short-term average above long-term average, price above both
+1	Short-term average above long-term average, price between
−2	Short-term average above long-term average, price below both
+2	Long-term average above short-term average, price above both
−1	Long-term average above short-term average, price between

(continued)

−3	Long-term average above short-term average, price below both
	S&P 500 Sentiment Score

3. Nasdaq 100 (ticker symbol: NDX)

+3	Short-term average above long-term average, price above both
+1	Short-term average above long-term average, price between
−2	Short-term average above long-term average, price below both
+2	Long-term average above short-term average, price above both
−1	Long-term average above short-term average, price between
−3	Long-term average above short-term average, price below both
	Nasdaq 100 Sentiment Score

4. S&P MidCap 400 (ticker symbol: MID)

+3	Short-term average above long-term average, price above both
+1	Short-term average above long-term average, price between
−2	Short-term average above long-term average, price below both
+2	Long-term average above short-term average, price above both
−1	Long-term average above short-term average, price between
−3	Long-term average above short-term average, price below both
	S&P MidCap 400 Sentiment Score

5. Russell 2000 (ticker symbol: RUT)

+3	Short-term average above long-term average, price above both
+1	Short-term average above long-term average, price between
−2	Short-term average above long-term average, price below both
+2	Long-term average above short-term average, price above both
−1	Long-term average above short-term average, price between
−3	Long-term average above short-term average, price below both
	Russell 2000 Sentiment Score

6. Market Sentiment Score

Line	Score	Index
1		Dow Jones Industrial Average Sentiment Score
2		S&P 500 Sentiment Score
3		Nasdaq 100 Sentiment Score
4		S&P MidCap 400 Sentiment Score
5		Russell 2000 Sentiment Score
		(Add lines 1 through 5) then (divide sum by 5) **Market Sentiment Score**

2. Stock Sentiment (−3 to +3) Stock sentiment is scored using exactly the same criteria as overall market sentiment. The relative position of the stock price to the short-term and long-term moving averages will dictate the trend score. The added significance of the stock price is weighted by assigning a score directly to the stock price performance, whereas the five indexes were averaged for a market sentiment score. It is possible to have a very weak stock with a trend score of −3 in a very strong market with an average market score of +3. In this example, the bullish market would be offset by the bearish stock and the other two legs of trend scoring would decide the overall trend score.

Scoring Template—Stock Sentiment For the stock trade candidate, select the current price and moving average position combination. Enter the corresponding score (−3 to +3) at the bottom of the table to score the stock sentiment.

+3	Short-term average above long-term average, price above both
+1	Short-term average above long-term average, price between
−2	Short-term average above long-term average, price below both
+2	Long-term average above short-term average, price above both
−1	Long-term average above short-term average, price between
−3	Long-term average above short-term average, price below both
	Stock Sentiment Score

3. Candle Pattern (−2 to +2)   There are several popular chart styles that traders may use to plot price movement and corresponding technical indicators. Among the more common are the line chart, bar chart, and candlestick chart. The line chart is useful for getting a quick look at the overall trend but is limited by the fact that it only plots one price—typically the closing price. The bar chart actually plots the same information as the candlestick chart. However, by adding the dimension of color, we find the candlestick chart easier to read. Ultimately, your goal as a trader and investor is to look at the chart and draw out the story of the market. Some pieces of the story that may be discerned through price charts include:

- Who is in control? Buyers, sellers, or neither?
- How strong are they?
- Is their strength increasing or decreasing?
- Where are the key price support and resistance levels?
- Is volatility high or low? Increasing or decreasing?
- Are there significant discrete price movements, such as gaps?

Candlestick Chart Construction   Candlestick (or simply "candle") charts provide you with four key price points. The relative position of these prices creates the shape of the candle, which is then plotted over time to yield a candle chart. Figure 2.5 illustrates the basic candle shape. The standard candle chart format uses a red/green or black/white scheme. In a black-and-white format, black and red have the same meaning and green and white are the same.

1. **Top shadow**

     You'll notice on both black and white candles that there is a line protruding toward the top. This is referred to as the top shadow or upper shadow. The top of this shadow line represents the highest trade

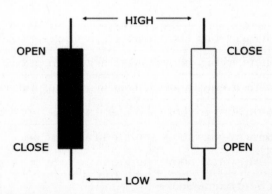

FIGURE 2.5   Candle Chart Construction

price achieved during the trading session. We're careful to define the trading session generally because any period may be a trading session. In other words, a candle chart may be constructed for a weekly, daily, or intraday time horizon. Whichever time horizon is chosen, each individual candle will reflect the length of the trading session. Most often, candle charts are created for daily charts, so an individual candle would reflect the prices for a single trading day.

Take note of the fact that you don't know when the highest trade price was reached during the trading session. That's okay. Part of the value of the candle chart is that it doesn't provide too much detail, which would tend to make it more difficult to quickly read the story of what's happening in the market. Nevertheless, a quick glance at the length of the top shadow will tell you where the top end of the trading range was for that session.

A note of caution is in order here. In our experience, we have seen more than a few instances where a candle displayed an unusually long shadow for a price that was never reached. Normally, that would indicate extreme volatility as the trading range reached to the end of the shadow before pulling back. As a prudent trader, you would do well to verify any extreme candle shadow by looking at a chart with a shorter time period to see if the stock actually traded at that extreme price. For example, if you see a very long shadow on a daily chart, zoom in to a 15-minute intraday chart to verify that the price actually traded to the price indicated. It is not unusual for a candle chart to display a very long shadow due to an error in the market data feed rather than a true trade. Reconciling your charts over two time horizons is often a quick and easy way to avoid making a trade decision based on faulty data.

2. Bottom shadow

Along with the top shadow, there is also a line that extends below the white and black candles. This is the bottom or lower shadow. In the same way that the top shadow gives you the highest trade price, the bottom shadow shows you the lowest trade price that was reached during the session. Both shadows taken together provide you with the full range of trading. You can begin to appreciate how the shadows tell you much about the volatility story. Candles with small, steady shadows tell a vastly different story than candles with long, wildly varying shadows. The latter shows a stock that is experiencing wide swings between the high and low prices and a battle for control between buyers and sellers.

3. Candle body

In addition to the shadows, the third part of a candle is the body. This is the rectangular portion of the candle and is either red (black) or green (white). The body represents the difference between the opening price and the closing price. The color of the body tells you where each price lies. For a red candle, the opening price is the top of the candle body and the closing price is the bottom of the candle body. A red candle tells the story of sellers in control. The only way that a stock can close the trading session lower than it opened is if the sellers were stronger than the buyers, sending the price to new lows. Similarly, a green candle body tells us that buyers are in control, advancing the price to new highs through the trading session. For a green body, the open is at the bottom of the body and the close is at the top of the body.

There are times when a candle body is missing the top shadow, the bottom shadow, or both. This occurs when the high or low is the same as the open or close. For example, consider a green candle with both the top and bottom shadows missing. In other words, the candle simply consists of the green body. You know that a green candle opens at the bottom of the body and closes at the top. Without shadows, this displays a trading session that opened at the low price and closed at the high. If the length of the green body were relatively long compared to recent candles, you would have a good idea that the buyers were solidly in control for that session. Looked at another way, from the opening bell, the sellers were not able to push the price any lower than the open and the buyers continued advancing the price higher right into the close. We look at that as a day when the market didn't run out of buyers, but the buyers ran out of time!

The scoring system assigns a neutral score of 0 to a candle body that represents an insignificant move. The extreme case would be a candle where the open and close are the same price. This is called a doji and has a body that is represented by a horizontal line rather than a filled rectangle. A doji shows indecision in the market. If the stock opens at a given price, moves higher to create a top shadow, lower to create a bottom shadow, and then ends the session exactly where it started, you know that neither the buyers nor the sellers had the strength to advance and hold the price during the trading session. We consider this indecision because it depicts a tug-of-war between the buyers and sellers.

Scoring Metric   For the candle pattern component of the trend score, you need to determine the color and relative length of the body. Although a further application of candle patterns uses a combination of body length, shadow lengths, and sequences, we will simplify the scoring by considering the two dimensions of body length and color. Appendix A provides a brief tutorial on the six common trend-reversal patterns that we frequently use in trading.

As we have already discussed, the body represents the difference between the open and the close. The color indicates direction, and the length of the body tells you how far the price advanced during the trading session. Ideally, a comprehensive scoring metric would account for the relative length of the body compared to previous candles over a specified time horizon. For example, if the current daily body were green and 0 to 10 percent greater than the average candle length over the previous 30 days, then you would score the candle as slightly bullish. However, recognizing that most readers don't have access to that level of data or would not invest the time to crunch the numbers anyway, the scoring system will instead score the candle body as a percentage of the stock price. This requires a quick two-step process: (1) Determine the candle length by taking the open and close and subtracting the lesser from the greater and (2) divide the candle length by the most recent closing price.

At this point we encourage you to experiment with tailoring the scoring system to the individual stocks that you trade. Our base scoring system rates a body length of 2 to 5 percent as a −1 or +1. A body length exceeding 5 percent of the stock price is scored as a −2 or +2. If you observe in your stock that an average body length is 8 to 10 percent of the stock price whereas a significant move is closer to 15 to 20 percent of the stock price, then adjust your scoring to better reflect the characteristics of your stock. In this example, you would score the candle as a +2 only if it is green and the body length is greater than 10 percent of the stock price. The important point to recognize is that you want to assign a score that reflects the strength of the move. An insignificant move should receive a neutral score of 0, a move of moderate significance should be scored as a −1 or +1, and a relatively strong move should receive the maximum score of −2 or +2.

Scoring Template—Candle Pattern

1. Subtract the lesser of the opening price or closing price from the greater. This is the body length.
2. Divide the body length by the closing price. Multiply the quotient by 100. This is the candle body length as a percentage of the closing price.
3. Select the correct line for either a red or green body. The column that corresponds to the body length relative to the closing price is the candle pattern trend score component.

Body Color	Body Length Relative to Closing Price		
	0–2%	2–5%	>5%
Red	0	−1	−2
Green	0	+1	+2

4. Volume (−2 to +2)   From a technical perspective, the two primary pieces of information that you're interested in are price and volume. Every other technical indicator and pattern is subordinate to price and volume. This part of the trend score will account for the latter.

Think of volume as market fuel. Volume displays the energy or drive behind a trend because it shows how much activity contributed to the price movement. It is generally understood that a trend that loses its volume will eventually also lose its direction and either flatten into a price channel or reverse direction. Upon a reversal, it is common to see volume rise once again as more trading activity jumps onto the new trend. In fact, there are some very good trading strategies that capitalize on this characteristic by watching flat, low-volume stocks and entering the trade just as a new direction breaks out on high volume.

The basic presentation of volume on most trading platforms is a histogram. A daily price chart may show price and moving averages in one chart panel with the volume histogram in a separate panel below. Each histogram bar displays the total volume for each trading day. The bars are typically red or green: red for those days that close lower than the previous day and green for the days that close higher than the previous day. Sometimes a moving average line is plotted over the histogram to show the volume trend over a specified time period. Ultimately, your objective in reviewing volume is to see if the price trends are supported by steady or rising volume or if the price trend is diverging from the volume trend.

On-Balance Volume   On-balance volume (OBV) is a composite volume indicator that accounts for both volume and price changes. OBV is plotted as a line chart that adds or subtracts each successive day's total volume based on whether that day closed higher or lower than the previous day. For example, if today's close is lower than yesterday's close, OBV for today is calculated as yesterday's OBV value minus today's total volume. As such, OBV is not a bounded indicator—it may assume any positive or negative value.

Our goal in the trend score is to quantify the OBV trend relative to the price trend. More experienced traders may visually analyze the OBV and price trends to determine the length and strength of the trend. This is truly one of those situations where a picture is worth a thousand words. Trends do not often neatly fit into steady cycles of consistent lengths. One trend may be very sharp and last only a week or two, whereas another may be slow and steady, extending for months. However, in keeping with our goal to score this component with objective binary criteria, we'll compare the current OBV value against the OBV from 10 days prior. We will do the same with the 20-day exponential moving average (EMA) on the closing price. This will serve as a fair proxy to the more subjective visual analysis.

You might note that we use the SMA in the market sentiment and stock sentiment scoring. However, for the volume component we're using the EMA. The EMA is considered a weighted moving average and is thus more sensitive to the most recent price data, whereas the SMA considers all price data to be of equal weighting. Because the volume scoring uses a shorter time frame (20 days versus 50 or 200), the EMA provides somewhat greater responsiveness to trend changes.

As you develop your skills and experience, we encourage you to adapt this scoring component to the individual characteristics of the stock you're trading. Although our default time period for measuring the trend is 10 days, you may either choose a different value or assign this score based on a subjective visual analysis. For example, if a visual review leads you to conclude that the OBV is trending lower while price is trending also trending lower, then assign a score of -2 (most bearish).

For this component of the trend score, we'll use the following data points:

1. OBV = current value of on-balance volume
2. OBV(10) = value of on-balance volume 10 days prior
3. EMA = current value of 20-day exponential moving average
4. EMA(10) = value of 20-day exponential moving average 10 days prior

The four possible combinations are (1) OBV and EMA trending higher, (2) OBV and EMA trending lower, (3) OBV trending higher and EMA trending lower and (4) OBV trending lower and EMA trending higher. If both OBV and EMA are trending higher, we'll assign the maximum bullish score of $+2$. This generally reflects a market where price is trending higher and volume is sufficient to maintain or accelerate the upward trend. If EMA is moving higher but OBV is falling, we'll assign a value of $+1$. This indicates that the momentum behind the uptrend may be diminishing. Without fuel, an uptrend will usually flatten or reverse. If the EMA is falling but OBV is trending higher, we'll assign a value of -1. This market scenario is bearish from a price perspective but does not have the added momentum of volume to accelerate the downtrend. Finally, if both OBV and EMA are trending lower, we'll assign the most bearish score of -2. This reflects a price that is trending lower and is supported by volume. In other words, the downtrend has the volume fuel to sustain or accelerate the fall.

Scoring Template—Volume

1. Subtract the current value of the 20-day EMA from the value of the 20-EMA from 10 days prior. If the difference is positive, the price trend is positive. If the difference is negative, the price trend is negative.

2. Subtract the current value of the OBV from the value of the OBV 10 from days prior. If the difference is positive, the OBV trend is positive. If the difference is negative, the OBV trend is negative.

	OBV Trend Positive	OBV Trend Negative
20-day EMA Trend Positive	+2	+1
20-day EMA Trend Negative	−1	−2

Composite Trend Score

You are now able to tally the results of the four individual legs of the trend-scoring system to arrive at a composite trend score for your trade candidate. Simply add the trend score for each leg for a total score. The most bearish score of −10 would be the result of scoring market sentiment −3, stock sentiment −3, candle pattern −2, and volume −2. Assigning the maximum bullish value to all four legs would produce the most bullish composite trend score of +10.

In the next chapter, we'll develop the second dimension of scoring: volatility. Trends tell you about direction, but volatility helps to describe the stability versus uncertainty in the trend. Both scores will go hand in hand to assist you in choosing the correct strategy for your greatest chance of market success.

CHAPTER 3

Volatility Scoring

*However, the fact is often lost sight of that there is
an important distinction between valid prediction
in the sense of a prediction being* true, *and valid
prediction in the sense of a prediction being* justifiable *upon the basis of the available evidence and
the accepted rules of inference.*
—Walter A. Shewart, *Statistical Method from
the Viewpoint of Quality Control*

When we employ a scoring system to quantify the market data available to us, our goal is to establish some structure around the current trading activity. Our decision of what and when to buy and
sell is guided in part by that structure. Though that may look like we're
attempting to predict the future, we're always careful to distinguish between careless prediction and thoughtful projection. This may sound like
we're parsing words, but it is an important distinction. As we've previously
noted, market pricing often tends to move in fairly well-defined waves. During those periods, if you can identify the direction and shape of the waves,
you are better able to make trading decisions while the wave lasts. As Walter A. Shewart indicates in the opening quote, being wrong does not negate
the validity of your analysis. It provides an opportunity for you to review
the available evidence (market data) and your rules of inference (analysis and application of market data). However, the fact that your prediction
may be justifiable yet incorrect is why every trader needs a strict risk management discipline.

In Chapter 2, we provided a framework for trend analysis and scoring. You might look at that as the direction of the wave. The other dimension to the wave is the shape. To help describe the shape, we'll analyze the second scoring component: volatility. Although the concept of trends is generally easy for people to wrap their heads around, volatility may not be so intuitive.

VOLATILITY OVERVIEW

It's helpful to have a common understanding of volatility before we proceed to a volatility scoring system. From a simple definition standpoint, volatility represents uncertainty. A highly volatile trend may move from point A to point B over a given time period, but it will swing wildly from extreme highs to extreme lows. The same trend with very low volatility will have a chart that shows small, steady steps between the same two points. For the trader, the latter trend has a much lower likelihood of stopping you out of your position due to price swings. In other words, the wave is well-defined and doesn't deviate significantly from its course.

The Bell Curve

To establish a benchmark for our discussions on volatility, let's review a bread-and-butter concept from the world of probability and statistics. You might remember the bell curve from your high school and college days. Young readers will doubtless encounter it soon enough! The bell curve is also known variously as the normal curve, normal distribution, or the Gaussian distribution, named after the nineteenth-century German mathematician Johann Carl Friedrich Gauss.

To set the stage for the normal curve, let's consider the following example. Suppose you wanted to make an inference about which age group represents the highest number of traders. Is a trader more likely to be a young twentysomething, middle aged, or an older retiree? One approach would be to find a representative group of traders and plot their ages. You could interview attendees at a stock trading expo as they arrive, simply asking them for their age. You might then have the following 27 ages: 19, 21, 23, 27, 28, 30, 32, 32, 36, 38, 39, 40, 43, 44, 44, 44, 46, 47, 49, 51, 55, 56, 56, 58, 62, 67, and 74. Granted, this is too small a sample for a proper analysis, but it serves our purposes of illustration. Once you have collected the individual ages, you then group them into age categories and observe the total number of observations within each category. An example table of this data might look like the following:

Age Group	Number of Observations
Under 20 years	1
20–29 years	4
30–39 years	6
40–49 years	8
50–59 years	5
60–69 years	2
70 years and above	1

If you take the table of data and plot a histogram to show the frequency of observation within each age group, you would have a chart that looks like Figure 3.1.

You can see how the number of observations is low at the beginning and rises to a peak near the middle before falling off at the end. A quick glance tells you that the greatest number of observations occurs in the 40–49-year-old age group. As you move farther below and above that age group, the number of observations within each group drops. If the total population of traders did, in fact, follow a normal or Gaussian distribution and you were able to collect enough data points, you would see that the histogram would eventually take the shape of the bell curve shown by the dashed line in Figure 3.2.

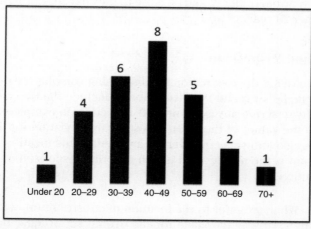

FIGURE 3.1 Histogram of Traders' Ages

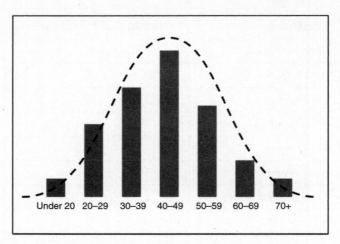

FIGURE 3.2 Normal Distribution of Traders' Ages

The resulting bell curve serves to describe the distribution of age data from any collection of traders. So long as you don't change the population from which the samples are drawn (i.e., only sampling ages of traders at a college or retirement village), you can reasonably expect that the ages you collect will follow your distribution curve. Once you have the curve, you can then assign probabilities to the occurrence of various ages. For example, without calculating specific probabilities, you can intuitively see that the likelihood of finding a 70-year-old trader is much lower than the likelihood of finding a 40-year-old trader. In fact, the chances of running across a 70-year-old trader would be close to the chances of running across a trader under 20 years of age.

Location and Dispersion

Now that we've set the foundation for discussing volatility by introducing the bell curve, let's expand the discussion to include the two characteristics that fully describe any bell curve. A bell curve is completely defined if you know the values of the mean and standard deviation for that curve. The mean is also known as the average and defines the location. The standard deviation is the metric we'll use to describe dispersion or, in trader terms, volatility.

Location   When we refer to the location of a distribution, we're talking about the mean or average value for the overall set of data. In statistics terms, this is known as a measure of central tendency; that is, the tendency of the data to centralize around a specific value. Location tells you where

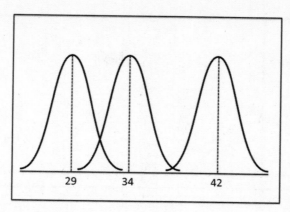

FIGURE 3.3 Constant Dispersion with Varying Location

the average of the data is most likely to occur. For traders, the location is best described by the moving average. A stock that is in an uptrend will have an increasing value of moving average, showing you that the location is moving higher. The reason moving averages appear as a flat line on a price chart is that the location isn't changing. The value of the average remains fairly constant.

Figure 3.3 illustrates a bell curve for uptrending data. You can see that the shape of the curve stays the same but the location moves higher as the trend continues. Suppose in our trader age example that the average age of a trader has been increasing over the last decade. Ten years ago the average age may have been 29, perhaps reflecting the acceptance of new trading technology. As the technology matured, it became more mainstream and attracted the attention of older traders. If you took three samples, drawn 10 years ago, 5 years ago, and last year, you might have seen that the average age jumped from 29 to 34 and then to 42. However, although the average age increased, the distribution of ages around the average remained the same. In other words, the spread or dispersion of the data was constant. The plot of each of your samples would look like the bell curves shown in Figure 3.3.

Dispersion Dispersion is the statistics term for trading volatility. It tells you how wide the swings are within the data that you're analyzing. In the bell curve example, dispersion describes the shape of the curve, or, to extend the wave analogy, it tells you the size and shape of the wave. Two waves may be moving in the same direction, but a fair-weather wave may be well-defined and stable whereas a wave in a storm is wild and ragged. Similarly, it is possible to look at two charts with identical moving averages, but one chart may have small candles with little or no shadows

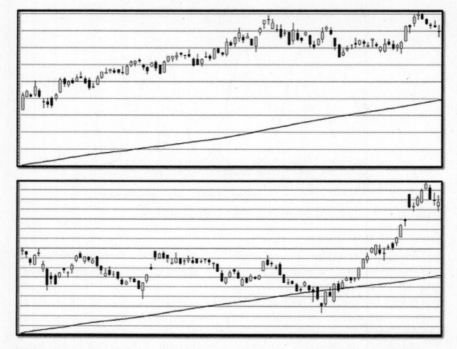

FIGURE 3.4 Chart Comparison Between Stocks with Different Volatility but Similar Trend

whereas another may have very long candles with extremely long shadows. You can appreciate the significance in volatility differences between the two. Figure 3.4 displays two stocks with approximately the same long-term trend. The up-sloping line on both charts is the 200-day simple moving average. You can see that the price in the top chart moves within a much tighter range than the bottom chart. The price movement in the bottom chart includes larger gaps and occasional dips below the moving average. Both charts represent similar locations but greatly different dispersions.

It may be helpful to look at an example of bell curves with the same location but varying levels of dispersion. As we said, the dispersion represents volatility and describes the shape of the curve. A bell curve with very little volatility will appear as a tall, narrow bell curve. This is shown as the solid line in Figure 3.5. A bell curve with very large dispersion, representing a stock with very high price volatility, appears as a low, wide curve as shown by the dashed line in Figure 3.5. A trader who has a position in a stock with high volatility is much more likely to observe price values farther away from the average (the peak of the bell curve) than a trader who has a low-volatility stock position.

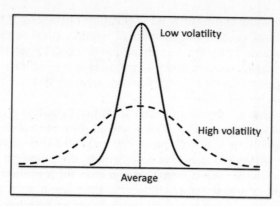

FIGURE 3.5 Constant Location with Varying Dispersion

Standard Deviation   Many traders are familiar with the moving average, which we've presented as a common measure of location. The metrics
that are commonly used for describing volatility are the variance and standard deviation. The other metric often used is the range, defined as the
difference between the high price and the low price for a trading session.
Although the range is a quick and easy calculation, it is too easily skewed
by an extreme data point. For example, if the stock should trade within a
narrow range for most of the day but momentarily trade higher, the day's
range is set by the extreme high value. To balance the influence of extreme
prices, we'll use the standard deviation.

The standard deviation is calculated as the square root of the variance.
The variance yields a value that is expressed as price-squared—not terri-
bly useful for us. Calculating the standard deviation as the square root of
variance gives us a measure of volatility that is expressed as simply price
(dollars instead of dollars-squared!). For the normal distribution, the equation for standard deviation is as follows.

$$\sqrt{\left\{ \sum_{i=1}^{n} (X_1 - X_{avg})^2 \right\} \Big/ n}$$

where X_i = closing price of period i
X_{avg} = average of n closing prices
n = number of periods

Most calculations use (n) in the denominator of the standard deviation
though others may use $(n - 1)$. The reason for the difference is that $(n - 1)$
subtracts one (degree of freedom, in statistical terms) from the sample size
to account for sampling error when the average is an estimate of the true
mean. For example, when we collected 27 traders' ages, we used that data

to draw conclusions about the total population of traders. If the true total number of traders were 10,000, then the 27 would represent a small sample from the population of 10,000. As our sample size gets larger, the difference between the sample average and the true population average (mean) gets smaller. This point is included only for statistical accuracy. From a trading standpoint, this is a nonissue.

Another point of clarification that we'll briefly address is the validity of the assumption of normality. The equation presented above is valid for the normal distribution or bell curve. Other probability distributions exist which use different equations to calculate the standard distribution. In order to use the standard deviation equation for a normal distribution, you would generally first establish that the data are, in fact, normally distributed. There have been many discussions about whether or not stock prices accurately follow a bell curve. We tend to discount this concern and focus on the pragmatic approach. Although this may not be theoretically pure, it tends to be empirically practical. Quite simply, whether stock prices are distributed strictly along the bell curve or not, using calculations based on that assumption tends to work well in the real world.

VOLATILITY SCORING SYSTEM

Unlike the trend score that could assume a value between -10 and $+10$, the volatility score can only be zero or positive. There is no significance to negative volatility. Therefore, the volatility scoring will help you quantify your trade between negligible volatility (zero score) and maximum volatility ($+10$ score). The final volatility score will be a combination of historical market volatility, historical stock volatility, and expected near-term market volatility.

Three Legs of Volatility Scoring

The three legs of volatility scoring will be added together to form the composite volatility score. In the same manner that we developed the trend score, we'll review how you'll approach the scoring, the technical metrics used to calculate the score, and, finally, we present a scoring template to make it easy to walk through the steps to arrive at the final score.

1. Historical Market Volatility (0 to +4)   Historical volatility provides a measure of recent price volatility that is then used as a gauge for future volatility. Clearly, there is no guarantee that volatility will remain the same, but it does offer a reasonable foundation for assessing a volatility score. Because we have discussed the role of the standard deviation as a measure of dispersion or volatility, you would expect that we use it for scoring. However, you can't apply the standard deviation directly, because you have no benchmark for determining whether the value is high or low. Standard deviation is given in the same units as the original data; in our application that would be dollars (or another price unit). But what constitutes high volatility? Would a standard deviation value of $5 represent high volatility? If the underlying stock price were $20, then a $5 standard deviation would represent a much greater level of volatility (relative to the stock price) than the same value for a $500 stock. Therefore, we have to measure historical volatility through a benchmark that has been normalized to the underlying share price.

Before we introduce the volatility scoring metric, we'll briefly digress to address the issue of volatility calculations. Market volatility as a historical and predictive tool has been studied for years at much deeper levels than we'll venture here. Keep in mind that the goal of volatility scoring is to provide an easy-to-use framework for choosing an appropriate option strategy. The strategies that are presented in this book are robust enough to accommodate any lack of precision in volatility estimation. More experienced traders may want to substitute another approach to volatility, such as average true range (ATR). The key is that you assign a score (between 0 and +4) to reflect your assessment of low versus high volatility.

Scoring Metric   The benchmark measure of historical volatility that we use for both the overall markets and the individual trade candidate is the coefficient of variation (CV). The CV is expressed as the current value of the standard deviation divided by the average value of the underlying stock. The average used in volatility scoring is the 50-day simple moving average of the closing price, the same average used in the short-term portion of the trend score. The standard deviation is calculated over a shorter time period to reduce the effect of trends. We base the volatility score on the standard deviation calculated on the closing price of 20 days. Coefficient of variation is then calculated as follows:

$$\text{CV\%} = (\text{standard deviation}_{20}/\text{simple moving average}_{50}) \times 100$$

where   Standard deviation$_{20}$ = 20-day standard deviation
Simple moving average$_{50}$ = 50-day simple moving average

Scoring Guide   Historical market volatility will be based on the average volatility of the five major indexes that were used in the trend score: Dow Jones Industrial Average (DJX), S&P 500 (SPX), Nasdaq 100 (NDX), Mid-Cap 400 (MID), and Russell 2000 (RUT).

The coefficient of variation for each of the five indexes will be averaged for an overall market CV. The average market CV determines this portion of the volatility score based on the following table.

Average Coefficient of Variation (%)	Volatility Score
0–2	0
2–4	+1
4–6	+2
6–8	+3
>8	+4

Scoring Template—Historical Market Volatility For each of the following five market indexes, complete the calculation table for the coefficient of variation. Many trading and charting programs (including some free online sites) include the standard deviation as a technical indicator choice. Though you may be able to run these calculations by hand, it would be tedious work to extract the data and crunch the numbers. In that case, we recommend substituting a volatility metric that you do have available.

1. Dow Jones Industrial Average (ticker symbol: DJX)

SD		20-day standard deviation of the closing price
SMA		50-day simple moving average of the closing price
CV		Coefficient of variation = (SD/SMA) × 100

Coefficient of Variation (%)	Volatility Score
0–2	0
2–4	+1
4–6	+2
6–8	+3
>8	+4
Dow Jones Industrial Average Volatility Score	

2. S&P 500 (ticker symbol: SPX)

SD		20-day standard deviation of the closing price
SMA		50-day simple moving average of the closing price
CV		Coefficient of variation = (SD/SMA) × 100

Coefficient of Variation (%)	Volatility Score
0–2	0
2–4	+1
4–6	+2
6–8	+3
>8	+4
S&P 500 Volatility Score	

3. Nasdaq 100 (ticker symbol: NDX)

SD		20-day standard deviation of the closing price
SMA		50-day simple moving average of the closing price
CV		Coefficient of variation = (SD/SMA) × 100

Coefficient of Variation (%)	Volatility Score
0–2	0
2–4	+1
4–6	+2
6–8	+3
>8	+4
Nasdaq 100 Volatility Score	

4. S&P MidCap 400 (ticker symbol: MID)

SD		20-day standard deviation of the closing price
SMA		50-day simple moving average of the closing price
CV		Coefficient of variation = (SD/SMA) × 100

(continued)

Coefficient of Variation (%)	Volatility Score
0–2	0
2–4	+1
4–6	+2
6–8	+3
>8	+4
S&P MidCap 400 Volatility Score	

5. **Russell 2000 (ticker symbol: RUT)**

SD		20-day standard deviation of the closing price
SMA		50-day simple moving average of the closing price
CV		Coefficient of variation = (SD/SMA) × 100

Coefficient of Variation (%)	Volatility Score
0–2	0
2–4	+1
4–6	+2
6–8	+3
>8	+4
Russell 2000 Volatility Score	

6. **Historical Market Volatility Score**

Line	Score	Index
1		Dow Jones Industrial Average Volatility Score
2		S&P 500 Volatility Score
3		Nasdaq 100 Volatility Score
4		S&P MidCap 400 Volatility Score
5		Russell 2000 Volatility Score
		(Add lines 1 through 5) then (divide sum by 5) **Historical Market Volatility Score**

2. Historical Stock Volatility (0 to +4)   Historical stock volatility is calculated separately and assigned its own weight in the overall volatility score. Historical stock volatility may range between zero and +4, based on the same criteria used in assessing historical market volatility.

Scoring Template—Historical Stock Volatility   For the stock candidate under consideration, complete the calculation table for the coefficient of variation.

SD		20-day standard deviation of the closing price
SMA		50-day simple moving average of the closing price
CV		Coefficient of variation = (SD/SMA) × 100

Coefficient of Variation (%)	Volatility Score
0–2	0
2–4	+1
4–6	+2
6–8	+3
>8	+4
Historical Stock Volatility Score	

3. Expected Market Volatility (0 to +2)   The final leg of volatility scoring accounts for the level of volatility expected in the overall market. The first two legs considered the historical volatility, which is measured from analyzing past price behavior. Expected market volatility is based on perceived levels of uncertainty through the analysis of option-trading activity. It is one of our best windows into upcoming volatility.

Scoring Metric   Many traders and investors who follow volatility refer to the VIX as the standard volatility metric. In 1993, the Chicago Board Options Exchange (CBOE) introduced the CBOE Volatility Index, VIX, which was originally designed to measure the market's expectation of 30-day volatility implied by at-the-money S&P 100 index (OEX) option prices. The current VIX is based on the S&P 500 index and estimates expected volatility by averaging the weighted prices of SPX puts and calls over a wide range of strike prices. VIX is a volatility index comprised of options rather than stocks, with the price of each option reflecting the market's expectation of future volatility. If you want to dig deeper into VIX calculation and trading strategies, we recommend *Trading VIX Derivatives: Trading and Hedging Strategies Using VIX Futures, Options, and Exchange Traded Notes* by Russell Rhoads (Wiley, 2011).

There are separate volatility indexes which track the Dow Jones Industrial Average (VXD), Nasdaq 100 (VXN), Russell 2000 (RVX), as well as some commodities. Although we captured all of the major indexes in previous scoring and averaged the result, we are going to focus only on the S&P 500 VIX for this portion of the scoring. We don't believe that adding additional layers to the forward-looking analysis will add significantly to the score. Once again, if you have more experience or if you are considering a candidate that is more closely aligned to another index, you may certainly substitute another volatility index in place of the VIX. For example, if you are considering a trade in the Oil Services ETF (OIH) or Schlumberger (SLB), you might choose to use the Crude Oil Volatility Index (OVX) instead of the VIX. The salient point is that you're trying to establish your best estimate of expected near-term volatility to balance your analysis of previous volatility.

Scoring Guide   Expected market volatility scoring is based on threshold scoring of the current value of the VIX. The VIX may be fairly complicated in its underlying calculation, but any trading software or site will provide you with the current VIX quote. Based on historical levels of low versus high market volatility, the VIX trading range will be divided into three layers:

- 0–20 low volatility score = 0
- 20–40 medium volatility score = 1
- Over 40 high volatility score = 2

The threshold levels that we recommend for scoring are based on historical levels of the VIX in high and low volatility markets. Many traders and investors consider VIX over 40 to be high volatility. The market drop of 2008 saw the VIX spike above 80 and that skewed opinions of what may be considered high volatility. Nevertheless, we'll continue to use the more common level of 40 to identify high levels of expected volatility.

You might be more familiar with other indicators that are based on threshold analysis. Among these are oscillating indicators such as the stochastic. This indicator measures overbought and oversold conditions based on the value of the indicator being above or below a specified threshold. For example, some traders consider a stochastic value above 80 percent to indicate that a stock is in an overbought condition and is signaling a pullback in price. Other traders may set the overbought level at 70 percent. You have the same latitude with the threshold in VIX. Although we set the scoring levels at 20 and 40, you are free to raise or lower the threshold based on your experience with the index as a forward-looking gauge.

Beta Weighting   An optional modification to the VIX scoring is to weight the VIX value based on the stock candidate's beta. Beta is a simple measure of a stock's volatility as compared to the volatility of the S&P 500 over the past five years. A beta value of 1 indicates that the stock moves in tandem with the overall market. If the S&P 500 increases 5 percent, you would expect that stock to also increase 5 percent. A negative beta value indicates an inverse correlation to the market. Therefore, a stock with a beta of −1 should drop 5 percent when the S&P 500 increases 5 percent. Beta may assume any continuous positive or negative value. So you may see a stock with a 1.5 beta that tells you that if the S&P 500 increases 5 percent, you would expect that stock to increase 7.5 percent.

Beta weighting allows you to adjust the VIX value to accommodate a stock's higher or lower correlation to the S&P 500. After obtaining the VIX quote, simply multiply the VIX by the stock's beta to arrive at a weighted VIX value. The weighted value is then used for this leg of volatility scoring.

Scoring Template—Expected Market Volatility   Obtain the current quote of the VIX (or alternative index for expected future volatility). Adjust the VIX value to account for the stock candidate's beta value by multiplying the VIX value by beta. Assign the corresponding volatility score based on the adjusted VIX value.

Current VIX value	
Stock beta value	
Adjusted VIX (VIX × beta)	

Adjusted VIX value	Score
0–20	0
20–40	+1
>40	+2
Expected Market Volatility Score	

Composite Volatility Score

You are now able to tally the results of the three individual legs of the volatility scoring system to arrive at a composite volatility score for your trade candidate. Simply add the volatility score for each leg for a total score. The lowest volatility scenario would be one in which the market average coefficient of variation, the stock coefficient of variation, and the adjusted VIX value are all in the scoring segment. If all three score at the highest values, the composite volatility score would be at the maximum value of +10.

KNOW THAT YOU DON'T KNOW

The lure of the market continues to reside in the challenge of navigating through uncertainty. As a trader, you don't have to navigate blindly. Although there are many opportunities for unexpected events to throw your trading plan off track, there is also some degree of structure in the markets to help guide your decisions. Volatility scoring is an approach to quantifying the level of uncertainty that you're operating within. That uncertainty, however, is what all the other traders must operate within, also. For that reason, we will present various option strategies that allow you to profit from the volatility that uncertainty generates.

At the same time, you must always approach the market with a defensive posture. Think about the worst-case scenario and be prepared to protect your capital against that scenario. We're not talking about eliminating risk; that's not possible or practical. We're talking about ensuring that the risks you face won't leave you with a catastrophic loss. That's the crucial topic we address in the next chapter.

CHAPTER 4

Protecting Your Position

The heart never takes the place of the head: but it can, and should, obey it.
—C. S. Lewis, *The Abolition of Man*

There is probably no more important topic in trading and investing than risk management. That's a pretty bold statement, considering how many different markets, strategies, products, and analyses you have available to you. However, the fact remains that the best strategy executed under seemingly ideal conditions may sometimes fail to play out per your expectations. When that happens, you must have a plan to defend against losses. The natural inclination is often to justify why you should be right or reason that if you hold the position a little longer, it may come back into alignment with you. At the moment you start to second-guess your risk management, you become an emotional decision maker. To paraphrase C. S. Lewis, the famous author of the *Chronicles of Narnia* series, your heart must yield to your head. You may not feel like taking a loss, but you must have a strict risk management discipline that cannot be compromised for even a single trade. We often point out that it only takes one catastrophic loss to wipe out years of accumulated earnings.

Since we're talking about making your emotions subservient to your intellect, let's start by making an appeal to your emotions. You'll find out soon enough that helping traders manage risk is one of the passions that drives us. We're often asked why we continue to write and speak about trading and investing. Why not just stay home and trade full-time? We understand the motivation of the person making the inquiry but the question betrays a need to realign priorities. We certainly continue to trade and invest, and extracting profits from the markets is very satisfying, but it's equally satisfying for us to help others navigate today's complex markets. The principles of risk management are not difficult to learn and can have a profound impact on your financial success.

You may recall Charles Dickens' *A Christmas Carol*, when Marley's ghost first visited Scrooge. After a brief exchange, Scrooge cries, "But you were always a good man of business!" To which Marley replies, "Business! Mankind was my business. The common welfare was my business; charity, mercy, forbearance, and benevolence, were, all, my business. The dealings of my trade were but a drop of water in the comprehensive ocean of my business!" Now let's get down to business.

SEVEN KEYS TO RISK MANAGEMENT SUCCESS

There are some important principles that help you understand the reasons as well as the mechanics behind managing trading risk. Whether you chalk it up to laziness, lack of preparation, not appreciating the importance, or any other excuse, you have to constantly defend against becoming slack in your risk management discipline. The following seven principles will help you understand and appreciate the need to protect every position, every time.

1. Risk Management Tempers Emotion

We'll start with the premise that your greatest obstacle to financial success is not that you don't know enough, but rather that you're not disciplined with what you know. To put it another way, your heart, not your head, is the problem. It is an observation from experience that few things generate the high level of emotional response that comes from dealing with money. Think about this from your own experience. Have you ever had a trade that performed surprisingly well? Do you remember the excitement of watching your equity go through the roof as profits added up with each tick of the market? If not, almost every trader has experienced that gut-wrenching feeling that attends the bad trade that you hold on to long after you should have stopped your loss. Both the excitement and the regret are emotions that can get you into trouble as a trader. Whether they make you feel invincible (you're smarter than the market) or cause you to deny reality (if you hold a little longer, it'll come back), emotions are bad foundations for trading decisions.

To illustrate this, let's look at a popular experimental economics game referred to as the ultimatum game. In the ultimatum game, two players are given the opportunity to divide a sum of money and there is no reciprocation. That is, each player only has to make one decision and the game is over. To start, player A is told to divide an amount, say $10, between player A and player B. The split can be any ratio with one exception: Player A cannot keep the entire amount. The worst-case split for player B is that player A will choose to keep $9 and give $1 to player B. The next step is for player B to decide whether to accept or reject player A's offer. If player B accepts the offer, then both players get the amount of money set forth in the offer. If player B chooses to reject the offer, then both players walk away empty-handed. Here's the key question: When is it advantageous for player B to reject an offer? The answer, of course, is never! In the worst-case scenario, if player B accepts the offer, he will still receive $1 that he otherwise wouldn't have. However, experimental results show that offers of less than 20 percent ($2 in our example) are often rejected. Subsequent investigation reveals that there is an element of fairness that's considered by player B and if the offer is perceived as unfair then the offer is rejected. Player B would choose the defense of perceived fairness rather than improve his financial condition if they appear to be mutually exclusive choices.

Since it is a well-established fact that people often act against their own best interests when it comes to financial decisions, risk management strategies are crucial to protect you against yourself.

2. Risk Management Keeps You in the Game

Daniel Kahneman and Amos Tversky analyzed an individual's response to profit and loss in their landmark research into prospect theory. Prospect theory states that people are much more willing to gamble with losses than with profits. This concept is actually quite familiar to traders because they are often quick to lock in a profit while allowing losses to continue in the hope that their patience will be rewarded by a rebound in the stock price. Gambling with a loss is known as loss aversion: the tendency for people to strongly prefer avoiding losses over acquiring gains. On the other hand, when you quickly lock in your profits, you're exercising risk aversion: You avoid any further risk when you have a profit in the position.

Some studies suggest that losses are as much as twice as psychologically powerful as gains. This phenomenon serves to dramatically increase the level of risk that a trader will accept with a losing position. You don't like the negative emotions that come with a loss and will go to great lengths to avoid it. You're surely familiar with the trader's maxim: "Don't get sore, just buy more!" This is where the doubling-down strategy was born. If the stock was a good buy at $50, it's a steal at $40. So you double your position size, with half at $50 and half at $40. Now your position only has to go up to $45 for you to break even on the trade. However, many times the losses are not avoided, but rather deferred. In fact, with a doubling-down strategy, losses are not only deferred, but also accelerated! When we practice loss aversion and watch the unrealized losses continue to grow, we'll eventually reach a point where even the unrealized loss becomes untenable and the position is closed.

You can survive many small losses but you often can't recover from a catastrophic loss. One of the rules we'll present is the position-sizing rule. Part of this process requires that you choose a maximum risk amount as a percentage of your trading capital. For example, if you decide that your maximum risk amount is 1 percent of your trading account and you have a $100,000 balance, then your goal is to keep your loss on any single trade at $1,000 or less. You then begin with $100,000 and your first trade is a loss, leaving you with a $99,000 balance. Your maximum risk amount drops to $990 (1 percent of $99,000). You can see in the following table that if you continue at this rate, after the twentieth consecutive loss, you'll still have almost $82,000 in your trading account.

Trade Number	Account Balance	Maximum Risk Amount
Starting	$100,000	$1,000
1	$99,000	$990
2	$98,010	$980
3	$97,030	$970
4	$96,060	$961
5	$95,099	$951
6	$94,148	$941
7	$93,207	$932
8	$92,274	$923
9	$91,352	$914
10	$90,438	$904
11	$89,534	$895
12	$88,638	$886
13	$87,752	$878
14	$86,875	$869

Trade Number	Account Balance	Maximum Risk Amount
15	$86,006	$860
16	$85,146	$851
17	$84,294	$843
18	$83,451	$835
19	$82,617	$826
20	$81,791	$818

3. Risk Management Requires Technical Analysis

We'll go so far as to say that you cannot effectively manage risk without an understanding of the core concepts of technical analysis. To be clear, we're not talking about knowing the Fibonacci retracement levels from memory or reciting the probability of observing a closing price beyond the 3-sigma Bollinger band. However, knowing how to identify key support and resistance levels, spotting important candle patterns, and being able to draw the story from the charts is crucial to sound risk management. They're what we call the bread-and-butter concepts of technical analysis. We have seen more than a few analysis methods presented from stage and in publications that appear to be satisfying a thesis requirement rather than helping you profit in the market. Our rule of thumb is this: If it doesn't tell you at least part of the story, then it isn't worth using. Every chart tells a story about whether the buyers or sellers are in control, how strong they are, whether their strength is increasing or decreasing, and much more. Your objective is to read that story. Any indicator or analysis that leads you closer to that goal is worthy of your attention. Any indicator or analysis that detracts from that objective should be discarded.

The reason that technical analysis is crucial for managing risk is that your profit and loss is entirely dependent on price movement. If you buy a stock or take a bullish option position, you don't make money if the underlying company performs well. You make money if the stock price rises. Yes, ultimately you would expect that the company fundamentals will be reflected in the stock price, but that isn't always the case and certainly not necessarily in your expected time frame. As we discussed in Chapter 1, fundamental analysis has a built-in time lag and that lag precludes its use as the sole risk management analysis. Your assessment of the fundamental strength or weakness of the company may or may not be reflected in the trading price. However, the trading price doesn't lie and when the price falls—for whatever reason—you need to be able to identify the fall quickly and move to protect your position. That can only be accomplished through technical analysis.

We suggest three key questions to which you should hold yourself accountable as a trader and investor. These questions will help ensure that you're using a proper technical analysis to enter and remain in any position.

1. **What is your reason for entering the trade?**
   This question may have any number of valid answers.
   - You bought the stock based on a bounce above support on a long green candle.
   - You set up a debit put spread because the price broke below channel support on rising volume.
   - You sold a covered call against your long stock position because volume has dried up and the stock started moving sideways.

   These are all examples of reasons why you might initiate a trade. The point is not necessarily what your reason may be, but rather that you have a reason that's based on some combination of fundamental and technical analysis. A good trading rule is to use your reason for entering a trade as your reason for exiting the trade. Whenever your reason for opening a position is no longer valid, then you should be ready to close the position. For example, if you sold a call against a long stock position based on the stock trading sideways (your entry reason) then if the stock breaks to a strong uptrend, you should consider rolling up or buying back the call. If the stock price breaks down, you should unwind the entire position by selling the long stock and buying the short call.

2. **What is your profit target?**
   This question also forces you to analyze the price history and make your best-guess estimate on where the price could reach if you're correct. We're not suggesting that you can predict the future or that you should tenaciously hold on unless and until your target is reached. Rather, you should perform a careful analysis of the trade potential in order to determine if it's worth the risk. Every trade and investment is a balance between risk and reward. If you haven't given any thought to the reward side of the equation, how do you know if it's worth the risk?

   There are a number of technical strategies for setting price targets. These include identifying key support and resistance, price gaps, and measured move strategies. A good example of a measured move is the channel breakout. A quick and easy target following a channel breakout is to project the channel range beyond the breakout point.

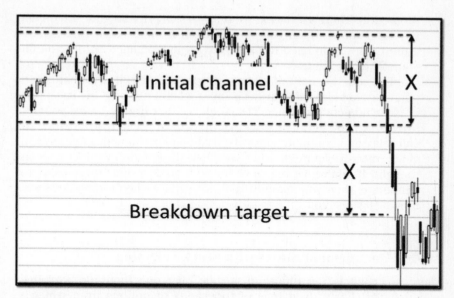

FIGURE 4.1 Channel Breakout Price Target

Figure 4.1 shows an established channel with a trading range of X. After the breakdown below channel support, the distance X below the previous channel support is the new price target.

Keep in mind that this step is for the initial trade evaluation only. Every minute of the trading day gives you new information about the market and you need to be ready to adjust your position and/or strategy accordingly. Once you've set your price target, you may very well revise it either higher or lower as you see the trade play out. That's not a case of bending the rules; that's smart trading.

3. **What is your exit price if you're wrong?**

This question is the most important of the three because it addresses the issue of risk management. You should not consider this a fuzzy concept, but rather a hard number. You can't set an approximate number in your mind for this question because you're then leaving yourself open to the hazards of emotional decision making. Unless you have a specific price—to the penny!—at which you'll exit the trade, you'll likely find yourself trying to justify holding on to a losing position when the moment of truth arrives.

It is also crucial that you decide on your stop exit price before you open your trade. After you enter the position and start dealing with the market volatility is not the time to be making the decision about your protection. There's a reason we refer to this price as your fire escape. It's the point at which you save yourself from disaster. And just like a fire escape, you need to have your escape planned before you find yourself in the flames.

The added benefit of setting a very specific exit price before you open the trade is that your decision of whether to hold the trade open or close it becomes binary. The stock is either trading above your exit price or it's not. Period. If your exit price hasn't been reached, then you can relax and continue with your trading plan. Immediately when the stock trades at your exit price, you close the position without a second thought. If you've set the rules for your trade when you're calm and deliberate, then you should trust those rules when the markets start moving against you.

4. Risk Management Starts with Stock Selection

There are roughly ten thousand stocks, over one thousand exchange-traded funds (ETFs), and tens of thousands of options from which to choose when it's time to open a trade. Nevertheless, from our observations with our audiences around the country, most people have traded less than 50, even less than 20, unique symbols over their last five years. We're not suggesting that there's any inherent virtue in trading hundreds of different stocks. But neither is there a benefit to falling into a rut and trading the same three stocks simply because you've developed a familiarity with them. In fact, trading a stock so often that you think you "know" the stock can be a fatal flaw for traders.

One of the worst losses we've observed in our collective years of training and consulting traders and investors occurred in the mid-1990s. We met a particular trader who came to us armed with charts from previous years to show the pattern he had spotted. Each year for the prior three years the stock fell around one point in the year and then rallied a short time later. After studying these patterns, he had convinced himself that he knew that stock (as if stocks possess personality traits that are inviolable from year to year). So he opened an account and committed his entire equity balance to that one stock when it dropped at his expected time. The only problem was that he didn't answer the third question we just posed: "What is your exit price if you're wrong?" He didn't have an exit price: He couldn't envision the need to exit because he knew how that stock behaved. He held on to the position as it continued to fall, even borrowing money to fund the account further when his balance dropped below maintenance minimums. Ultimately, he ended up losing everything simply because he thought he knew better than what the market was telling him.

You will always be able to find a trade in any market. Strong markets have weak stocks and vice versa. The latest rally that you missed will not be the last strong rally given to you by the market. You can find dividend stocks in solid channels as well as uptrends that are more stable than you thought possible. Risk management begins by targeting the stocks that match your trading objectives and strategies. Too many traders constantly go back to the same trough to feed and end up forcing trades that aren't really there. We like rules of thumb. Here's another one: If the trade doesn't jump out at you when you look at a chart, don't jump in after it!

5. Risk Management Is Dynamic

There are actually two dimensions to this point. The first is that your trade is dynamic in the sense that you have to respond to changes in the market after you enter the trade. It's intuitively clear that you have to make the best risk management choices based on available information when you first enter the trade. However, there are countless forces driving the market, including economic reports, trading activity, shifts in company fundamentals, and more. As the markets digest each of these variables, you have to be prepared to respond when your position changes, for better or worse. One of the most common forms of dynamic risk management is the trailing stop. Simply, this involves resetting your stop price as the charts establish new support or resistance levels. This allows you to simultaneously protect against loss while locking in gains based on your technical analysis.

The second dimension is that you have to remain dynamic as a trader. This involves staying on top of changes in the market rules, products, technology, and strategies through ongoing education. Don't assume that benevolent gurus always have your best interests as their top priority. We certainly hope you trust us and we'll do our best to give you that confidence, but trust is earned, not assumed. As the English writer and philosopher G. K. Chesterton once said, "Without education, we are in a horrible and deadly danger of taking educated people seriously."

Consider some of the changes that traders have seen in the last 10 or 15 years and how these have impacted how you trade and manage risk:

- Moving from fractional quotes to decimal quotes.
- Trading rooms giving way to electronic communication networks (ECNs) giving way to online direct-access trading.
- Sub-$10 commissions.
- Conditional orders, including fully contingent stock-option orders.
- Comprehensive charting with scores of indicators.
- Screening tools with real-time streaming results.

- ETFs for markets, industries, currencies, and more.
- Standard options, long-term equity anticipation securities (LEAPS), and weeklies.

The list goes on and highlights the fact that you need to know what you have at your disposal and how to effectively use it for profit and protection.

6. Risk Management Is Probabilistic

Perhaps a better way to phrase this point is to say that the markets are probabilistic and, therefore, risk management needs to accommodate this. If the market were deterministic, then every time event A occurs, we should see event B as a result. In a deterministic world, for example, you would be able to say something like, "Every sequence of five green candles will be followed by a red candle." And then if you observe a chart with five green candles you could count on the next candle being red. But we know the markets don't operate that way. You may see event A occur and then often observe event B, but not always.

The next logical step would be to recognize the uncertainty but attempt to quantify it. After all, there are well-established rules for quantifying uncertainty through probability theory. If you're a bit more familiar with the normal distribution we discussed in Chapter 3, then you know that if you draw a line three standard deviations above the mean and another line three standard deviations below the mean, you can take a slice out of the bell curve and expect to find about 99.7 percent of all observations. This should happen every time for every normal curve.

So if we understand the markets to be probabilistic, why not assign probability theory to trading? The first reason is that trading doesn't lend itself to clean definitions—a requirement for building on theory. For example, if you want to determine how often a bullish engulfing candle pattern results in a reversal of the trend, you would have to account for various scenarios in which you observe the pattern. At a minimum, you would need to provide standard definitions for the following:

- What defines the initial downtrend?
- Is volume rising, falling, or remaining steady?
- Does the pattern include shadows, and of what length?
- What magnitude of price rise constitutes a reversal and in what time frame?
- What are the extenuating market conditions?
- Does the pattern occur at a clearly identifiable support level? How is the support identified?

With just this short list you can appreciate that not all bullish engulfing candles are created equal. In the absence of strictly defined conditions for the pattern, it would be downright misleading to claim, for example, that this pattern results in a trend reversal 80 percent of the time.

Another consideration is that the assumptions for applying probability theory simply don't hold up. That is, stock prices do not consistently follow the normal, or any other, distribution. It is, of course, possible to take a finite set of historical stock prices and fit a distribution to those prices, but there is little reason to expect that the conditions that yielded that distribution will remain unchanged, allowing you to predict future prices.

We suspect that the culprit behind trying to predict stock prices with quantifiable certainty is the volume of data available. If there are numbers, there must be an algorithm. Nassim Nicholas Taleb (*Fooled by Randomness: The Hidden Role of Chance in Life and in the Markets*, p. 162) light-heartedly describes this phenomenon from his own experience:

A programmer helped me build a backtester. It is a software program connected to a database of historical prices, which allows me to check the hypothetical past performance of any trading rule of average complexity. I can just apply a mechanical trading rule, like buy NASDAQ stocks if they close more than 1.83 percent above their average of the previous week, and immediately get an idea of its past-performance. The screen will flash my hypothetical track record associated with the trading rule. If I do not like the results, I can change the percentage to, say, 1.2 percent. I can also make the rule more complex. I will keep trying until I find something that works well.

What am I doing? The exact same task of looking for the survivor within the set of rules that can possibly work. I am fitting the rule on the data. This activity is called data snooping. *The more I try, the more I am likely, by mere luck, to find a rule that worked on past data. A random series will always present some detectable pattern. I am convinced that there exists a tradable security in the Western world that would be 100 percent correlated with the changes in temperature in Ulan Bator, Mongolia.*

Do your best analysis, choose an appropriate strategy, and execute according to a disciplined, well-defined plan. And then recognize that you'll sometimes totally miss the trade. Those are the trades that require your fire escape.

7. Risk Management Is Nonnegotiable

You don't get to pick and choose when you'll exercise risk management strategies. This should be a nonnegotiable practice; one that is part and parcel with every trade and investment you make. It is true that you only need one substantially errant trade to erase years of profits. For that reason, you should identify your exit price just as surely as you identify your entry. Every time.

You may be tempted to only apply risk management principles to those trades that you deem high risk. The problem with that approach is that most people are notoriously bad at estimating the likelihood of an event occurring. In 1662, Antoine Arnauld and Pierre Nicole published *Port-Royal Logic*, showing how people overestimated the probability of being struck by lightning in a thunderstorm. Statistically, the odds of a lightning strike may be very low, but the consequences are high and, therefore, add weight to the fears beyond the mere likelihood of occurrence. An important aspect to their work is that any experience with a lightning strike (having witnessed a strike, knowing an acquaintance that experienced a strike, etc.) only added to the fears. The underlying probability didn't change, but the perception was greatly influenced by these other factors.

We know a hunter who has some timber property in central Georgia. It is well known that the region is home to several species of poisonous snakes. Late one night, outside his camp, the hunter walked across the path of a large timber rattlesnake. Within two weeks, he had traded his hiking boots for snake-proof boots. Now, do you think the likelihood of running across a poisonous snake increased? No; rather, his perception of the risk of running across a poisonous snake increased, based on his recent experience.

If you have never experienced a brush-with-death sort of trade, the kind that has you lying awake in bed at night, then your perception of that risk is very low. We know plenty of traders who have lost thousands and millions of dollars in bad trades. They're the ones who are most attentive to managing risk because they've felt the pain of not managing risk.

THREE LEGS OF MANAGING RISK

Now that you have an understanding of the reasons why risk management is essential to your trading success, let's move on to the application. There are three checks you should perform for each trade that will help ensure that your risk management is complete and that you're minimizing your exposure to undue loss. Balancing risk and reward lets you know if the trade is worth your attention. The concentration check helps you diversify your risk so that any one risk factor doesn't have a disproportionate influence on your success. Finally, position sizing is a calculated approach to determining the correct amount of money to place into the trade based on your technical analysis.

1. Risk/Reward

Would you play the lottery if the probability of winning didn't change (about 1 in 175 million for some lotteries!), yet the ticket price rose from $1 to $100 or $1,000? What if the probability and the ticket price stayed the same but the payout dropped to $50? If your answer changes with the scenario, then you're evaluating risk and reward. Lotteries draw in millions of gamblers because they offer the chance to win tens of millions of dollars for the cost of a ticket—usually a single dollar. Although the odds against winning are so large as to be virtually incomprehensible, people will still buy tickets because the risk (cost of the ticket) is so small compared to the reward (tens or hundreds of millions of dollars).

Here's an analogy to help you understand lottery odds. Let's assume that you purchased enough 12-inch rulers to lay end-to-end along the equator to create a line of rulers measuring 24,900 miles long. On the back of one of these rulers, you place a red dot and then you turn the ruler back over. Your friend comes along and starts at any point on the equator and begins to walk. His objective is to select a stopping point, bend down and turn over the ruler. After walking 10 miles or 100 miles or 10,000 miles he randomly stops, turns over a single ruler, and discovers the red dot. Actually, your friend has a much greater chance of finding the red dot ruler by mere luck than he has of winning the Mega Millions lottery, played in 12 U.S. states.

Every financial endeavor entails some degree of risk, whether you're looking at a trade, a new business, or changing careers. Your choice is to determine if the potential gain justifies the risk you'll assume. The first part of the consideration is the magnitude of risk versus payout. It's easy to risk a dollar to win millions, even though the likelihood of success is very low. Losing that dollar will have no material impact on your lifestyle. Regardless of the probability of success, though, you would likely not risk $1 million if your total net worth were $100,000. Why? Because even though the chance of losing may be small, a loss would be catastrophic and you may not ever be able to recover.

The second aspect to consider is the probability of success. The greater the likelihood of winning, the more risk you can assume. Most people would place a $1 bet for the chance to win $10 if the outcome were the result of a coin flip. This can easily be explained though an expected value analysis. Simply, the expected value of a probability-based payout is the amount of the payout multiplied by the likelihood of winning. Assuming that a coin flip gives you a 50 percent chance of success and the payout is $10, your expected value for the bet would be $5. In effect, you're paying $1 for a $5 expected return. That's a good risk for the reward.

With trading decisions, you have to make a judgment call on the risk-reward evaluation for two reasons. First, we've already discussed the fact that the markets don't give you quantifiable probabilities. You can't state with a high degree of confidence that a trade has a 50 percent, 75 percent, or 90 percent likelihood of success. There are guidelines and rules of thumb that are helpful but not cast in stone. For example, many traders use the option delta as an estimate of the likelihood of that option expiring in-the-money. For example, an at-the-money option has a delta of roughly .50, so a covered-call writer selling an at-the-money call can estimate that there will be a 50-50 chance of getting assigned at expiration. Second, the payout is not assured. You may estimate the likelihood of a stock rising, but how can you determine if it will rise 2 percent or 20 percent? Some strategies with capped profits make it a little easier to determine the payout. A covered call in a very bullish trend has a high probability of assignment that would leave you with the premium collected plus the proceeds from the stock sale at the strike price.

The goal of the risk-reward step of risk management is not to force you into fuzzy calculations around your probability of success and the size of your profit. Rather, it's to encourage you to make sure that you allocate your limited funds to the best trade possible. If you have a choice among three separate trades, the risk-reward evaluation should help steer you toward the best trade, even though your estimates of both risk and reward may be slightly flawed because you would expect that any bias or flaw in your evaluation would influence all three equally.

2. Concentration Check

As a general rule, we don't recommend actively trading with more than about 20 percent of your net investable assets. This would exclude home, cars, and so on but would include retirement, savings, and brokerage accounts. Even though we are proponents of trading and technical analysis, every asset class and strategy carries its own set of risks and we think it's a good idea to participate in multiple areas of the market. This book primarily addresses the portion of your investments with which you're actively timing the market.

With that said, the next step in the risk management process is to ensure that you don't place your trading account on red one. If you're not familiar with the roulette wheel, you can choose to place a bet on a single number—red 1, for example—and get the maximum payout (35 to 1) if you win. However, you have the lowest chance of winning (2.63%). Even with higher odds, it still doesn't make sense to concentrate your risk in any one position.

The rule we work with is that no more than about a third of your trading account should be held in any single position. If you trade with only about 20 percent (.2) of your investable assets and you limit your position to a third (.33) of your trading account, then any one trade doesn't represent more than about 7 percent (.33 × .2 = .66 or 6.7 percent) of your investable assets. In the worst-case scenario, a catastrophic loss in one position would leave you with 93 percent of your assets intact.

Part of your responsibility with the concentration check is to make sure that you don't have excessive correlation in your positions. For example, if your trading account is evenly divided among positions in Barrick Gold (ticker symbol: ABX), Goldcorp Inc. (ticker symbol: GG), and Newmont Mining (ticker symbol: NEM), you may be following the letter of the concentration law but certainly not the spirit. You don't have to run correlation studies, but be sure that you don't expose yourself to industry, geographic, or other specific risk factors that could affect multiple positions.

3. Position Sizing

Position sizing involves the balance between managing your account equity and managing your specific trade. Too many traders decide on a position size based on how many shares or contracts they can afford, how good they feel about the prospects for the trade, or some other subjective criteria. When deciding how large or small a position to open, you should follow some basic rules.

1. Determine your risk amount.

Determining your risk amount is the first step in proper position sizing and is completely independent of the actual trade setup. You don't need to know anything about the specifics of the trade because this step deals only with your account. We refer to this as the money management step. Because it is not dependent on the trade, you should know what your risk amount is before you ever find your trade candidate.

The risk amount is generally established as a percentage of your trading account. We recommend setting your risk amount to a value between 1 and 3 percent of your account equity. Shorter-term traders should lean toward the lower number whereas longer-term traders and investors may use a higher value. In fact, very short-term traders such as day traders may elect to use .5 percent. The value for the risk amount percentage you select is not as important as sticking to your discipline. In other words, it is better to use 2 percent consistently than 1 percent occasionally. The percentage you choose then becomes the maximum allowable loss you're willing to accept on any single trade. So if you have a $100,000 trading account and you're using 2 percent as your risk amount, then you don't want to lose more than $2,000 (2% of $100,000) on any single trade. Expressed as an equation, you have:

$$\text{Risk amount} = \text{Risk percentage} \times \text{Account equity}$$

The first point to note with this is that you're applying the risk amount to each unique trade. If you have three open trades, then each trade is managed to the 2 percent limit. You do not have to divide the $2,000 risk amount into thirds and use $667 for each. The second point we want to emphasize is that the 2 percent applies to the maximum acceptable loss for the trade. It does not indicate how far the underlying share price may move to reach that loss. Sometimes traders misunderstand this point and tell us that they can't use a 2 percent risk amount because their stock moves more than 2 percent every day. We're not talking about how much the stock moves. You may let the stock move 2 percent, 10 percent, or 30 percent. The point is that for whatever amount the stock price moves, the net effect on your account should not exceed a 2 percent loss.

You can see that your risk amount will drop as you lose and increase as you profit. If you start with $100,000 and a 2 percent risk amount, after three losing trades you'll have about $94,000 remaining and your risk amount has dropped from $2,000 per trade to about $1,882. If you do well and increase your account by 5 percent, your risk amount rises to $2,100 per trade. This forces you to do what you should practice anyway: Back off your position size when you're not trading well and add to your positions when you're successful.

2. **Determine your risk per share.**

In the first step you deal with money management. You next move to the step that addresses trade management: determining your risk per share. The chart gives this to you. The basic equation for risk per share follows.

$$\text{Risk per share} = \text{Entry price} - \text{Exit price}$$

Keep that equation in mind, because you'll use it for both direct stock trading as well as option trading, adjusting for the option characteristics.

The entry price is easy. That's the price at which you open the position. For example, in Figure 4.2 you can see a stock that has

FIGURE 4.2 Entry Price as Stock Bounces above Support

established a role reversal support. The current candles show the price bouncing up from support, giving you an opportunity to buy this stock as it rallies from the support price. Ideally, you want your entry price to be close above support for a bullish trade or close below resistance for a bearish trade so that you can quickly identify when you need to exit the trade.

Once you've identified your entry price, you need to choose your exit price. This is the stop price at which you'll close the position if it moves against you. Figure 4.3 shows the area at which you would place your sell stop on a long stock trade from the example.

Deciding how far below support to set your stop is based on your experience and risk tolerance. Some traders opt for a rules-based approach, such as placing the stop 5 percent below the support or a distance related to a volatility indicator. Other traders simply make a subjective call based on a visual analysis of the recent trading patterns. We have another rule of thumb that we like to apply. Set your stop far enough below support (or above resistance for a bear strategy) so that it's difficult for your stock to hit your stop price. In other words, err on the side of too far rather than too close. This is still subjective but it helps you decide which way to lean. That way, if your stop price is reached you can be confident that you should be out of the trade.

FIGURE 4.3   Stop Price Range for Long Stock Trade

Contrary to what you might guess, you are not being extra conservative if you place your stop very close to support. Although you will likely lose less on a per-share basis, you're increasing the probability of losing. Also, as you'll see in the next step, your position size is adjusted based on your choice of stop price, so you'll actually end up accelerating your losses if you deliberately place your stops excessively tight.

3. **Calculate your position size.**

The third step reconciles money management from step 1 with trade management from step 2. This is accomplished by adjusting the size of your position based on your risk amount and the risk level of the trade. Simply, the equation for position size is:

$$\text{Position size} = \text{Risk amount}/\text{Risk per share}$$

You can see that as the uncertainty in the trade increases, you have a higher risk per share, which results in a smaller position size.

For example, suppose you have $100,000 and are using 2 percent as your risk percentage. You know you need to cap your risk amount at $2,000 (2% × $100,000) per trade. If you decided to buy the stock from Figure 4.2 at the current trading price of $50, that would represent your entry price. Looking at the chart, you might determine that support is at $46 so $42 would be a good place to set your sell stop. Your entry of $50 minus your stop of $42 gives you a risk per share of $8. You can then calculate your position size by dividing $2,000 by $8 to give you a maximum trade of 250 shares.

In the preceding example, suppose that support stayed the same but volatility was lower and you were able to tighten your stop to $45 rather than $42. Your risk per share drops from $8 to $5, which increases your allowable position size to 400 shares. You see that both examples limit your loss to $2,000 but still accommodate varying levels of volatility.

Please make note of what you *don't* do with position sizing. You don't look at your account and see that you can afford to buy 2,000 shares (2,000 shares × $50 per share = $100,000). However, you know you don't want to lose more than $2,000, so you set your stop at $49. Since your stop is only a dollar below your entry, if you sell at $49 you're limiting your loss to 2 percent. That means you're following the risk rules, right? Absolutely not! What you're doing, in effect, is telling the market where you need to get out rather than letting the market tell you where you should get out. I'm sure we don't need to remind you what the market thinks about your needs or opinions. Although you would be limiting your loss to 2 percent, you're ignoring the fact that the stock has support at $46. With a stop at $49, you're placing your exit price $3 above support, significantly increasing the likelihood of being stopped out on the trade. Furthermore, 2,000 shares use your full account value in a single trade, breaking the concentration check we discussed earlier.

Adjusting Position Size for Options   Calculating position size for option trades is not quite as straightforward as for stock trades. The two pieces that require additional attention are the bid/ask spread and the option delta for estimating the exit price. Let's walk through an example based on the previous stock trade. Suppose that you choose to replace the stock with something that acts like the stock: a deep in-the-money call.

You know that the first step is to determine your risk amount. In fact, this doesn't change at all with an option trade. So to continue the example, you will enter the trade knowing that you want to cap your loss at $2,000.

The next step is to determine your risk per share. Remember that risk per share equals entry minus exit. You look at the option chain for a call option that has about five months until expiration and you see the following:

Strike	Bid	Ask	Delta
$50	$13.30	$13.60	0.81

The entry price is simply the price you pay for the option right now. We'll assume that you don't use limit orders to try to get price improvement, which means you buy at the ask and sell at the bid. Any price improvement will only improve your overall position. Therefore, your entry price is $13.60.

The big question is, what is your exit price? You have to answer this question by estimating where the option will be trading if the stock reaches its stop level. Recall that the stock's stop price was set at $42, representing a drop of $8. Using the option delta, you can estimate how much the option will drop based on an $8 drop in the stock price. A delta of 0.81 tells you that the option should drop about $0.81 for every $1 drop in the stock price. Therefore, if the stock drops $8, the option premium should drop about $6.48 ($8 × 0.81). Because you would have to sell at the bid, your projected exit price is the current bid premium minus the estimated premium drop. That leaves you with an exit price of $6.82 ($13.30 current premium bid – $6.48 estimated premium change). Your risk per share is then $6.78 ($13.60 entry price – $6.82 exit price).

You can now calculate your position size because you know both the risk amount and the risk per share. Dividing $2,000 by $6.78 leaves you with a position size of 295 shares, or three call contracts. Most of the time, you'll have an odd lot position size (other than 100-share increments). If the odd lot size is about 80 or higher, then you can round up to the next contract. Otherwise, truncate your position to the lower number of contracts. For example, if you calculate your position size to be 453 shares, 53 is less than 80 so drop down to four contracts. In our example, 95 was the odd lot number so it's fine to round up.

We recognize that there are other variables that influence the exit price of the option. For example, theta, or time decay, is working to reduce the premium. However, it's generally not practical to estimate *when* the stock may reach its stop price. That's a contingency you protect against from a price standpoint, not a time standpoint. If the stop were reached quickly, then theta would have a negligible effect on the exit price. If the stop were hit closer to expiration then the option would have experienced greater time decay and your estimate would likely be high. Also, the option delta is not constant as the underlying price changes. As the stock price drops toward the stop level, delta will decrease because delta drops as an option becomes farther out-the-money. This is the option gamma. Using a static delta (ignoring gamma) in the exit price estimate is a more conservative approach to risk management. The point we want to emphasize here is that there are a number of refinements that may be included in the estimate, but don't lose sight of the fact that it is an estimate. A third coat of wax on a '72 Pinto won't make it a Mercedes.

This approach may be extended to multileg strategies such as spreads by calculating the net risk per share for the entire position. For example, suppose you decided to open a debit call spread that requires that you buy a lower strike call and sell a higher strike call with the same expiration. You can follow the previous example to calculate the entry price for the long call (current ask) as well as the entry price for the short call (current bid). Using each option delta, you are then able to estimate the exit price of both options for a given drop in the price of the underlying. Finding the difference between entry and exit will give you a risk per share for the long call and a gain per share for the short call. The long call will have a loss that is partially offset by a profit in the short call. The risk per share is the net loss per share after accounting for both legs.

SETTING STOPS

We've been using stops throughout this chapter, so it's a good idea to turn our attention toward the task of setting stops. By definition, a stop is an order that exists to close your position when a trade moves against you and protects you from further loss. To avoid redundancy in the following discussion, any mention of a stop below support for a bull trade may be also read as a stop above resistance for a bear trade.

Limit versus Market

Before we talk about various forms of stop orders, we think it's important to contrast the two order type choices that you have with various stops. If your stop price is reached, you have the choice between a limit order and a market order. A limit order guarantees price but doesn't guarantee execution. A market order guarantees execution but doesn't guarantee price. Our recommendation is to always use market orders when setting stops for protection. The reason is simple: If you place a limit stop order and then your stock drops below the limit you set, you no longer have any protection. Sometimes stop orders are useful for entering trades but our discussion here is limited to stops as risk management tools.

Fixed Stop

A fixed stop sets the exit price at a fixed level below the entry price. This may be a specific dollar amount or a specific percentage. For example, if you use a 5 percent stop and you open your position at $50, then your stop will be set at $47.50. Fixed dollar or percentage stops are staples on most trading platforms.

There's an inherent weakness in fixed stops, though, in that they don't account for the uniqueness of the trade setup. Suppose you choose to diligently apply a 5 percent fixed stop to every trade. That works great if the stock's support is 3 percent or 4 percent below your entry price. But what happens if support is 6 percent or even 15 percent below your entry? You can clearly see that a fixed stop is the most rigid and the least adaptable to individual trades.

Trailing Stop

A variation to the fixed stop is the trailing stop, which is designed to protect against loss while incrementally locking in profits. The basic trailing stop also uses either a fixed dollar amount or percentage. Unlike the fixed stop that remains at the initial stop level regardless of where the price moves, the trailing stop will adjust in the direction of profit. As the stock price rises, the stop price will also rise, following the stock by the specified amount. If the stock never trades higher than the entry price, then the trailing stop would act exactly like a fixed stop. For example, suppose you buy a stock at $50 and set a $2 trailing stop. Upon placing the stop order, the stop price is initially set at $48—the entry price less the trailing stop amount. If the stock were to rise to $52, the stop would rise to $50. If the stock then rises to $53 and then falls to $51, the trailing stop would be triggered and your position would be closed at $51.

You may also use a technical trailing stop that sets the trail distance based on chart technicals rather than a fixed dollar or percentage. A common example of a technical trailing stop is to use a moving average in a trending stock. Figure 4.4 shows a stock with an uptrending moving average indicated by the solid line. Below the moving average is a dashed line, indicating where the trailing stop would follow. The figure shows you where the stop would execute based on a technical trailing stop.

Any technical indicator or pattern may be used as the basis for a trailing stop. Your goal is to think through the conditions under which you would exit the trade and then use the technical tools and indicators with which you're familiar to alert you to those conditions.

Calendar Stop

All traders are familiar with the fact that charts have two axes: vertical for price and horizontal for time. However, most traders only consider the price axis when determining stop points to exit a trade. The time axis may also be used to help you know when to close your position.

Stop executes

FIGURE 4.4 Trailing Stop Using a Moving Average

The first application of the calendar stop is to estimate a time frame for reaching your price target and close your position if that time frame is exceeded. For example, suppose you're trading a channeling stock and you see that the average time to move from support to resistance is about three weeks. You may buy that stock on a bounce above support and then set your calendar stop at five or six weeks. Even though the average time may have been three weeks, you need to allow for the fact that cycles are loose at best. There is no hard-and-fast rule that three weeks must be the time to hit the other side of the channel. At the same time, the stock may drift just above support, not dropping below the channel to trigger your stop but neither rising to your profit target. Oftentimes, it's better to take the trade off the table and find an opportunity that will give you a return for your risk. The premise behind a calendar stop is that not losing money is not the same thing as making money.

A variation of the calendar stop is a discrete event stop. This may be used for any known event: earnings, company news, mergers or acquisitions, and so on. If your trade is based in part on what you expect the stock to do following a key event, then you should evaluate your reasons for holding the stock after the event passes. For example, let's say you bought a stock based on an expectation of a key merger that you think will be addressed during an upcoming shareholder conference call. Sure enough, the issue is discussed and the next week the stock trades flat. It may not have fallen to your stop, but the reason for your trade—the event—is no longer valid. At that point, the best action is to close the trade.

SAFETY IN NUMBERS

You may have heard it said that it's better to have a mediocre trading strategy with great risk management than a great strategy with mediocre risk management. There's a lot of truth there, because one bad trade, left to a catastrophic loss, can more than offset many successful trades. Charts tell you a story and technical analysis quantifies the measure of that story. We want you to use technical analysis as a guide in managing your risk, but don't become enamored with the myriad indicators, patterns, and chart styles. Contemporary trading tools and analysis make it easy to get caught up in the *process* of managing risk and lose sight of the objective. Use technical analysis the way a drunk uses a lamppost: for support, not illumination.

CHAPTER 5

Covered Calls

Selling a call option against an existing stock position is known by a few common names: covered call, buy-write, and covered write. Generally speaking, the terms are synonymous with a few subtle differences. We will discuss how you can use covered calls in bullish and neutral markets. Before getting into the various strategies, it's important to understand the rationale behind a covered call.

Using covered calls can be a viable strategy in bull and range-bound markets. Covered calls are not advisable in bear markets for two reasons. First, the premiums on call options are reduced during bearish trends, generating lower rates of return and increasing risk. Second, the owner of the actual shares will always have a higher delta than the owner of the call, even with deep in-the-money options. That means the gains in the short position (calls) will never equal the losses of the long position (shares).

One of the most common mistakes of the covered call trader is to ignore a falling stock, believing she can eventually recoup the loss in share value by selling another covered call down the road. Utilizing conditional orders to automate your exit will help keep you disciplined and close out the position when the price behavior warrants.

Another common mistake of a bullish covered call seller is the unwillingness to be assigned. This mistake is made when you buy back the call option at a substantially higher price than it was sold for in an attempt to retain the underlying shares. This emotional attachment to a stock is dangerous. You should enter every covered call transaction looking forward to the day you are assigned and you get to sell your shares for the maximum profit. Covered calls may be an excellent way to generate consistent, conservative returns on stock and exchange-traded fund (ETF) positions trading in a range or to enhance and harvest profits from bullish positions.

GETTING TO KNOW THE STRATEGY

A useful analogy for a covered call is a real estate option to buy a specific property. For this example, let's consider a small coastal town in California that has experienced exponential growth. Two friends, Kathy and Jim, live in the area. Kathy owns a small cottage near the ocean. She purchased the home five years ago for $300,000 and it has since increased to a current valuation of $500,000. Jim has never purchased a home and, although he has been saving for one, the prices have increased faster than his savings rate.

One day Jim and Kathy were discussing real estate values in their area. Jim expressed his belief that the market should continue growing at an accelerated rate, with baby boomers retiring and wanting to live near the coast. Kathy agreed that her property will likely continue to grow in value, but thinks the rate of growth will slow down substantially. Jim disagreed and said, "I bet your house will be worth at least $600,000 by this time next year!" Kathy replied, "If you're that confident in your bet, then I'll sell you a one-year option to purchase my house for $600,000." Although Jim still didn't have enough money to buy a house outright, he had saved up enough to consider this a reasonable investment that he could afford. Jim decided to take Kathy up on her offer.

The two agreed on terms that would allow Jim to buy Kathy's house for $600,000 at any time of his choosing over the next 365 days. For this contract, Jim agreed to pay Kathy $10,000. The two engaged an attorney friend to draw up a legal contract that obligates Kathy to sell her home to Jim at a price of $600,000. The term of the contract is one year, after which time the contract expires. Although Kathy isn't looking to sell her home right now, she wouldn't mind selling it for $600,000 in the next year. She reasons that she could use the money and buy a larger, modern home, even if it meant moving inland a few miles. The $10,000 Jim agreed to pay allows her to take the African safari she's always dreamed about. Because she doesn't believe the prices will increase 25 percent in the next year, she thinks this is a good way to pay for her safari.

Jim, on the other hand, is delighted that he now controls a $500,000 parcel of real estate with an option to purchase it for $600,000. He fully anticipates that within a year the price will reach $625,000. At that point, he will be able to buy Kathy's house for $600,000 and immediately turn around and sell it for $625,000. In the end, Jim will realize a $15,000 profit because he paid $10,000 for the option and will receive a net profit of $25,000 from the sale of the house.

Three possible outcomes in this scenario are outlined in the following table.

1. The house value falls to $450,000.
2. The house value increases to $600,000.
3. The house value dramatically increases to $800,000.

	$450,000	**$600,000**	**$800,000**
Jim	Option expires worthless, Jim loses $10,000.	Option expires worthless, Jim loses $10,000.	Jim buys Kathy's home for $600,000, then sells it to a retiring surgeon for $800,000.
Kathy	Kathy keeps her home, uses Jim's money for her safari, but skimps on souvenirs due to falling home values.	Kathy keeps her home, uses Jim's money for her safari, and brings back a souvenir for Jim.	Kathy sells her home to Jim for $600,000 and finds a nice place five miles inland.

Essentially, Kathy was a covered call writer in this example. Using the language of options, Kathy sold a one-year, $600,000-strike, American-style option for a total premium of $10,000. Kathy was then obligated to sell her home within the terms specified in the contract for the life of the contract. This was a "covered" call because Kathy was in possession of the home in the same way that a shareholder who sells a covered call owns the shares that he is obligated to deliver.

Occasionally, traders will sell calls in which they do not own the underlying stock. This is referred to as trading "naked" or "uncovered" and is very risky because the losses are potentially unlimited. If Kathy had sold Jim an uncovered option to buy the ocean cottage and the price soared to $800,000, she would be obligated to buy the cottage on the open market at $800,000 and then turn around and sell it to Jim for $600,000. The result would have been a $190,000 net loss for Kathy ($200,000 loss from the sale of the house offset by a $10,000 gain through the premium received).

Keep in mind that during the length of the contract, Kathy continued to own her cottage and enjoyed the benefits of home ownership. The only difference is that during the term of the contract, she would have been required to sell her home for $600,000 if Jim had decided to exercise his rights under the contract. The same is true for a covered call seller. She continues to own the underlying shares and enjoys dividends and voting privileges, but she cannot sell the position unless she buys back the contract, thereby removing her obligation to sell her shares.

STRATEGY IN ACTION

Covered call writing is typically the first option strategy that novice option traders learn to execute. A type of covered call strategy often used by shorter-term option traders is called the buy-write. The ideal condition for this strategy is when the overall market sentiment is mildly bullish. During this period you want to employ a conservative bullish trade setup. We'll walk through an example with our model trader, Frank.

Frank has been watching a stock that has been moving up slowly and decides the time is right to buy the stock. Although he could use a call option to control the underlying shares, Frank recognizes that the stock is going to pay a dividend of $0.15 per share with an ex-date one week from today. Therefore, he decides to buy shares instead of call options in order to receive the dividend.

Through his analysis, he has observed that the stock has support around $17 and resistance at $18. He looks at the option chain and sees that the near-term $18 call option with 14 days remaining until expiration is trading at a premium of $0.22. He decides to execute a buy-write in which he will buy 1,000 shares of the underlying stock at $17.23 while simultaneously selling (writing) the $18 call option for $0.22 for a net debit of $17.01 per share.

He now owns 1,000 shares of the stock, but he also has an obligation to the buyer of the call option to sell the 1,000 shares for $18 at any time during the next 14 days. Frank recognizes that by selling the call option at the same time he bought the stock, he has placed an upper limit on his trade profit if the stock moves above $18 during the next 14 days. Frank accepts that, because he doesn't believe the stock will be able to make it to $18 in the next 14 days and he has a $0.15 dividend coming as well. In fact, the dividend of $0.15 plus the premium of $0.22 will provide $0.37 per share or $370 on the 1,000-share position in just the first 14 days of owning it. This represents a 2.1 percent return on investment (ROI) ($0.37 divided by $17.23) in just two weeks.

Frank then starts to think about how great it would be if, in fact, the stock did rise above $18 in the next 14 days and his calls were assigned to him. He would then sell all 1,000 shares at the $18 strike price.

If that were to happen, he would receive the $150 dividend, the options premium of $220, and the $770 appreciation recognized from the stock sale ($18 − $17.23 = $0.77 per share or $770) for a total of $1,140. That represents a 6.6 percent ROI in two weeks' time.

Ideally, the stock would go up to $18 and he would sell it and experience the maximum profit a buy-write strategy can deliver. If the stock doesn't rally up but remains at $17.23, he will still receive the dividend and keep the option premium. In 14 days and will have earned 2.1 percent on his money. Upon expiration of the call option, he could then sell another call for the following month. Because the premium from the option contract Frank sells offsets his total cost of buying shares, he has a cost basis of $17.01. The buy-write lowers his cost basis that subsequently helps to lower the overall risk.

Frank will hold his position until expiration, unless the stock trades below the identified support of $17 or he receives an early assignment, at which point he will be obligated to sell his shares. If Frank gets an early assignment, he will keep the premium, sell the stock at $18, and receive the dividend if the assignment was before the ex-dividend date. If the stock does trade below $17, he would close out the entire position by buying back the call option at a lower price and then liquidating the shares to protect his trading capital. Again, he would still receive the dividend if he sold the underlying shares on or after the ex-dividend date.

STRATEGY MANAGEMENT

In the buy-write example above, Frank sells a call that is out-the-money. This allows him to profit from price appreciation if the stock increases in value. If the stock is trading above the $18 strike price at expiration, he will be assigned and will sell the stock at the strike price. His total profit at assignment will have three components: dividend yield, time premium, and price appreciation. Take note that the majority of the profit potential in Frank's buy-write example comes from price appreciation. Price appreciation is the one element of the strategy that is the most uncertain. The time premium decay is certain (time only goes one way), the dividend is almost certain (except for an early assignment), but the price appreciation is anything but certain.

Adjusting the Strike Price

Let's adjust the strike prices on a stock that doesn't pay a dividend to see how selling in-the-money, at-the-money, and out-the-money call options affect our risk, reward, and probability of success. Consider a $50 stock and five strike prices: two in-the-money, one at-the-money, and two out-the-money. An example option chain is shown in the following table.

Current Trading Price = $50 with 32 Days until Expiration			
Strike	**Premium**	**Time Value**	**Intrinsic Value**
$45.00	5.25	0.25	5.00
$47.50	3.25	0.75	2.50
$50.00	1.65	1.65	0
$52.50	0.75	0.75	0
$55.00	0.25	0.25	0

1. In-the-Money

We'll start off by looking at an in-the-money covered call strategy in which we sell a strike price that is lower than the current stock price.

Why would you ever want to obligate yourself to sell a stock at a price lower than the current price? Wouldn't it make sense to sell the strike price higher than the current price? It seems counterintuitive until two factors are explained: premium received and probability of success.

Looking at the example option chain, you can see that the $45 strike is selling for $5.25, the $47.50 strike is selling for $3.25, and the $55 strike is selling for $25. Ask yourself this question: In the remaining 32 days before expiration, is the probability higher that the $50 stock will be above $45, $47.5, $50, $52.50, or $55? Logically, the highest probability is that the stock will be above $45, with each successively higher strike price having a successively lower probability. In fact, the $45 strike is 10 percent lower than the current price, whereas $47.50 is 5 percent lower and $55 is 10 percent above the current price. If you believe there is the potential for some downside volatility, you can adjust for that risk by selecting a strike with a built-in cushion. The cushion comes from the fact that a lower strike price generates a higher premium, which serves to lower your overall cost basis of the stock.

In this example, which option is better if your goal is providing downside cushion? The $45, $47.50, or $50? You have to decide how much downside protection you need, if any. That decision is made easier by using the trend and volatility scoring system to help determine the right strike price for the current situation. A neutral trend with high volatility will require more downside cushion than a bullish trend with lower volatility. Please remember that this strategy is not recommended for bearish trends, regardless of the level of volatility.

If you see that the stock has a significant support level at $48, you would select the $47.50 because support should keep stock above this level. If you are correct and the price remains above $47.50 for 32 days, then upon expiration you will be assigned and required to sell the stock at $47.50. Because you purchased the stock for $50 and received a premium of $3.25, your cost basis is $46.75. If you are then assigned to sell your stock at the $47.50 strike price, you will have a $0.75 profit (1.5 percent).

If your analysis determines that support isn't at $48 but rather it is at $45.50, then you would be wise to sell the $45 strike for $5.25. If in 32 days the stock is trading above $45, you will be assigned and required to sell the shares at $45. Your cost basis is $44.75 and you will sell the stock at the $45 strike price, yielding a $0.25 profit (0.5 percent). This trade has a high probability of success and a downside cushion greater than 10 percent but a rather low return on investment.

2. At-the-Money

Let's now assume a slightly more bullish market sentiment. Suppose the stock has just broken through resistance and created support at $50, which is the price at which you purchased the stock. You could consider selling the at-the-money $50 strike for $1.65. Because time premium is highest with at-the-money strike prices, this is an optimal opportunity to capture the greatest time decay. Assuming the stock trades at or higher than $50 for the next 32 days, you will be assigned and required to sell your shares at $50. Your cost basis is $48.35, leaving you with the premium received as your total profit when you sell the stock at the $50 strike price. This trade returns 3.3 percent, still provides some downside cushion, has an average probability of success, and has no price appreciation potential. However, it does allow you to capture the maximum amount of time premium. Selling in-the-money and at-the-money covered calls is a way to adjust for a neutral to slightly bullish market while adjusting for probability.

3. Out-the-Money

If the trend is moderately to strongly bullish, the strategy shifts from selling in-the-money and at-the-money covered calls to selling out-the-money covered calls. If resistance is at $52 then selling the $52.50 strike would be the logical choice. If the stock rises to trade above $52.50 at expiration, it would trigger an assignment and require you to sell your shares at the $52.50 strike price. Your cost basis of $49.25 ($50 purchase minus $0.75 premium received) would allow you to recognize a return of 6.5 percent. Of the $3.25 total profit on the trade, $0.75 was time premium and $2.50 was price appreciation. In order to receive the full price appreciation, the stock must increase in value from the current price of $50 to at least $52.50, which is a 5 percent move upward.

If there is no overhead resistance, then you might want to sell the $55 strike call that has a lower probability of being assigned. The $55 strike call gives you a $0.25 premium. The stock would need to appreciate 10 percent in 32 days before you would anticipate an assignment. As you can see, this has a lower probability of assignment, very little downside protection, and a realistic expectation that your profit will only be the time premium of $0.25 (0.5 percent) in 32 days.

In the five strike price examples above, we are adjusting the covered call/buy-write strategy to accommodate various market conditions and support and resistance levels while balancing risk, reward, and probability of success.

This strategy is attractive because it allows you to profit in both a sideways move and an upward move. You may also potentially receive dividends while building in some downside protection.

However, it is not designed for a bear market because the downside protection is limited. Although you receive a credit from the sale of the of the call option, it will not make up for the greater loss you'll incur if the share price experiences a significant drop. The most common error we see with covered calls is that traders fail to protect their positions when the market falls, assuming that the credit received from the covered call was sufficient. Too often we see investors with healthy, diversified portfolios sell covered calls on their positions without a risk management strategy. Eventually, the good stocks get called away when their price appreciates and the poorly performing stocks stay in the portfolio as their prices depreciate. When this happens, the investor is often left with small profits from the good performers that are no longer in the portfolio and big paper losses from the poor performers. Poorly performing stocks do not yield good returns using a covered call strategy. It is a fool's logic to think otherwise and assume a covered call strategy will make up for substantial losses over time. We've watched investors write covered calls on Kmart, General Motors, and Lehman Brothers all the way down to zero.

Theta Analysis

The theta analysis on a covered call position is very simple. Because you own outright the shares of the underlying (long the shares), you will not experience any time decay on your long position. The calls you write (short the calls) will experience time decay, but you are on the receiving end of the time decay. Therefore, in an uptrending or sideways trending market the covered call writer has the advantage.

Delta Analysis

Although we usually refer to deltas when discussing option contracts, we can also discuss delta as it relates to the owner of shares and the net delta of an overall position. Because delta is the relationship of the contract to the shares, a share position will have a 1-to-1 relationship to itself. Owning 100 shares will then have a value of 100 deltas and owning 300 shares can be described as 300 deltas.

If a covered call writer has a 1,000-share position and he writes 10 contracts of an out-the-money option with a delta of .25, he would have a net position of 750 deltas (1,000 − 250 = 750). Of course, as the price moves up and down the delta of the short leg will change, but the delta of the long leg will always remain at 1,000. Therefore, a covered call position will always be delta positive. The level of delta positive of the overall position at any point in time depends on the relationship of the underlying to the short leg.

The calls you write (short the calls) will experience time decay, but you are on the receiving end of the time decay. Therefore, in an uptrending or sideways trending market the covered call writer has the advantage.

Roll Out

You roll out a position when you buy back the short and then immediately sell the same strike for another month or longer. You'll receive a premium higher than your cost to buy back the initial short leg. Roll outs are best done early in the week of the option's expiration week. An important point to remember: If you are assigned at or before expiration, you will have realized the maximum profit of the strategy. Early assignment simply gives you the added benefit of receiving your maximum profit early. Roll out strategies are defensive in nature. Instead of defending the position, we prefer to take the assignment and move on to the next trade.

Roll Up

A roll up is almost identical to a roll out except that you sell a higher strike price rather than a longer expiration. This is usually done when the stock price has moved up enough so that the short leg is now in-the-money. A roll up helps you capture more of the underlying price movement.

For example, if an owner of a stock trading at $30 sells the $33 strike price with three weeks to expiration, he may receive a $1 premium. Suppose there are four days remaining until expiration, the stock is trading at $33.50, and his option is trading at $0.75. He has a few choices at this point.

- Do nothing and take the chance that the stock will stay above $33. This will determine if he gets assigned or not.
- Roll out by selling the next month's $33 strike price for $1.25 and capture some additional time premium but no further price appreciation.
- Roll up and roll out in order to capture more time premium and the potential for further price appreciation. The next month's $35 strike is bid at $1.00. He can enter an order to buy back this month's $33 strike for $0.75 and immediately sell next month's $35 strike for $1.00 for a net credit of $0.25. Although he only captured $0.25 of time premium, he is still theta positive and has increased his price appreciation potential from $33 to $35. Rolling up and rolling out is a strategic way to continue to take advantage of time decay while adjusting a bullish position for continued upside price appreciation.

Calculations

Max profit	Maximum profit should be calculated for the time the covered call is in place. Therefore, the calculation is the difference between the strike price of the call and the purchase price of the shares plus the premium received less fees.
Max loss	Purchase price of the shares minus the premium received plus fees.
Break even	Purchase price of the shares plus premium received minus fees.
Capital required	Total purchase of the shares less the total premium received plus fees.

STRATEGY APPLICATION

The covered call is best suited for neutral to slightly bullish positions. The trend score should be zero or positive. This strategy will apply to strong bullish positions with trend scores approaching +10. However, the likelihood of being assigned increases as the bullishness of the trend increases. Covered calls may be applied to any level of volatility, recognizing that higher volatility risk may be cushioned with the in-the-money variation of the strategy (see Figure 5.1).

Market Score Trade

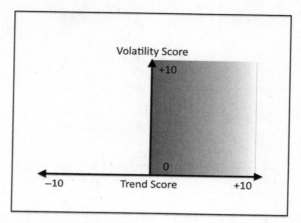

FIGURE 5.1 Market Score Application

Channels

A channel is a price pattern where you observe prices bouncing between highs and lows with the peaks running fairly parallel to the valleys. The price may be trending upward, as in Figure 5.2, or simply running sideways, but the highs can be connected by a trend line and the lows can be connected by another, parallel line. The approach for drawing the trend lines is to look for is a best-fit line that connects as many highs as possible. A second best-fit line is then drawn connecting the lows. The upper and lower channel lines should run approximately parallel to each other. Taken together, the upper and lower trend lines create the channel lines. The upper channel line is considered resistance and the lower line is support.

Channeling goes by various names, including oscillating, channeling, sideways, and consolidating. Essentially, a channel represents a sort of equilibrium between buyers and sellers. The distance that buyers are able to move the price to reach the upper resistance line is approximately the same distance that the sellers move the price when it retreats to support. Eventually, the market dynamics change and the channel is broken. Sometimes a new channel with a new trend forms. In any event, the channel serves as a useful price guide so long as it remains intact. Once you've identified a channel, it is your responsibility to know when the channel is no longer valid. That's a simple matter of following the price movement relative to the channel lines on your chart.

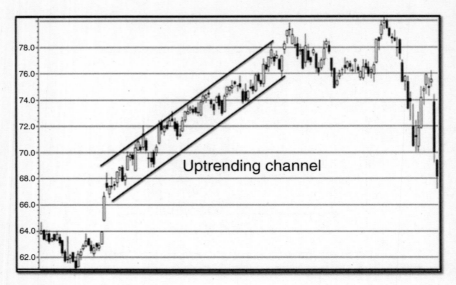

FIGURE 5.2 Channeling Price

For the covered call trader, the key point is that there is not a strong bullish directional move. If the channel occurs without any underlying trend—that is, the price moves sideways without a change in the highs or lows—many traders will look for a breakout from the channel before taking on a new position. For the covered call strategy, you expect the price to either stay within the channel or move slightly higher. It's not bad if the stock breaks out and trades above channel resistance. If the price drops below the lower channel support line, you should exit your entire position by closing the short call option and selling the stock.

If you're selling a call option for an underlying position that is in a price channel, you can use the channel as a guide for which strike to sell. If you want a low probability of getting assigned and are willing to accept a lower premium in return, then you should write a call with a strike at or slightly above the channel resistance. If you sell a call with a strike between the channel lines, then you can monitor the trading cycle as expiration approaches. If necessary, roll the position or simply accept assignment if the stock trades above your strike.

Basing Channels

A variation of the channel discussed previously is the basing channel. Channels may occur for numerous reasons, but a common scenario is

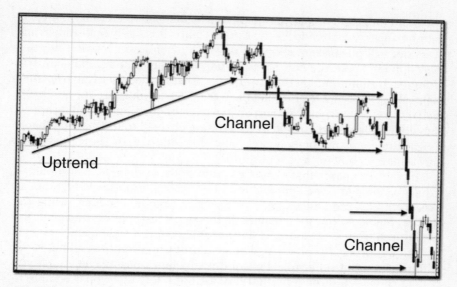

FIGURE 5.3 Basing Channel

when prices move sideways following a trend. Essentially, a base shows you that the market is taking a breather.

For example, consider the price pattern shown in Figure 5.3. You'll see that the stock initially moved higher during the uptrend noted on the left side of the chart. Toward the middle of the chart, the price broke down below the channel support. Following the breakdown, the price moved sideways within a channel for a short time. You can then see how the price clearly broke the sideways channel again and fell sharply, as evidenced by the long black (red) candles. Eventually, the downtrend ran out of steam and the price formed a new channel at the lower right corner of the chart. Both of the channels depicted on this chart are basing channels that follow pullbacks in the price. They represent the sellers taking a break. You can also see this pattern develop in uptrends. Buyers may push the price sharply higher and then take a break before resuming the uptrend. During the break, the sellers are not strong enough to reverse the trend and push the price lower but the buyers aren't taking it higher, either. The result is a sideways channel, showing the temporary balance between buyers and sellers.

Basing channels can be attractive market conditions for covered call traders because these channels may sometimes last for months or years. This is especially true if there has been a significant pullback following an extended uptrend. Suppose a stock has been in a steady uptrend for several years and then the company announces a significant deleterious change in their business, which reduces their profitability. It is likely that traders and investors will push the stock price down to much lower levels, reflecting their opinion about the new stock value. Once the price has fallen, it will often reach equilibrium at the lower price. That is, the sellers have finished their selling and the buyers won't push the price any higher. The stock will then trade within a relatively narrow range, neither rising nor falling appreciably. This shows up on a chart as a basing channel following a pullback. Unless the company fundamentals suddenly improve, the new price level may remain steady for a year or more.

If you buy a stock that's trading within a basing channel, you shouldn't expect significant price appreciation in the short term. However, you can execute a covered call strategy to generate premium income while the stock remains within the channel. If the stock also pays a dividend, the total return from a stock in a basing channel could be significant.

It's important to note that you should not hold on to a falling stock with the intent of selling calls when it finally hits a basing channel. If you bought the stock during the uptrend, it's not likely that you'll be able to recover your loss in equity through covered call premium collection. If you own a stock and it breaks support and falls, the best strategy is to sell your stock and unwind any associated options. This strategy is recommended for traders who buy the stock once the basing channel has begun and then sell the covered calls to collect premiums within the channel.

CHAPTER 6

Long Calls

B uying calls (long calls) is one of the most common option strategies utilized by retail traders. There are two key reasons why this strategy is so popular: (1) unlimited profit potential and (2) smaller capital at risk. Unfortunately, it is also the strategy that we see most often misused by traders. Traders frequently buy call options as a way to supersize their rewards and minimize risk while throwing the probability of profit out the window.

A long call can serve as a stock replacement strategy or as a way to speculate on the upside movement of a stock, exchange-traded fund (ETF), or index. Understanding a call option and the correct use of this leveraged product is the first step in setting the foundation for more advanced strategies with higher probabilities of success discussed in other chapters. Fortunately, most traders can readily grasp the concepts behind long calls because they are intuitively very similar to the traditional long stock trade.

GETTING TO KNOW THE STRATEGY

In order to explain the concept in practical, everyday terms, let's use an example that hits close to home: the price of gas. Imagine for a moment a local gas station was selling fuel coupons for $25. The coupon allows the bearer to purchase 100 gallons of unleaded fuel at a price that is locked in to the market price at the time the coupon was purchased. The coupon expires on December 31. On the day you decided to purchase a coupon, the price of a gallon of unleaded fuel was $3.00 and it was exactly six months before expiration. For your $25 payment, you received the right to purchase 100 gallons of unleaded fuel at any time over the next six months for $3.00 per gallon.

Let's convert the terms of this fuel coupon into the language of options. The coupon is a call option that represents the right to buy a specific asset at a defined price for a defined amount of time. The terms of this right are specified in a contract. In this case, the contract represents 100 gallons of unleaded gasoline as the deliverable. As the holder of the fuel coupon, you can exercise your right to the deliverables of that contract any time you choose. The price at which the 100 gallons of gasoline can be purchased is called the strike price. Your coupon has a strike price of $3.00, giving you the right to make your purchase at a cost of $3.00 per gallon. The expiration date is December 31, six months from the date of purchase. The six months remaining until expiration represents the life of the contract. Finally, the $25 you paid for the coupon is called the premium. With the coupon in hand, you have the right to buy but you are not obligated to buy any gas at all. You may choose not to use the coupon. The seller of the coupon, on the other hand, has an obligation to meet. By selling the coupon, he has obligated himself to sell 100 gallons of gas to the bearer of the coupon at $3.00 per gallon at any time up until December 31. In exchange for this obligation, the seller received $25. At the time you purchased the coupon, unleaded fuel was $3.00 per gallon and the coupon's strike price was also $3.00, making this an at-the-money (ATM) coupon. Because you have the right to buy at $3.00 and the current market price is also $3.00, this coupon has no intrinsic or "true" value. The $25 you paid for the coupon is the price you were willing to pay for a future value—the possibility that gas prices would rise before expiration. This is referred to as time value and is represented in option language by the Greek theta.

Unlike most coupons, which are free, your fuel coupon cost money. The coupon is really a small investment. Like any investment, you need to know at what point you will make money, lose money, or break even. We'll start with the break-even point. The break-even price for this coupon is when the price of unleaded reaches $3.25 per gallon. It's simply the strike price of the coupon ($3.00 per gallon) plus the premium per gallon ($25/100 gallons = $0.25 per gallon). Because you paid $25 for the coupon, your coupon purchase would save you money if gas exceeds $3.25 per gallon. As long as gas prices stay below $3.25, you simply hold on to your coupon and just pay the price at the pump. There is little reason to exercise your right to buy gas at $3.00 as long as there is still time left in the coupon. The gas station owner will not expect to see anyone redeeming (exercising) his or her coupon (call option) until the price of unleaded exceeds $3.25 (break-even).

If fuel prices increase and the price of a gallon exceeds $3.25, the gas station owner should expect to be required to fulfill (be assigned) his obligation to sell 100 gallons at $3.00. He must meet his obligation by selling fuel at $3.00 per gallon, even if that same fuel costs him $2.50, $3.00, $4.00, or whatever the price of a gallon may be at the time the coupon is redeemed. As the expiration date draws near, he should expect to see coupons redeemed if unleaded is at $3.01 or higher. This is because the holders of the coupons will salvage any value left in the coupon, even if it only saves the holder a few cents per gallon, prior to the coupon's expiration. If they don't use the coupon by expiration then their $25 will be a total loss when the coupon expires.

Let's look at a few examples as the coupon expiration approaches. Imagine you have the fuel coupon in your car and gas prices have fallen. The current price of a gallon of unleaded is $2.85 and the coupon is valid for just one more day. Is there any reason to drive into town and present the coupon to the gas station attendant and demand that he deliver your 100 gallons to you at $3.00 when the price at the pump is $2.85? Of course, the answer is no. Even though you have the right, there is no financial benefit to exercising your right, so you choose to not use the coupon. The fuel coupon expires worthless tomorrow and you will lose $25.

Let's change this up just a bit and say unleaded is selling for $3.15 and today is the last day to redeem your coupon. If you do nothing, then your coupon will expire tomorrow and your $25 will be a total loss. In order to salvage some of the intrinsic value of the coupon, you decide to drive your car loaded with several large gas cans down to the station to get your 100 gallons of unleaded at $3.00. You present your coupon to the gas station attendant and tell him you want to redeem your coupon. He says to you, "The owner told me to buy back the coupons for what they are worth at today's prices. Do you want the 100 gallons at $3.00 or would you rather just have $15 cash for your coupon?" Because you really didn't need the gas, you see the logic in taking the $15. You decide to sell the coupon to close out the deal. By taking the $15 intrinsic value for the fuel coupon, you no longer have a right and the gas station owner no longer has an obligation. Tomorrow the coupon will reach expiration unexercised. Unexercised does not mean unprofitable. You, the coupon buyer, realized a $10 loss because you bought it for $25 and sold it for $15. If you hadn't driven to the station to exercise your right, then you never would have salvaged the $15. The seller of the coupon realized a $10 gain because he sold the coupon to you for $25 and bought it back for $15.

Let's look at what happens if the price of unleaded were to increase to $4.50 per gallon. At that price, the coupon becomes far more valuable. Suppose it is December 30, the coupon expires tomorrow, and unleaded is selling for $4.50 per gallon. The market cost of 100 gallons is $450. Because the coupon represents the right to buy 100 gallons at $3.00 per gallon, you could exercise the full contract for a cost of $300. The intrinsic value of the coupon is the difference between the current price $4.50 minus the strike price $3.00. The coupon is in-the-money by $1.50 per gallon. The coupon is valid for 100 gallons, so the intrinsic value is now $150.

Imagine you are planning a fishing trip in a few weeks and you've read that gasoline prices are expected to continue to rise. Your coupon has just one day left prior to expiring, so you drive your RV and boat down to the station to exercise your coupon. This time when you hand the attendant the coupon and tell him you want to exercise your right and fill your tanks up he offers you the $150 intrinsic value of the coupon. You have the choice to either take delivery of 100 gallons or take the money. Because you believe the price is going to continue to increase and you know you have the upcoming fishing trip a few weeks away, you turn down the offer and instead exercise your right to purchase 100 gallons at $3.00 per gallon. The attendant reduces the price on your pump from $4.50 to $3.00 and you fill up, thinking how smart you were six months ago to have purchased the $25 fuel coupon. That $25 purchase saved $150, yielding a net savings of $125.

We've just discussed three examples of how an option may, upon reaching expiration, (1) expire worthless, (2) be sold back at intrinsic value, or (3) be exercised, depending on the market price and objective of the call buyer. The options market is highly liquid, meaning that the holder does not need to exercise the contract to realize a profit. He can simply sell it in the open market for the intrinsic value. If the fuel coupon market were as liquid, the buyer of the coupon could buy and sell fuel coupons at any time, based on the current price of unleaded fuel and where he anticipates the price will move.

Suppose that during the six months the coupon was valid, the price of unleaded fluctuated dramatically. At one time during this period, it went as high as $5.00 and later as low as $1.00. Because the coupon could be redeemed at any time during this period, the intrinsic value would have fluctuated with the price of unleaded. When unleaded was at $5.00, the coupon would have been worth at least $200 ($2.00 per gallon) on the fictitious Fuel Coupon Exchange.

Suppose fuel prices went to $1.00 in October. The Fuel Coupon Exchange may have had a listed price of $8 for the coupon. How would a coupon that had no intrinsic value be worth anything at all? The answer is that time provides extrinsic (nontangible) value. Although the $3.00 coupon was far out-of-the-money in October, there were still two months left before the coupon expired. The $8 represents the remaining value of the time before the coupon expires, or extrinsic value.

STRATEGY IN ACTION

Now that the parallels have been drawn from the fuel coupon to a call option, let's look at the strategy of buying a call on a bullish stock or ETF. Figure 6.1 is a chart of the Gold ETF (GLD). This ETF attempts to mirror the movement of gold, with each share representing approximately .1 ounce of gold. Based on economic uncertainty and global recession, gold prices had been fluctuating dramatically and GLD was $92.40. The 50-day simple moving average (thin line) was above the 200-day simple moving average (thick line) and the price of the ETF was above both moving averages.

We will compare how a stock trader versus an option trader would analyze a potential short-term trade of GLD. Based on a review of recent price behavior, support appears to be around $86 and resistance around $98. A stock trader who wants to purchase 100 shares of GLD would need to have $9,240 plus commissions to execute this order. Based on the support at $86, a trader might choose to protect his position with a stop order just below $86; possibly $85.40. With a stop order at $85.40, the trader would risk $7.00 per share or $700 for a 100-share position. His trade is based on his expectation of GLD continuing to move toward the resistance level of $98. If he is correct and GLD reaches $98, he will have a profit of just over $500. This profit represents a return on his investment (ROI) of 5.4 percent.

FIGURE 6.1 Price Chart of GLD

Let's consider an option trader who has done the same analysis on GLD and has come to the same conclusions about support and resistance levels. He recognizes that with a price per share $92.40, 100 shares would place nearly $10,000 at risk. He also notices that GLD has a history of gapping at the open and that makes him nervous about using a stop order for protection. Further, he observes that GLD is trading right in the middle of support and resistance. This makes the risk-reward ratio unattractive to a buyer of the GLD shares, but he believes he can improve the ratio, lower his risk, and conserve capital by purchasing a call option.

The following option chain displays five months of call options that are ATM or close to ATM, including the delta and theta for each contract.

Month	Strike	Bid	Ask	Delta	Theta
Mar	$92	2.70	2.80	.543	−.073
Apr	$92	4.80	5.00	.540	−.053
May	$92	6.40	6.70	.542	−.037
Jun	$92	8.00	8.30	.544	−.029
Sep	$92	11.10	11.50	.552	−.020

The delta represents the theoretical price movement of the option relative to the underlying or, in this case, GLD. Note that the delta for each month is roughly the same, at approximately .54 to .55. In simple terms, when GLD moves up $1.00, each of these options should move up approximately $0.54. The options will also move down about $0.54 for every $1.00 GLD drops.

These values, like all the option Greeks, will change frequently. Greeks help with a side-by-side comparison of option characteristics. Theta is a good example of this. Note that the theta for the March $92 strike price is −.073, −.053 for the April $92 strike, and −.037 for May (about half the theta of March). Theta is the cost per share per day for the contract. It is the loss of time value and helps the option trader determine how much time decay to expect. A buyer of a March $92 call option should expect the total value of his contract to decline $7.30 each day, assuming the price and all other variables in the stock market remain constant. A buyer of a May $92 call option would expect his total contract value to decline at a rate of $3.70 per day. Time decay increases as an option approaches its expiration date.

Notice that the ask price for the March $92 call is $2.80 whereas the same contract for May is $6.70. The deltas are almost the same but the thetas are quite different. The key difference is the length of the contracts, with just 14 calendar days remaining in the March contract and 70 days remaining in the May contract. An option trader must weigh the costs and benefits of these variables when deciding which and how many contracts to trade.

One of the most common mistakes that a novice trader makes is to decide how much money he is willing to lose and then buy as many option contracts as he can afford. This usually means he is buying an option that has a high theta and low delta, because the cheapest options are those with the lowest time and intrinsic value. In the previous example, the entry price for the GLD trade was $92.40 and the stop was set at $85.40. If the trade stopped out, the loss would be $700 based on a 100-share position size. Referring to the following option chain, he might decide to buy $700 of the March $96 strike for $130 per contract, allowing him to buy five contracts. The delta on the March $96 is .269 and theta is −.060 or $6.00 per day per contract.

Month	Strike	Bid	Ask	Delta	Theta
Mar	$96	1.20	1.30	.269	−.060

Let's compare the novice trader's choice with the GLD strategy used by a more experienced, conservative option trader. Although the experienced trader thinks GLD could achieve a price of $98 per share, she believes it might take a few weeks. She also believes $98 could be the high point, but $94 is a more accurate near-term possibility. Because of this, she is looking to keep her delta high for the near-term moves and theta low for the lower cost of a longer-term position hold. As a result of these factors, she decides to buy one contract of the May $92 call option for $670 plus commissions. This contract has a .652 delta and a −.037 theta, or just $3.70 per day to hold the contract. Now we can compare the strategy results of the share owner, the novice option trader, and the experienced option trader for the three following scenarios (fees excluded for illustration).

Scenario 1: One Day before March Expiration, GLD Closes at $96				
Trade	Cost	Current Value per Share	Profit/ Loss	Profit/ Loss (%)
100 shs @ $92.40	$9,240	$96	$360	3.9%
5 Mar $96 calls	$650	$0.03	($635)	(98%)
1 May $92 call	$670	$8.29	$159	24%

Scenario 2: One Day before March Expiration, GLD Closes at $86				
Trade	Cost	Current Value per Share	Profit/ Loss	Profit/ Loss (%)
100 shs @ $92.40	$9,240	$86	($640)	(6.9%)
5 Mar $96 calls	$650	$0.01	($645)	(99%)
1 May $92 call	$670	$3.24	($346)	(52%)

Scenario 3 is based on GLD closing at $86 at the March expiration and subsequently rallying to $100 for the May expiration.

Scenario 3: One Day before May Expiration, GLD Closes at $100				
Trade	Cost	Current Value per Share	Profit/ Loss	Profit/ Loss (%)
100 shs @ $92.40	$9,240	$100	$760	8.2%
5 Mar $96 calls	$650	N/A (expired)	($650)	(100%)
1 May $92 call	$670	$8.00	$130	19%

By comparing the three scenarios side-by-side, it's easy to see that each one has advantages and disadvantages. The share buyer has a much larger capital requirement and the concern about a gap down below his stop price. The advantages are that he has unlimited time, enjoys point-for-point movement, and has the possibility of earning dividends. The out-the-money March call buyer has the advantage of controlling 500 shares for a smaller sum, but the trade-off is a very short amount of time for the price to move up beyond the strike price. This is a do-or-die type of trade and highlights the contrast between risk and reward. This trade has high risk and the potential for high reward. The at-the-money May call buyer's strategy is a compromise between the two. Her single at-the-money call option contract controls the same number of shares as the shares buyer but with a smaller capital outlay.

Although the experienced trader does not have point-for-point movement, her starting delta of .542 will improve as the position moves in-the-money and will decrease as it moves out-the-money. This means she will make money faster when GLD goes up and will lose money slower when GLD goes down. This is because delta increases when an option moves in-the-money and decreases when it moves out-the-money. The change in delta is represented by the Greek gamma. Gamma represents the theoretical change in delta for each point the underlying moves higher or lower.

For example, consider a call option with a delta of .5 and a gamma of .03 when an ETF is trading at $122. If the price increases to $123, we expect the delta to change to .53. If the price declines to $121, the delta should change to .47. Gamma is highest in at-the-money options and increases as time decreases. These concepts are illustrated in Scenario 2 in the previous option chain. The share position lost $640 (6.9%) and the 5 March $96 calls position lost $645, or 99 percent of its value. However, the 1 May $92 call position is down just over 50 percent from its opening value, with $324 remaining.

Although each of the three strategies has advantages, the nature of trading involves risk, and the ability to manage and mitigate risk is often the distinguishing characteristic of a successful trader. The conservative option trade affords the trader more control of risk as compared to the share purchase, even though the profit potential is limited by time. Some investors believe unlimited time is the cure for an investment gone wrong and rely on it to overcome bad decisions and the absence of an exit strategy. For the options buyer, time works against him and forces action. Buying a call option is a balancing act between time, control, risk, reward, and probability.

In the previous example, we looked at using calls as a stock substitution strategy. In this next example, let's look at how our model trader, Frank, utilizes calls to speculate. Obviously, the word speculation should indicate that Frank is going to utilize a strategy that depends on a combination of luck and skill. Most investors take a speculative trade from time to time and often treat these trades as binary; either they go big or go broke. Although the trade might rely on Frank's luck for success, there is still a correct way to speculate with call options.

Frank is willing to risk 1 percent of his $100,000 account, so he decides to take a $1,000 option position as a speculative trade. Assume Frank's stock has increased in value from $72 to $87 over the past 12 months with a consistent growth rate averaging around $1.25 per month. However, in the past 30 days the stock's rate of growth has accelerated with a $2.50 move confirmed by increasing volume. Frank believes this stock is being accumulated by large institutions in anticipation of a product announcement that is expected in the next few weeks. He feels the stock has more upside potential, but he's nervous about buying at such a high level. He's also hesitant to risk significant capital. He'd like to take an option position that maximizes upside potential and minimizes the downside risk.

Because this trade is more speculative, he decides to buy an out-the-money call and focus on the $90 strike price. By purchasing an out-the-money option, Frank is able to buy more contracts than if he bought an in-the-money option that had some intrinsic value.

Month	Strike	Bid	Ask	Days Remaining
Sep	$90	0.5	0.75	26
Oct	$90	1.10	1.25	61
Jan	$90	2.05	2.25	151

Which one should Frank buy? This is a question many new option traders struggle with. Unfortunately, new traders often make the wrong decision and purchase the September $90 strike for $0.75. To explain why this is a mistake, even when speculating, we go back to the price history. In the past year, the stock has shown a consistent rate of price appreciation of about $1.25 per month, with a recent increase in that rate of growth. The assumption is that the upward trend will continue at a rate of about $1.25 per month.

Because the September $90 strike price is the cheapest, Frank could buy 13 contracts for a total investment of $975. The break-even on this position is the strike price plus the premium or $90.75. At the 12-month growth rate of $1.25 per month, the analysis indicates that price should only reach $88.25 in the next 26 days. Even at the short-term rate of price appreciation ($2.50 per month), the price will only reach $89.50. Should Frank go with the shorter-term rate of growth or the longer-term rate of growth when deciding which option to purchase? It will be to his advantage to base his analysis off the slower rate of growth, to increase his probability of success even in a speculative position. If Frank were to buy the short-term out-the-money option, the stock would have to further accelerate the rate of price appreciation in order to reach the break-even point. This option contract has a very low probability of success. In order to simply break even, the stock would have to increase from $87 to $90.75 (a $3.75 jump) over the remaining 26 days. This growth rate exceeds both the short-term and long-term growth rates and would represent a tripling of the 12-month rate of price appreciation observed on the price chart.

This short-term position is also very expensive as a result of the recent volatility. Volatility is represented by the Greek vega. Vega is the measurement of the value of volatility in an option's price. Because the recent price move represented a significant increase over the historical price movement, the option premium increased to account for higher volatility. The desire to control as many shares as possible by maximizing the number of contracts $1,000 could purchase too often leads the trader into a high-risk, low-probability trade.

Let's assume that Frank recognizes the September $90 option would be a mistake and considers buying an in-the-money option instead. He looks at the September $85 strike price and sees that it is selling at $3.25. He calculates his break-even price to be $88.25 and his trend analysis projects the price to be $88.25 at expiration. He is not interested in a trade that puts him right at break-even. Taking into account the accelerated trend, he can expect the stock to reach $89.50 at expiration, but that is based on a short-term jump in the longer trend. He reasons that the accelerated trend will likely not continue for another month.

It's clear to Frank that he is going to need to purchase an option with more time. He recognizes that by buying a longer expiration, he not only gets more time at a lower per-day cost (low theta), but he also gives the stock more time to reach the break-even point. He considers the October $90 strike that is two months from expiration and priced at $1.25. Break-even for the October $90 is $91.25. The measured move analysis places the stock in two months at $89.50. This is still shy of the break-even point.

Recognizing that the earlier month expirations would yield a low probability of success, Frank focuses his analysis on the January $90 strike with 151 days trading at $2.25. The break-even point is $92.25. Based on five months of projected growth, Frank determines that the stock should reach $93.25. Frank decides to take this trade and is able to buy four contracts at $2.25. Based on his analysis and the call options Frank purchased, the position should be profitable as long as the stock continues on the slow uptrend it has been on for the past 12 months.

STRATEGY MANAGEMENT

Let's look at what would happen if the stock did indeed move up the first month but then started to slip back. One month into the position, the stock increased as expected, up $1.25 to $88.25. One day, Frank observed a shooting star pattern with the stock closing at $88.50. The next day the stock dropped $0.50 on increased volume, closing at $88.00. That night he decided to close out his option position to protect his remaining equity. The position was still out-the-money and well away from the break-even point. It's important to remember there was another reason Frank purchased the January expiration instead of the September or October expiration: to avoid excessive time decay if the position didn't go as planned. Because the longer-term option contracts have lower time decay, Frank's position has decayed at a much slower rate than if he had purchased the shorter-term options. As a result, Frank was able to liquidate the four contracts at $2.34, making just a few dollars.

When Frank opened the trade, theta on the call was −.010, so his four-contract position was losing time value at a rate of approximately $4 per day. The position lost just over $120 for the 30-day period. If he had bought the October option, he would have lost about $8 per day or $240 for the period. Assuming that delta for the January option was .391 and the price increased from $87 to $88.00, the price of the option increased by $39 per contract or $156 for the position. Although the October and January calls had similar deltas, the difference in theta values meant the difference between closing out a trade with a small profit versus a loss.

We'll summarize the differences between a stock replacement strategy and a speculative strategy. When using calls as a stock replacement strategy, the investor wants to keep delta high and theta low. The only way to accomplish this is to buy in-the-money options with deltas greater than .70 and at least three months of time remaining. A speculative call buyer seeking to maximize control over shares needs to purchase enough time to allow the underlying to exceed the break-even point regardless of the delta. It's fine to buy an out-the-money call option if the time remaining until expiration is sufficient to allow the share price to exceed the break-even point. A speculative call buyer would have a position with low theta and low delta. He would rely on a price movement and an increase in delta to recognize profits. If the underlying begins to move against the trader, the remaining time value may be sold to salvage some of the position value.

Calculations

Max profit	Unlimited
Max loss	Premium paid for calls plus fees
Break-even	Option strike price plus premium paid plus fees
Capital required	Cost of the contracts plus fees

LEAPS

Long-term equity anticipation securities (LEAPS) are nothing more than standard calls and puts with one exception: Their expiration dates are up to 2.5 years in the future. Due to these attributes, LEAPS can serve as long-term insurance on investments or more commonly as a stock replacement vehicle for buy-and-hold investors.

Advantages

- Using LEAPS requires less capital to control a stock or ETF position for an extended period, allowing smaller accounts to control positions that otherwise exceed the available capital.
- Because an investor can use existing capital to control a position, he does not need to borrow funds from his broker (a margin loan) and pay interest. On the other hand, time decay should be looked at as a form of interest payment.
- Most brokers do not require that a buyer of either a LEAPS call or put contract have the funds to exercise the call nor the shares to deliver on a put contract.
- Because purchasing a LEAPS contract involves a significant amount of time, the theta is typically very low.
- Deep in-the-money LEAPS contracts closely mirror the movement of the underlying instrument, so investors can use LEAPS for both bull and bear trends in the market.
- LEAPS may be useful in IRA accounts that have annual contribution limits. The contribution limits typically result in lower account balances for younger investors. This advantage also holds true for accounts for minors, such as Coverdell educational savings accounts (ESAs) and custodial accounts.
- LEAPS can be used for complex multileg strategies like diagonal and calendar spreads, in which a short-term contract is sold to offset the costs of a long-term LEAPS contract.

Disadvantages

- Even though LEAPS can be active for up to 30 months, they are still a decaying asset with a finite amount of time and will ultimately expire. This will require the LEAPS investor to either exercise or liquidate the position.
- Like all option contracts, LEAPS represent control but not ownership. An owner of a LEAPS call option on a dividend-paying stock will not receive any dividends due a shareholder.
- LEAPS are thinly traded instruments and often have large spreads between the bid and ask, making transactions expensive to reverse.

LEAPS as a Stock Replacement Strategy

A couple with investment experience wants to save for their newborn daughter's future education expenses, so they open a Coverdell ESA. In January they fund the account with $2,000 for the previous year and $2,000 for the current year. With an account balance of $4,000, they begin to look at their choices. They believe the greatest growth opportunities are in the technology stocks that make up the Nasdaq 100 index. They consider the Nasdaq 100 tracking ETF (QQQ) that was trading around $50.

Investing the entire $4,000 in QQQ would only allow them to buy 80 shares. Instead of purchasing shares, they decide to buy LEAPS as a way to leverage the $4,000. As they review the option chain, they take note of the value of theta, delta, and the time premium versus intrinsic value. Based on their analysis, they decide to buy a LEAPS call option with a $45 strike that has a delta of 0.75. Like most LEAPS, the spread between the bid and ask is large: in this case, $0.80. They believe they will be able to split the spread and execute an order at the midpoint between the bid and ask at $10.00.

Because their objective is to control as many shares of QQQ as possible, it would be tempting to use the $4,000 to buy as many contracts as possible. As an example, assume they could buy 40 contracts of the $70 strike for $1.00. With a strike that is $20 out-of-the-money, this option would be very cheap as compared to the $45 strike that has $5 of intrinsic value. Although the account would control 4,000 shares, or $200,000 worth, of QQQ for 533 days, this trade is highly speculative with a very low probability of success. After all, QQQ would need to be trading at $71.00, or 42 percent higher, upon expiration to be profitable.

When choosing between the $45 strike or the $70 strike, neither strategy is right or wrong, per se. Baseball is an appropriate analogy for these two trades. There's a time to swing for the fences to win the game and a time to bunt or look for a walk. Because this is a new account, it may be best to get a few singles and walks to build up momentum. Once the account has grown, it may be fine to allocate some of the profits toward the home-run swing. It's the slow and deliberate approach to trading options that will, over time, provide the educated and experienced trader with consistent profits in all market conditions.

Six Steps to Trading LEAPS as a Stock Replacement Strategy

Managing a LEAPS trade is very similar to managing a long stock trade. As the LEAPS contract gets closer to expiration, though, the LEAPS will act more like a traditional option because theta, or time decay, begins to accelerate.

1. Choose your stock or ETF based on your selection criteria.
2. Analyze a long-term (5-year weekly, for example) chart to determine key support and resistance prices.

3. Choose a LEAPS contract with a delta of 0.7 or higher when the stock or ETF is trading close to support.

4. Use conditional orders to exit your position or alert you if the underlying breaks below key support.

5. Monitor the position in the same manner as a Long Stock trade. If the trade becomes profitable, consider trailing your conditional stop higher.

6. Six to eight weeks prior to expiration, consider closing the position because the time decay will start to accelerate. If the analysis on the underlying indicates a continuation of trend, consider using some of the funds to purchase another LEAPS position.

STRATEGY APPLICATION

The long call is best suited for bullish positions. The trend score should be positive and the higher the score, the better. This strategy is best applied to strong bullish positions with trend scores approaching +10. Long calls may be applied to any level of volatility, although higher volatility scores will likely translate into higher premiums paid for the contract (see Figure 6.2).

Market Score Trade

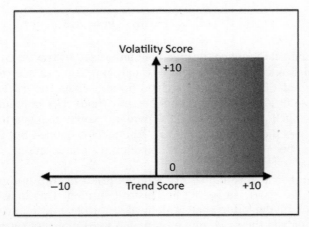

FIGURE 6.2 Market Score Application

Fibonacci Retracement

The objective of using Fibonacci retracement lines is to identify levels of support when a stock pulls back following a rally or, alternately, to identify levels of resistance when a stock rallies following a drop. Fibonacci retracement lines are based on the Fibonacci number sequence. The sequence is as follows:

1, 2, 3, 5, 8, 13, 21, 34, 55, 89, . . .

You'll observe that each number is the sum of the previous two numbers. The quotient of very two successive numbers in the sequence approaches the golden ratio. As the sequence gets higher, the ratio is more closely followed. The golden ratio is 1.618 and is observed as follows:

$$3 \div 2 = 1.5$$
$$5 \div 3 = 1.67$$
$$8 \div 5 = 1.6$$
$$13 \div 8 = 1.625$$
$$21 \div 13 = 1.615$$
$$34 \div 21 = 1.619$$
$$55 \div 34 = 1.618$$
$$89 \div 55 = 1.618$$

An interesting characteristic of the golden ratio is that its inverse is equal to the golden ratio minus one. This is shown as

$$(1 \div 1.618) = (1.618 - 1) = .618$$

The standard Fibonacci retracement lines used by traders are 23.6 percent, 38.2 percent, 50 percent and 61.8 percent. You can see from the introduction that 61.8 percent is derived directly from the golden ratio of .618. One hundred percent less 61.8 percent yields 38.2 percent, and 61.8 percent less 38.2 percent yields 23.6 percent. You'll also see that 50 percent is not a standard number in the Fibonacci sequence but it is generally included because 50 percent is considered a common retracement for stock prices.

The chart in Figure 6.3 shows a stock in an overall uptrend. At the left side of the chart, an up leg has been identified. This is a short-term move higher in the price that is defined by a clear low and high. The leg in the chart is the price move on which the Fibonacci retracement is based. Because this trend is higher, the top of the trend is considered the zero percent retracement level and the starting point is the 100 percent

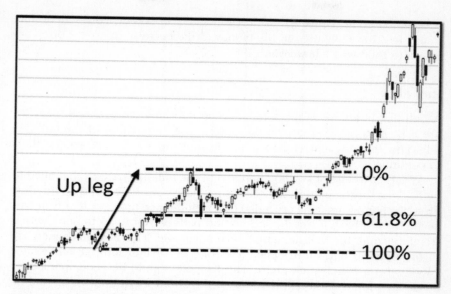

FIGURE 6.3 Fibonacci Retracement Setup

retracement. To think of it another way, if the price pulls back all the way to the start of the trend, it has retraced the entire distance of the leg.

In order to not clutter the illustration, the only Fibonacci line shown in the example is the 61.8 percent retracement. It should be easy to see in the chart that at the 61.8 percent line, the price has pulled back a little more than halfway from the top to the starting point. Following the start of the pullback from the initial leg up, the price retraced to the 61.8 percent line three separate times. Each time it reached that retracement level it found support and rallied higher. As expected, the Fibonacci retracement held as support following a rally in price. Furthermore, notice how the price moved up to approach the 0 percent level and found resistance.

The trade setup is based on the stock making a new high above the 0 percent (high point on the initial up leg) level at the right side of the chart. When the Fibonacci retracement levels have been holding as support and/or resistance and then are broken to new highs or lows, the breakout point makes for a suitable trade entry. In this example, the breakout to a new high above the 0 percent level is the reason for entering into a new bull directional trade.

A long call trade would be appropriate in this setup. Once again, you need to balance the probability of success with the other factors presented earlier in this chapter. For example, normally an out-the-money strike is more speculative because the stock has to move farther to reach your break-even point. However, with a Fibonacci breakout, you may be fine to pay less for a slightly out-the-money strike because the trend often accelerates following a breakout.

Bull Flag

A bull flag is one of more popular trend continuation patterns (see Figure 6.4). As a trend continuation pattern, the completion of the bull flag tells you that the uptrend in place leading up to the pattern is likely to continue.

There are several key components of the bull flag pattern that need to be in place for the pattern to serve as an indicator of the trend continuing. First, the pattern must be preceded by a well-defined uptrend. It only makes sense that to have a trend continuation pattern you need to start with a trend. Second, the bull flag must have a flagpole. This is a sharp increase in the uptrend and often appears as one or several long green (white) candles on a candlestick chart. The flagpole should be accompanied by a rise in volume. Although there is no threshold for volume, it should be clear that the flagpole was not created by only a handful of traders. You want to see plenty of participation to show that the increase represents buying pressure. The flag is created when the flagpole reaches a high and

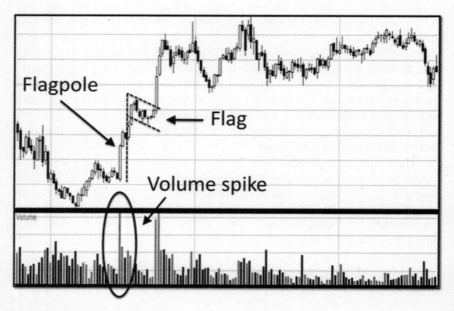

FIGURE 6.4   Bull Flag Pattern

then gives way to sideways or slightly lower trading. This tells you that the buyers are taking a breather but the sellers are not able to pull the price back to significantly lower levels. Together, the flagpole and flag create the bull flag pattern.

The pattern alone does not indicate a continuation of the trend, however. The final step is that the pattern must complete. This happens when the price breaks out above the flag. You can see in Figure 6.4 that the breakout above the flag yielded more long green (white) candles and volume once again rose sharply.

The long call trade with a bull flag is to buy a strike that is just above the top of the flag as soon as you identify the pattern completing. This trade setup anticipates a sharp move on sharp volume in a relatively short period of time. As such, you wouldn't need to buy a LEAPS, but you should make sure that you don't buy too little time, either. There are few things worse than being right but not being right quickly enough!

CHAPTER 7

Long Puts

For most traders, call option strategies are more intuitive and more readily understood than put option strategies. We'll ease into the concepts by comparing the rights of a call buyer with the rights of a put buyer. Buying a call option involves the right to purchase shares at a specific price for a fixed amount of time. Unlike a call option, where the buyer has the right to purchase a stock, the put buyer has the right to sell a stock at a specified price for a fixed amount of time.

GETTING TO KNOW THE STRATEGY

For investors with shares of a stock or exchange-traded fund (ETF) in their portfolio, puts can be used as a way to protect against downside risk in much the same way that insurance policies protect home and auto owners against property losses. Because put contracts share similarities with insurance policies, we will start to explain the concepts on that basis. Let's say a homeowner buys a vacation property on the coast of a low-lying island in the Gulf of Mexico for $300,000. He recognizes the potential for a hurricane to devastate the property, so he purchases insurance to protect the full value of the structure for $300,000. For this insurance he pays a premium of $3,000 for one year's worth of coverage with zero deductible.

During the first year of ownership, no hurricanes hit the island and, therefore, there's no damage. His insurance policy expires unused and worthless. The homeowner renews the policy for a second year of coverage at a cost of $3,000 for $300,000 of coverage with a zero deductible. This year the homeowner is not so fortunate and a hurricane hits the island and destroys the house completely. The homeowner collects $300,000 under the terms of the policy. He has not profited $300,000, but rather he was reimbursed most of the cost to rebuild the structure. This is the essential purpose of insurance.

To further the analogy, let's suppose that a third party does not have any ownership interest in the same house but, nevertheless, recognizes the threat to the house from a hurricane. He is interested in buying an insurance policy on the house for speculation. The insurance company is willing to sell the same $300,000 policy on the house in order to receive the $3,000 premium payment. He will profit from this speculative policy if the house incurs damage that exceeds the $3,000 he paid in premiums. During the first year of this speculative policy, a small hurricane does strike the island but only incurs minor damage amounting to $20,000. The insurance company pays the speculator $20,000 cash. His profit is $17,000 ($20,000 damage payment minus $3,000 premium) from the hurricane. Compare the speculator to the homeowner, who is also paid $20,000, but the owner's $20,000 is not profit. It's reimbursement for the $20,000 in damages to his home. Although an insurance company might not allow a policy to be written for speculative purposes, the options market allows puts to be used for both protection and speculation. In this chapter we'll consider put options as market strategies for both protection and speculation.

STRATEGY IN ACTION

Our model trader, Frank, has been watching the stock of ABC Company and decided to purchase 1,000 shares of the common stock at $92.60 per share on March 11. This is a large transaction for his account, but he believes ABC will continue to release new, innovative products over the next few months. He expects this to fuel a strong upside movement in the stock price, pushing it toward previous resistance of $175. He is basing this on the overall bullish trend of the markets and his technical analysis of ABC stock. He thinks that over the next few months ABC will continue to trend higher with increasing volatility due to the nature of their business model and sector. Based on his analysis, Frank thinks ABC has the potential to reach $175 within six months while remaining above the key support level of $85, shown in Figure 7.1. At the same time, Frank recognizes the aggressive nature of this trade and the fact that near-term support of $85 is more than $7 lower than his entry at $92.60. As a result of the perceived risk, he decides to buy a put option to hedge his position.

FIGURE 7.1 Uptrending Chart for Protective Put

Frank's total investment for his 1,000 shares is $92,600 plus fees. His cost basis is $92.60 per share, which makes his maximum risk $92.60 per share, because theoretically the stock could go to zero and he would lose his entire investment. To hedge this position, Frank decides to purchase 10 contracts of the ABC July $85 put option at the ask price of $7.75, for a total cost of $7,750 plus fees.

Frank's purchase of both the underlying shares and the put option is analogous to the owner of a $92,600 home purchasing a four-month insurance policy with a replacement value of $85,000 and a four-month premium of $7,750. In Frank's case, his 1,000 shares of ABC purchased for $92,600 are now insured for $85,000 through the July expiration. The strike price ($85) represents the insured value of the position. Frank knows with certainty that he has the right to sell his 1,000 shares at $85 per share at any time he chooses until the put option expires in July.

It's important to understand that when Frank purchased the put option for protection, he increased his cost basis in the trade. Frank paid $92.60 per share, then added another $7.75 per share with the put contract purchase to bring his net cost per share up to $100.35. Although he increased his cost basis, he has lowered the maximum loss of the position. With the $85 strike put contracts acting as an insurance policy, Frank's maximum potential loss has been reduced from $92.60 per share to $15.35 per share. The difference between what he paid for the shares ($92.60) and where he has the right to sell the shares ($85) plus the cost of the put premium ($7.75) is $15.35. If the stock price were to experience a catastrophic drop, Frank's worst-case scenario would be a loss of $15,350. Because the strike price is $7.60 less than the stock purchase price, Frank will incur the first $7,600 in losses on top of the $7,750 he paid in premium to arrive at a maximum loss of $15,350. The first $7,600 is similar to the deductible on an insurance policy.

With all option positions, it's important to determine your max gain, max loss, and break-even price. Although Frank believes $175 is a point of resistance, his position has an unlimited maximum gain. That's because he owns the shares directly and will recognize a dollar-for-dollar profit as the stock price increases. The maximum he can lose during the life of the put option is $15,350. The maximum loss will be recognized at or below $85 (the strike price) upon expiration. Keep in mind that if Frank holds his shares past the expiration date of his put options, his maximum loss increases once again to the purchase price of the shares plus the premium he paid for the expired options. Finally, he needs to know at what point he will break even. When a put is purchased as a position hedge, the break-even price is the purchase price of the stock position plus the put option premium. For Frank's position, break-even is $100.35 per share ($92.60 plus $7.75). If his analysis is correct and ABC reaches $175, he will easily overcome the break-even price and move into a profitable position.

Another variable to look at is the price at which the put contract pays for itself as an insurance policy by offsetting the premium paid. To calculate this, the premium is subtracted from the strike price, or $85 − $7.75 = $77.25. If ABC were to fall below $77.25, the premium would have paid for itself. As is the case with most insurance policies, Frank is hopeful that he will not be in a situation in which he needs to exercise his puts. They serve as protection against an unexpected, yet possible, negative trade outcome.

STRATEGY MANAGEMENT

Let's consider three possible scenarios of this hedged position during the life of the put contracts: (1) ABC moves significantly higher, (2) ABC price remains unchanged, and (3) ABC moves significantly lower. Because Frank is an astute technical trader, we'll first look at what happens when the stock moves higher. In this example, let's suppose that Frank's analysis of resistance at $175 was accurate and the stock moves up to $170 before reaching a technical plateau the day prior to his put contracts expiring. Frank's 1,000-share position is now worth $170,000. Because the stock is well above the $85 strike, Frank has no interest in exercising his right to sell his shares at $85 when the market value is $170. Therefore, he simply lets the puts expire worthless. His total cost basis for the position was $100,350 so his net profit is $69,650.

Many investors in this situation will simply sell their shares and be happy with the nearly $70,000 profit. We've often heard folks say, "Bulls make money, bears make money, pigs get slaughtered," to imply that there is stock market karma that will penalize the trader for staying in a position any longer to try to extract further gains. This concept falls into the category of market mythology and limits a trader's ability to maximize his potential for financial gain. Frank recognizes this and decides on another course of action that will protect his profits and not limit his upside. Because ABC started showing signs of a plateau at $170, Frank recognizes that a plateau is not the same as a reversal. There is not yet any technical evidence that the stock is going to retrace at this point. So why sell if there is little evidence of a reversal? In fact, this plateau has created a bit of a technical channel in which ABC has found support at $165 and resistance at $170. ABC is right at the top of the channel. It may just as easily break through $170 as it could pull back to the $165 support. If Frank simply sells the position, he is limiting any further upside potential. Instead, Frank decides to continue his put protection strategy and elects to buy 10 more contracts of the $165 strike. This time he chooses an expiration of only one month in order to allow the stock to either break through the $170 resistance or break down through the $165 support. If the cost of 1 August $165 put is $2.50 per share, Frank will spend another $2,500 to protect the position for another month. Frank's decision to stay in the position and utilize some of his profits to further hedge against any loss below $165 helps to maximize his profit and minimize his loss.

Now let's turn our attention to what happens when the price moves flat and reaches the July expiration trading at the original purchase price of $92.60. First of all, we should point out that a trade that spends four months going neither higher nor lower should often be sold long before the four-month put contract expires. However, for the sake of explaining what would happen, we'll assume the position is held right up to the last trading day prior to expiration. Because the July $85 strike was purchased with no intrinsic value, the entire $7,750 was extrinsic (time) value. Because the four months has now elapsed and the put is still out-the-money, the option reaches expiration worthless. Frank loss is the full $7,750 premium. His 1,000 shares are still worth $92,600, however. If Frank sells his shares just prior to Friday's close, he will suffer a $7,750 loss.

The capital required to execute this combination (shares and put option) trade was over $100,000. Buying shares and then buying a put contract defines the risk of the investment for a defined period of time. What if ABC didn't pay any dividends? What is the benefit of owning the shares over using long calls? The upside potential of both is unlimited. The downside loss potential is defined and time decay works against the trader in both strategies. The capital requirements for the protective put are much higher than the long call. For an investment that does not pay a dividend, a long stock with a protective put is essentially the same as an out-the-money long call. This is why a trade consisting of long stock and a protective put is often referred to as a synthetic call. It's important to understand the gain and trade-off of each strategy. Protective put strategies make the most sense on stocks that pay dividends or stocks that an investor intends to hold for longer periods but require an occasional hedge against technical or fundamental risk. Otherwise, a long call strategy works just as well without the higher capital requirements.

In the third scenario, let's consider what happens when the stock drops dramatically during the four months prior to expiration. Once again, we'll consider the day prior to the July option expiration and ABC is trading at $50. Frank's 1,000-share position of ABC is now only worth $50,000. However, the 10 July $85 strike price put contracts have an intrinsic value of $35 per share or $35,000. Frank is obviously not happy about the dramatic collapse in the value of his ABC shares but neither is he going to suffer a catastrophic loss. Although Frank could close out the stock and option contracts as the market closes on Friday, that's really not necessary. The following day, Frank's in-the-money puts will auto-exercise and his 1,000 shares will be automatically sold at $85 per share. This transaction brings $85,000 into his account. Because Frank's total cost basis on the trade was $100,350, he is left with a $15,350 loss on the position. Although this is not the outcome Frank had hoped for, the loss was substantially reduced from what it would have been if he had not purchased the puts. Without the puts acting as a hedge, his loss from the original investment of $92,600 would have been $42,600. To reiterate an earlier point: If Frank was willing to accept this $15,350 loss in a four-month period, he could have allocated the same $15,350 into long calls and used the remaining capital to invest in relatively conservative products such as high-quality corporate bonds or tradable certificates of deposit. The decisions about using appropriate leverage, utilizing capital, and preserving capital should go hand in hand with strategy decisions.

Delta Analysis

Although owning the puts guarantees the buyer that he can sell his shares at the strike price at any time during the life of the contracts, the position is not a 1:1 hedge. The puts will have a lower delta than the underlying shares right up until expiration. This means that if an investor owns 1,000 shares of stock and an at-the-money put with a delta of .50, a $1 drop in the stock will reduce the value of the shares by $1,000 and will increase the value of the puts by $500 for a net loss of $500. If the position continues to fall, the delta on the puts will increase (which decreases the loss) until the puts gain $1 for every $1 lost in the stock price. The initial delta to stock difference can be thought of as an insurance deductible before total coverage begins.

Theta Analysis

Because protective puts are a hedging strategy in which the puts provide a guaranteed selling price during the life of the contract, the position suffers from time decay. Therefore, it is best to buy more time than anticipated to keep theta costs to a minimum.

Calculations

Max profit	Because protective puts are a hedge strategy, the downside is limited and the upside is unlimited.
Max loss	During the life of the protective puts contracts, the maximum loss would occur if the price of the underlying were to fall below the strike price and remain below upon expiration. Maximum loss is calculated as the purchase price of the underlying plus the option premium plus fees minus the strike price.
Break-even	Purchase price of shares plus option premium paid plus fees.
Capital required	The cost of purchasing the shares plus the cost to buy the put contracts plus fees.

SPECULATIVE PUTS

A concept that can be difficult for the novice trader to grasp is that money can be made when the market goes down. Although the long-term market direction is generally up, there have been plenty of periods when the market has gone sideways or down for extended periods. In fact, prices tend to edge upward rather slowly compared to the rate at which they fall. When the market does pull back, it tends to happen quickly and aggressively, and that's where speculative puts come into play.

Markets tend to drop faster than they rise because investors react to their fear of losing their money by selling more aggressively than they bought. Fear and greed are the two primary emotions that drive market direction and, of the two, fear is stronger. The speed and force in which markets retrace is often indicative of this fact. For the levelheaded and educated option trader, market pullbacks or corrections are significant opportunities to profit using short-term bearish strategies like buying puts for speculation. You recall the example of a speculator who buys an insurance policy on a home he does not own, anticipating a profit if a hurricane should inflict damage. In the same way, a trader who anticipates a price drop in a stock, ETF, or index may profit from the decline.

A few years back a trader was on a business trip and found himself stuck at the airport with a delayed flight. He called his wife to tell her he was going to be delayed a few hours and would be grabbing dinner. She quickly advised him to stay away from chicken. "All the news stations are warning people against eating chicken due to an outbreak of avian flu that may be contagious to humans," she told him. The news reported that tens of thousands of birds had already been destroyed due to this outbreak and more were expected. Over a large salad, he pulled up a price chart on a major supplier of chicken products. He could see that the news was starting to hit the wires just as the market was closing and that the stock was picking up downside momentum on increasing volume into the closing bell. The stock closed at the low for the day around $18 after opening around $19.

Based on the price behavior and the fact that the stock had support around $14.50, he decided to set up a speculative trade for the next day. However, his work schedule was full when the markets were to open the next morning so he would be unable to do any analysis in the morning. The trader created a conditional order that would purchase put contracts if the stock price were to trade below $18. The conditional order was set up to buy near-term out-the-money puts.

This order would seem to be counter to the notion of buying more time and intrinsic value. So why did he take this trade? The market can act like an emotional creature that dislikes uncertainty and reacts quickly to fear. The conditions were right for a speculative trade; a calculated gamble. In fact, the news had just been released, the facts had yet to be confirmed, and the company had not even released an official statement. The trader saw an opportunity for a speculative trade and wanted to risk as little capital as possible while positioning the trade to potentially capture more of the downside.

He calculated his risk per position and bought as many contracts as he could afford. He chose the front month (14 days to expiration) out-the-money ($17.50) puts. This trade was treated as a binary position: either he was going to lose it all or he would turn a quick profit. Go big or go home; nothing in between. The next day the stock opened up just below $18, triggering his order. With an ask price of $0.50, he was able to purchase 20 contracts. As the day wore on, several more farms reported outbreaks and the stock fell further.

People weren't just afraid to eat chicken, they were demanding recalls on the chicken they had in their freezer and were not buying any more. Meanwhile, the outbreak started popping up in multiple locations, prompting the company to destroy more birds in an attempt to control the spreading virus. The next week the company announced a national recall and the stock fell to $13. Each day as the news played out he adjusted his conditional orders to close out his position if the stock rallied above short-term resistance.

As the story wore on, it was reported that avian flu could not be contracted from eating chicken, provided the chicken was properly cooked. Furthermore, the spread appeared to be contained, causing the stock to slowly rebound. Several days prior to expiration, the stock rallied past $14 and his conditional order sold the puts at just under $4 per share to close out the position. His puts traded from $0.50 to $4 in less than 14 days based on bird flu news and rumors.

This is an example of a trade that was driven by news but supported by technical analysis. Because technical analysis assumes that all things known have already been factored into the price, you might think that the trade was totally dependent on future news stories and that his strategy was based on luck. Because the directional movement would be determined by the unfolding news, he had no way to determine probability of success. As a result of the unknown factors, he elected to go in as a binary trader and use the charts to manage the position day to day without any clearly defined expectation of outcome. Speculative puts are well suited for this type of trading because the trader can define his risk through position sizing, purchase short-term out-the-money contracts, manage the position technically on a daily basis, and treat the outcome as binary.

Delta Analysis

It's often said that stocks take the stairs up and the elevator (or the window!) down. Simply put, stocks usually fall faster than they rise. As such, a speculative put buyer can usually get away with buying less time and a lower delta than a long call buyer. For a news-driven event, an at-the-money or even a slightly out-the-money put is acceptable. Less time may be purchased, but when in doubt, err on the side of buying extra time rather than too little.

Theta Analysis

With a typically shorter time to expiration, the speculative put has high negative theta. This trade is not intended for being moderately correct; it's for winning big or missing entirely.

Calculations

Max profit	Occurs at expiration when the stock is trading at zero. Theoretical max profit is the premium and fees subtracted from the strike price.
Max loss	Occurs at expiration when stock is at or above strike. Premium paid plus fees.
Break-even	At expiration the break-even is strike minus premium and fees.
Capital required	Premium paid plus fees.

COLLARS

Now that you have a couple of strategies under your belt, let's start to explore how some of the strategies can be combined to help accommodate the ever-changing market conditions. We are regularly approached by long-term investors with a question similar to this: "I have a large position of XYZ stock in my portfolio, it's doubled in the past few years, and I'm wondering if I should just take my money and run."

A collar strategy allows an investor to have continued upside potential along with the guarantee that profits will not turn to losses. As with all strategies, there are trade-offs that must be considered. A collar is a combination of two strategies, a covered call and a protective put. A collar will place a cap on profits through the use of a covered call. The protective put will ensure that the majority of the unrealized profit is protected.

Let's look at this strategy in action. A stock in an upward trend has doubled over the past two years and is currently trading at $90. Because the price appreciation has been consistent, the strike price for the covered call is based on a projection of the trend continuing at its current rate. The covered call writer wants to sell a strike price that is unlikely to be surpassed during the life of the contract. Suppose our example stock moves about 3 percent per month on average. The investor should sell a short-term option that is about 3 percent higher than the current price. Because the stock is trading at $90, she should sell the $93 strike call no more than one month out.

Let's assume the $93 call is trading at $1.68. The proceeds from the sale of the covered call will then be used to purchase a protective put with the same expiration. Suppose the funds would allow the investor to purchase the $86 strike price for approximately the same price as the covered call credit. Based on this collar, the stock now has upside potential of $3 per share and downside protection beyond any drop that exceeds $4 per share. Notice the skew to the downside with $3 upside and $4 downside. Ideally, the collar would be $3 upside and $3 downside but, as mentioned before, because stocks tend to drop faster than they increase, the puts are priced slightly higher.

There is another piece to this puzzle. This stock also pays a quarterly dividend of $0.60 in the next month. On the ex-dividend date the stock will automatically be reduced by the amount of the dividend, which will also decrease the value of the call and increase the value of the put, partially counterbalancing the skew to the downside. If the stock did not pay a dividend, then the skew would be smaller but would still exist to the downside.

As the collar approaches expiration, the ideal position for the investor is to have her stock trading just below the $93 strike price of the covered call. If her analysis is correct and the stock continues at the 3 percent rate of growth, then she would anticipate a price of around $92 and a dividend of $0.60. The collar would then expire worthless, allowing her to build a collar for the next month at the $95 call and the $91 put. Of course, if the stock moves up too quickly and the price exceeds $93, her shares will be sold at $93. She may or may not get the dividend, depending on if and when the price moves beyond $93. If the price moves lower, she has price protection at $86 at expiration. She also receives the $0.60 dividend, setting the effective sales price of shares under this scenario at $86.60.

The three outcomes to the collar strategy are (1) continue to own shares between $86.60 and $93, (2) sell shares at $93, or (3) sell shares at $86.60. Both losses and gains are constrained, or collared. The collar strategy provides investors a way to slowly ratchet up the exit price. This helps to maximize profits along with the possibility to enjoy future dividend payouts while limiting the downside risk.

STRATEGY APPLICATION

The long put is best suited for bearish positions when used as a speculative trade. Long puts may also be used for protecting against possible negative trends, even with a positive trend score. Typically, the trend score should be negative and the higher the score, the better. Speculative long puts are best applied to strong bearish positions with trend scores approaching −10. Long puts may be applied to any level of volatility and are especially useful as protection in volatile markets where the risk of a gap makes a stop order undesirable (see Figure 7.2).

Market Score Trade

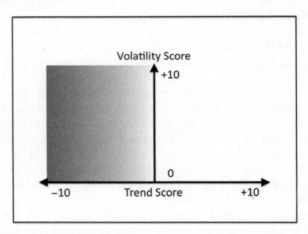

FIGURE 7.2 Market Score Application

Double Top

The double top reversal is a common chart pattern because it has a relatively simple setup (see Figure 7.3). It is one of the first patterns that novice traders learn and may be used effectively with the long put strategy. It is also known as the "M" reversal because it takes the shape of an "M" on the chart. The double top signals a bearish reversal.

The creation of the double top begins with an initial uptrend. This establishes the first leg in the "M" shape. The first leg peaks at first top, setting the resistance level. If the price is not setting new highs, you may be able to look back on the chart and see the same resistance level previously confirmed. This is the case in Figure 7.3, where the resistance at the double top had been reached earlier in the chart. After hitting the peak, the stock pulls back to the middle of the pattern, where it finds temporary support. The price then rallies a second time, once again hitting resistance at the previous high. It is at this point that the double top gets its name. The final leg is created when the price falls from the second peak and creates the last leg of the "M" shape. It is preferred, although not required, for the pattern

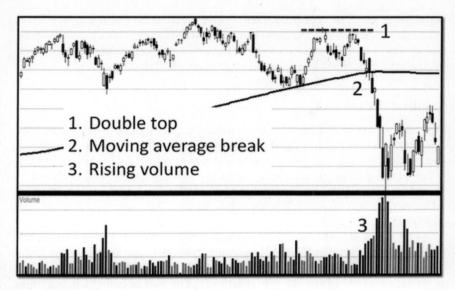

1. Double top
2. Moving average break
3. Rising volume

FIGURE 7.3 Double Top Reversal

to have time symmetry as well. Both halves of the "M" shape should take approximately the same length of time to form.

You have to appreciate the difference between a price pattern being created and a pattern completing. The double top pattern is complete—indicating the reversal—only when the price breaks down below the support level set by the middle of the pattern. Or, to look at it another way, the pattern completes when the stock trades below the bottom of the "M".

In the example shown in Figure 7.3, the pattern actually completed with a red (black) candle that came to rest on the 200-day simple moving average. As a trader, you have to consider every pattern in context. Although it's true that this double top pattern technically completed, the price is resting firmly on a key moving average. Because moving averages often act as support when the stock is trading above them, it would be prudent to allow the trading to play out just a little longer to see if the moving average will provide a base for the stock to rally. As it turned out, the illustration shows the price falling through the moving average the next day. The break below the moving average was also confirmed by rising volume, telling you that the sellers were strengthening on the downtrend.

The long put trade with a double top is a straightforward setup. If you don't have a long position in the stock, you can open a speculative put trade when the pattern completes. Taking the trade prior to completion of the pattern carries the risk of the trade moving into a channel rather than breaking lower. The second trade scenario with the double top is when you own the stock and use the long put for downside protection. Double tops can be good indicators of an impending price drop and may help you exit your long stock trade very near the top of an extended uptrend.

Trailing Protection

One feature of put options that makes them superior to stop orders in some applications is the guaranteed selling price. Stop orders are great in an orderly market when the price trades through the stop price and allows for efficient execution. However, markets are not always as well behaved as we'd like. When you own a stock and you want the additional confidence of knowing that your selling price is guaranteed, you can open a protective put trade.

Figure 7.4 shows a stock that is in a steady uptrend. When a trend has been in place for an extended time, many traders begin to get increasingly nervous about their profits. The "it's too high" mentality kicks in and often forces traders out of the trade prematurely. The fear of losing a profit often results in the trade being closed long before the charts actually signal that the trade should be closed.

Rather than project a fixed price target at which the trade will be closed, it is better to let the chart tell you when it's time to exit the trade.

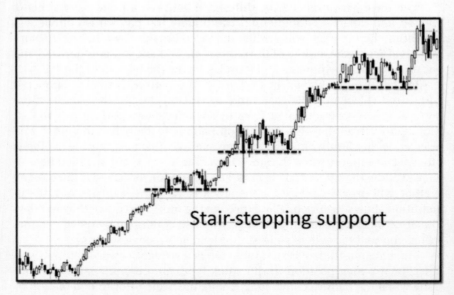

FIGURE 7.4 Support Levels for Protective Puts

With an uptrend, as you see in the example, a good strategy is to identify each new support level that's created on the way up. You can see in the chart that, as the stock rises, it creates a stair step of higher support levels. Recognize that the stock is telling you where the new floor is and then use that information to your advantage.

It is certainly acceptable to use a trailing stop in this case, where the stop price is adjusted higher with each new support level. However, there is always the possibility of a gap down that would bypass your stop order. That's where the protective put is helpful. An appropriate strategy would be to replace the trailing stop with a put option with a strike price just below the most recent support level. Even though you may be adjusting your support every few weeks, you still want to buy a put with a little extra time. In other words, don't always buy the front month because you expect to adjust it higher in a month or less. The better approach is to buy a little extra time (reducing your theta) and then recoup some of the option value when you sell it to adjust your strike price higher.

You understand that the trade-off with a protective put rather than a stop order is that the protective put requires you to pay a premium for the protection whereas a stop order may be entered and adjusted without cost. You have to balance the cost of protective puts against the uncertainty of the protection you get from stop orders. If your trade has performed well for you and you're willing to cap further growth, you may then consider offsetting the cost of protection with a covered call to create the collar we described earlier.

CHAPTER 8

Straddles and Strangles

W e've found over the years that there are three things rookie investors and traders love in the markets:

1. A good story
2. An opportunity to make big money
3. A clearly defined time frame (the shorter, the better!) to make big money

We've had many long flights made longer by sitting next to a self-proclaimed expert investor regaling us with his claims of knowing the next big thing in the stock market. Typically, after a few cursory greetings and comments about modern air travel, said seatmate will ask, "So, what do you do?" After a brief explanation, the conversation usually moves in one of two directions: (1) "What's your opinion of XYZ?" or (2) "Do I have a hot stock pick for you!"

Traders love hot stock tips. They love to get them and they love to give them, even though they almost always prove worthless. We refer to traders who base their entire strategy on these tips as lottery ticket traders. They'll suffer through hundreds of losing trades while tenaciously clinging to the hope that one day they will scratch the right ticket and hit it big. They usually start off with a short story about a cure for cancer, a discovery of a new energy source, or a revolutionary product about to be released. Not surprisingly, the stock is unusually cheap; as in $.0001 (add zeros to taste) cheap. They tell us that if we were to invest a few thousand dollars into this company's stock (like they did), by (insert specific date here) our investment would be worth (choose the largest number you know and double it).

We always listen politely while we jockey our noise-canceling headphones out of the bag to ensure that this one story is not followed by a dozen more. Although these get-rich stories are almost always bogus, there are occasionally opportunities for big, fast market moves. These moves are often based on a clearly definable event that a trader believes will send the stock either soaring to the financial stratosphere or have it crashing down closer to bankruptcy. These events aren't tips; they are anticipated and even orchestrated to elicit a response from the investment community. It is this type of known event on optionable securities that we will focus on as we explore the strategies known as straddles and strangles.

GETTING TO KNOW THE STRATEGY

Traders have always attempted to step in front of big news that would drive the markets before anyone else could capture the opportunity. That's what drives people to risk prison time for insider information. Today we are living in the hyper-information age with live updates streaming to our smart phones, tablets, and laptops. Information is a catalyst for big moves in a compressed time frame. A trader can take advantage of this by positioning himself ahead of the information and in the direction of the move. The challenge is in anticipating the correct direction of the move. What's a trader to do if he cannot answer this question? He's confident that a significant move is highly probable but he's not sure whether the direction will be up or down.

This is when the straddle or strangle can be put to work. For example, when the late Steve Jobs, former CEO of Apple Inc., was unveiling the new iPad to the public on January 27, 2010, we watched the announcement stream over a cell phone video link to a MacBook that displayed three charts and trading windows. The first display was a one-minute candlestick chart with quotes on AAPL (Apple Inc.), the second was T (AT&T), and the third was VZ (Verizon Communications Inc.).

No one knew the pricing on the iPad, so there was the potential for both a bull and a bear trade on AAPL, depending on how the market reacted to the pricing announcement. There was also some speculation that Mr. Jobs would announce a new iPhone and iPad partnership with Verizon, which could mean a bull trade on VZ and a bear trade on T. We were positioned to trade in either direction, based on the reaction to the announcement.

This type of quick-draw trading is reminiscent of the early days of day trading. We were looking for news-driven, emotional reactions in the market that translated into fast price swings. Execute your trade in the right direction as the swing developed and you could reap the trader's equivalent of the winning lottery ticket. In this case, we were receiving the information real-time along with the rest of the trading and investing community. However, we were able not only to watch for the information but also to analyze the reaction and trade in the direction of the action using directional options. When you have a direction, you're able to buy a call for an upward move or a put for a downward move. This is not usually the case; an option trader rarely knows the precise day or time in which information is released.

When a move is anticipated but the direction is not, straddles and strangles are well suited for this type of speculation (note that we used the word *speculation* versus *investment* or *trade*). A straddle or strangle is buying both a call and a put simultaneously. Because a stock cannot increase and decrease at the same time, with both of these strategies you will be wrong on at least one side of the trade. In fact, you could be wrong on both sides of the trade if the move doesn't materialize at all or to a lesser degree than anticipated. In other words, there is a guaranteed losing component to the trade in both strategies and no guarantee of even one winner. This is what makes these strategies more speculative than others covered thus far.

STRATEGY IN ACTION—STRADDLE

A straddle utilizes the purchase of both a call and a put with the same expiration date and the same strike price. The straddle does not attempt to identify a direction in which the stock is going to move. It simply sets up an opportunity to profit if and when the stock makes a substantial move up or down. The straddle depends on volatility, either implied or realized.

Straddles afford the trader a few advantages over buying stock to speculate on a move. Because the long straddle relies on volatility, it is relatively easy to identify when an opportunity might exist. Newsworthy events that are scheduled and anticipated are ideal:

- Earnings releases
- Product launches
- Lawsuits
- Drug trials
- Approval or denial of a merger or acquisition
- Announcements from the Fed
- Political decisions, speeches, and elections
- Virtually any anticipated announcement in which the resulting information has the ability to move the stock significantly

Because most of these are scheduled and anticipated, trading long straddles can be an easy way to play an event. Another advantage is that a long straddle has unlimited profit potential. Through the long call side, the upside is unlimited and the put is limited by the fact that a stock can only go as low as zero. The final advantage is that a long straddle is a defined risk trade, meaning a trader can only lose the amount of money it took to get into the long straddle. Because options use leverage, this amount will always be less than what a stock buyer is risking.

Let's look at an example of a straddle based on increased stock and option activity around an upcoming and much-anticipated earnings announcement. Frank had been following both the news and the chart of a former stock market technology darling. This stock was experiencing a great deal of publicity from the financial media, which added to its volatility. The price chart indicated a bearish pattern over the prior three months as the price dropped from $30 to $25. Frank also noticed that the downside volume appeared to be increasing while the upside volume was decreasing; further evidence that the sellers were controlling the price movement.

From his broker's site research, Frank saw that earnings were to be released before the market opened on April 19. Because the earnings were seven days away, Frank needed to look at options that would expire after the earnings were announced. The April options ceased trading April 16, so he had to consider the May options for this long straddle. Although Frank was trying to purchase options that had a life span just long enough to capture the anticipated event but no more, he was disappointed by the fact that he must buy an additional month's worth of time. That was necessary for him to align his strategy to the earnings date.

However, that may have been avoided if the underlying stock had participated in the weekly option series. The weeklies are short-term contracts that originate Thursday morning and expire on Saturday (and cease trading on Friday) of the next week. Although not every stock currently has a weekly option, the exchanges continue to add weekly contracts for stocks that have the greatest trader interest. This means that if you are looking for a short-term trade on a known event like earnings or a product announcement, you might have contracts available to you with expirations as short as a day, a week, or a month.

Strike Selection

Because a straddle uses the same strike price for both the call and the put, strike selection is simple. However, there will be plenty of times when the stock is trading somewhere between the available strike levels. When that happens, it's best to buy one strike that is in-the-money and the other that is out-the-money. The in-the-money strike should be the one that is in the direction of the short-term trend. For example, if the stock is trending lower, you should choose the in-the-money put.

Frank found himself in the position of having his stock trading at $25.69 while his option choices were the $25 strike and the $26 strike. Frank recognized that his stock had been trading in a bearish pattern so the logical decision was to build the straddle around the $26 strike. That made the put in-the-money by $0.31 and the call out-the-money by $0.31. He chose the May $26 put with an ask price of $0.65 ($0.31 of this is intrinsic value and $0.34 is time value) and a 0.59 delta.

The other leg of the straddle was the May $26 call which was out-the-money by $0.31 and had a 0.41 delta. He paid the ask price of $0.34 and, therefore, executed the straddle for a net debit of $0.99 plus fees. Frank had entered into a bearish long straddle. Because he owned both a call and a put, he was positioned to capture profits in either direction, provided the stock "pops or drops" upon release of the earnings announcement. The straddle will fail if the stock price fails to move a significant distance. The degree to which the stock moves determines the trade's profit or loss.

Because the straddle cost $0.99 and the stock was trading at $25.69, the stock needed to move at least a dollar either up or down in order for this position to become profitable by expiration. That represented about a 4 percent move. Prior to entering into this trade, Frank would have been wise to review the chart, overlaying the earnings announcements, and determine whether the stock's historical reaction typically exceeded a 4 percent move. If the stock only moved 2 to 3 percent on earnings over the previous year or two, then it would have been wise to pass on the trade. However, if the stock had shown that it frequently made moves that exceeded 4 percent, then this was probably a viable strategy and trade setup. Because Frank's straddle had over a month of time value left, the trade could have become profitable much sooner than expiration if the price had moved or if the volatility increased.

The Volatility Effect

Volatility plays a key role in straddles and strangles. Options pricing models are based on four variables: (1) intrinsic value, (2) time to expiration, (3) volatility, and (4) interest rates. Volatility is measured by the option Greek, vega. Vega measures how much an option's value will change when its implied volatility changes. A change in the volatility of the underlying can have a surprisingly high effect on the value of an option contract. When there is increased speculation about a stock's future move, there is more interest in options as a vehicle to capture that move. This pushes implied volatility higher and increases the value of the option contracts. If the stock's movement is lethargic or there is little interest in the options, prices will decline. Vega is always highest with at-the-money options where there is the most time premium and drops as you move further in-the-money or out-the-money.

Because Frank's straddle involved options that were placed nearly at-the-money, his position was highly influenced by vega. There are many other books that thoroughly cover the topic of option pricing but, for the sake of practice over theory, we will keep this topic limited to some trader basics. Frank anticipated increased volatility and price movement when earnings were to be announced. His premise was that future volatility would be greater than past volatility. Future volatility is called implied volatility. Past volatility is called historical volatility. When implied volatility increases, the price of options increases for both calls and puts. Because Frank was a buyer of both calls and puts, the cost of his straddle was comparatively expensive relative to a period in which earnings were not going to be released. Frank's calls and puts would both increase in value with the increase of implied volatility as the earnings date approached. In other words, it's possible that he could recognize a profit in his straddle based solely on an increase in volatility.

On the day earnings were announced, all that was unknown became known, which meant much of the implied volatility vanished. When the volatility vanished, so did some of the value of the straddle. Without the implied volatility, the value of the straddle became dependent on a directional move. This is the "pop or drop" situation mentioned earlier. If the stock didn't make a substantial move when the earnings were announced, Frank should have expected a loss of value in the straddle.

STRATEGY MANAGEMENT

Without an increase in volatility or a directional price move large enough to offset the drop in implied volatility, the straddle will succumb to time decay as it marches toward expiration. If you own a straddle and you don't get higher volatility or a sharp price move, you would be wise to close the straddle and move on to another opportunity. When you're trading straddles and strangles, it's important to understand how volatility, directional movement, and time decay factor into the strategy. These three elements make up the primary valuation of each option contract. Volatility and direction are dynamic—constantly increasing and decreasing—but time is a constant.

Break-Even

The long straddle actually has two break-even points: one for the call side and one for the put side. You calculate the upside break-even point by adding the net debit for the position to the strike price of the call. In our example we had a $26 strike plus a $0.99 net debit for a break-even on the call side of $26.99 (plus fees). The break-even for the put side is calculated by subtracting the net debit for the position from the strike price of the put. Our example trade had a $26 strike and a $0.99 net debit for a downside break-even of $25.01. Because the stock was trading at $25.68, the example straddle was biased to the bear side, meaning the straddle would become profitable faster with a stock price decrease versus increase.

Maximum Loss

A straddle is simply a combination of a long call and a long put. Maximum loss is limited to the total premium paid, or the net debit for the position. In our example, the max loss is $0.99 plus fees.

Maximum Gain

The maximum gain is the greater of the maximum call gain or the maximum put gain. With a long call, the maximum gain is theoretically unlimited because the call option would eventually rise almost dollar for dollar with the stock. A long put reaches its maximum gain when the stock price falls to zero. In the example trade, the break-even on the put side was $25.01. This is the price at which the position starts to profit. From $25.01, the stock could theoretically drop to zero, yielding a max gain of $25.01. Regardless of the stock price, therefore, the maximum gain for a straddle is unlimited based on the call side max gain.

Closing with a Profit

Because this trade has a bearish bias, you would expect the price of the stock to make a strong move to the downside around the time of earnings. When the puts start to increase in value, you need to protect the position. You could create a conditional order that automates a sell to close trade on the put if the stock should reverse course and start to rally. Because the call in the example was priced so low initially, it would be just as well to hold on to it and allow it to expire worthless. However, there are times when the call may still have enough time value to salvage to make a closing trade worthwhile. If so, then you would close the call side and turn the straddle into a long put position.

Closing with a Loss

Most straddles end up being biased to one side or another, just like our example. Risk management is always important, and because this straddle was skewed bearish, the trader needed to be prepared to quickly close out the put side if the price had become bullish. Remember, the maximum loss is the net debit, but you are often able to reduce the effect of the losing side by closing that side when the price moves in the opposite direction.

STRATEGY IN ACTION—STRANGLE

As we observed in the example of the long straddle, the trade skewed to the bear side. Because an event-driven trade has the potential to send price movement either up or down, having a bias toward one side or the other may not necessarily be where the trader wants to position himself. The long strangle helps to balance out the directional bias. The balance is achieved through a call and a put of differing strikes versus the same strike.

Let's assume our model trader, Frank, elected to use a strangle over a straddle to avoid the bearish bias. He could have purchased a call and a put that were both slightly out-the-money (OTM). Because his stock was trading at $25.68, he could have set up the trade by purchasing the May $26 call for $0.34 and the May $25 put for $0.30. The net debit for this OTM long strangle would have been $0.64 plus fees. Take note that the straddle was $0.99 and the strangle was $0.64. For every strategy there is a gain and a give-up. By using the strangle over the straddle, the cost of the trade is reduced by $0.35. What's the give-up? The following break-even analysis will provide the answer.

Break-Even

Like the straddle, the long strangle has two break-even points: one for the call side and one for the put side. The calculations are the same as the straddle. The break-even for the call is now $26.64 and $24.36 for the put. The stock will have to move a considerable amount in either direction in order for this strangle to come out profitable—approximately 5 percent per side. Using the straddle, the put side only requires a decline in the stock's price of about 2.6 percent to reach the break-even point, whereas with the strangle a 5 percent move is required. The call side actually benefits slightly under the strangle because it requires only about a 4 percent move to break even rather than about a 5 percent move with the straddle.

Maximum Loss

A strangle is also simply a combination of a long call and a long put. Maximum loss is limited to the total premium paid, or the net debit for the position. In our example, the max loss is $0.64 plus fees.

Maximum Gain

The maximum gain is theoretically unlimited on the call side and limited to the difference between the break-even point and zero on the put side, or $24.36 per share.

Closing with a Profit

Unlike the straddle, our example strangle trade has a slight bullish bias, although it's very close to being neutral. In this strangle, an increase in volatility can increase the value of both the call and the put option without an associated change in the value of the shares. You may very well see a profit on the overall position as the earnings release date draws near. If the option value increases due to higher volatility, you could sell the position prior to the earnings event and capture some profit. You need to be aware that after the earnings announcement release, the increased premium based on implied volatility will vanish like air leaving a bursting balloon. At that point, you would be relying solely on directional price movement to profit from the position.

Closing with a Loss

Because the strangle is not as directionally skewed as the straddle example, it may be viewed more as a binary trade in which it either produces a profit or it produces a loss. Both the call and the put are out of the money; therefore, once the earnings date has passed, the greatest risk to the position is no movement at all. With time decaying very quickly, implied volatility vanishing, and no price movement, there would be very little premium to salvage.

STRATEGY APPLICATION

Strangles and straddles are a little bit like trips to Las Vegas. You start your trip with a predetermined amount of money that you are prepared to lose—but you hope to score a win, anyway. Having an understanding of the proper use of speculative strategies like straddles and strangles allows you to gamble on news events, earnings, and hot tips from well-meaning friends (and fellow airplane passengers) without endangering significant capital. When you trade speculative market strategies, the odds may not necessarily be against you, but you must still approach the market with an amount of money you are both willing and able to lose in the event the trade goes against you. It's okay to put your money on black or red every once in a while, but don't bet your retirement on it.

Bollinger Band Breakout

Bollinger Bands are moving average envelopes that surround the price and become wider or narrower as the price volatility increases or decreases. There are two bands: the upper Bollinger Band and the lower Bollinger Band. Because the bands change with volatility and trend, the price doesn't often break through the bands, although it will on occasion. When you view Bollinger Bands on a price chart, you'll see that in periods of high volatility or strong trends, the bands will be comparatively far apart. During periods of both low volatility and sideways trading, the bands will draw close together.

Bollinger Bands are constructed around a moving average, although the moving average itself is typically not plotted with the bands. The most common moving average used in the construction of the Bollinger Bands is the 20-period simple moving average (SMA). Although the 20-period SMA isn't drawn, the upper Bollinger Band and the lower Bollinger Band are drawn a specified distance above and below the 20-period SMA. The distance from the 20-period SMA the bands are drawn is based on a standard deviation of the data. You recall from the discussion in the volatility-scoring chapter that standard deviation is one measure you can use to describe the volatility in price.

Given the standard deviation, the upper Bollinger Band is then drawn at two standard deviations above the 20-period SMA. Likewise, the lower Bollinger Band is drawn at two standard deviations below the 20-period SMA. Based on normal probability theory, you would expect that about 95 percent of all closing prices will fall between the two-standard-deviation Bollinger Bands. Though two standard deviations is a common default setting, this value may be adjusted. If the bands are tightened to one standard deviation, for example, the bands will be very narrow and will tend to generate many more buy and sell signals that won't be very useful. On the other hand, widening the bands by using three or four standard deviations will capture almost all of the price data but won't generate signals very often.

The Bollinger Band squeeze is a setup that begins with a significant tightening of the bands. Because *tight* does not have a textbook definition here, you need to make that assessment based on how close the bands appear compared to previous distances. The relative distance of the bands will change as the time horizon on your chart changes. For that reason, our recommendation is to use a 180-day daily chart for Bollinger Band analysis. You may choose to use other time horizons, but it's important that you

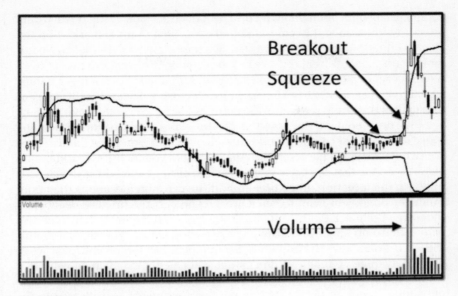

FIGURE 8.1 Bollinger Band Squeeze

don't change your chart time frame once you've started your analysis. In other words, don't identify a Bollinger Band squeeze on a 180-day daily chart and then switch to a three-year weekly chart to manage your trade. Figure 8.1 shows an example of a Bollinger Band squeeze and subsequent breakout.

Notice how close the bands are to each other in the area identified in the illustration as the squeeze. Relative to the rest of the chart, the distance between the bands is as close as any you can observe. Another characteristic that we look for is the length of the squeeze. Again, there is no textbook definition for a minimum required length; however, the longer, the better. Let's talk for a minute about the story that's being told by the squeeze. You know that in order for a squeeze to form, price needs to have very little trend and volatility. If you have significant values for either, the value of the standard deviation will increase, thus widening the distance between the bands. So with an absence of trend and volatility, what conclusions can we reasonably make about the trading activity? Simply, the buyers and sellers are quiet and neither side is willing to battle for control. If buyers and sellers were battling, but in equilibrium, then you'd see no trend, yet high volatility. If either side were winning, then you'd at least see a trend, with or without volatility.

So now you have a squeeze, telling you that the buyers and sellers are in a quiet period. Unless everyone has completely lost interest in that company, at some point you would expect that one side or the other would break the impasse and begin to take control. That point is marked on the chart by the Bollinger Band breakout. It's important to note that we're not looking for just any breakout: We're interested in the breakout that follows the squeeze. Remember, based on two-standard-deviation Bollinger Bands, a breakout is expected from 5 percent of all closing prices. It's the squeeze that makes this trade setup significant to us.

The next step of the trade is the breakout. This occurs when the squeeze is broken by the stock price closing outside either band. There are two confirming characteristics that will help you identify a valid breakout. The first is that the price closes beyond either band with a candle that trades in the direction of the breakout. If the price breaks above the upper Bollinger Band, you want to see a green candle. If the price breaks below the lower Bollinger Band, you should look for a red candle. Long candles with little to no shadows at the close are even better. The second confirmation is volume on the breakout day compared to the recent (past week or two) average volume. We don't want you calculating average volume if it's not immediately available; a visual analysis is sufficient. A true breakout should generate higher trading interest that would be reflected in the volume histogram. There is no minimum volume increase percentage here but, once again, the higher the better. The key point for volume is that it certainly should not be lower with the breakout.

Bollinger Band breakouts following a squeeze tend to be very sharp and fast trades. Many times the trade runs its course in only a few days. You can see in the illustration that the example trade reached its peak only three days after the breakout. For that reason, we don't recommend looking for Bollinger Band squeezes on weekly or monthly charts. By the time those time frames identify the breakout, it very likely will have already passed you by.

You may now recognize why the Bollinger Band squeeze and breakout is a suitable trade setup for a straddle or strangle. Both of these strategies require a sharp direction move and/or an increase in volatility. The Bollinger Band breakout provides both. The one factor that you have to work with when you're basing your trade on a Bollinger Band squeeze is timing. With a news or event trade setup, you know in advance the date of the event. There is really no way to anticipate when a breakout may occur with a Bollinger Band squeeze. Nor is there any way to accurately anticipate the direction of the breakout, although these strategies do not require that you correctly guess the direction.

However, the flip side that works in your favor is that option premiums during a Bollinger Band squeeze should be very low, because historical and implied volatility should both be at a minimum. As opposed to news or event-driven trades where implied volatility rises as the event date approaches, Bollinger Band squeezes are quiet periods with no market anticipation. As such, you should err on the side of buying too much time. You need to give yourself as much time as possible to allow the breakout to occur during the life of your straddle or strangle. If you're still holding your position as the options approach their expiration month, you should be able to roll out the position for a relatively little debit. Unless the volatility has slowly expanded, premiums based on volatility should still be fairly low.

The ideal scenario for a straddle or strangle based on a Bollinger Band breakout is that you open the position for a very small debit based on a minimum volatility level and then you close the position shortly after the breakout based on a sharp move in price accompanied by an expansion of volatility. Then take a break and enjoy the fruits of your success!

CHAPTER 9

Debit Spreads

A debit spread strategy is one of the most common launching points into intermediate option trading. It's certainly important to have a comprehensive understanding of single-leg option strategies for those market conditions that allow for aggressive bull or bear positioning. In addition, though, the use of spread strategies will often increase the probability of success and help further mitigate risk during times of less market certainty.

The key advantage of a spread strategy is that it gives you the ability to move away from having to rely solely on the direction of the underlying and allows you to modulate your risk/reward in a more diverse range of market conditions. Put more concisely, your goal is to risk less and profit more often. Take note that the last sentence was phrased as *profit more often* versus *more profit*.

As with all strategies, not just spreads, you have to choose the balance between the strategy's strengths and weaknesses. Many traders fail to appreciate this fact. When we present at live events, we're constantly asked, "What's the best strategy?" The questioner is confused when we reply, "All of them!" We've always found it interesting to observe the progression of an investor or trader as she grows her skills and evolves into a skilled technical option trader. The typical evolutionary path we've observed is that a long-term fundamental stock investor first steps into the short-term technical world and becomes a stock trader. Then she moves on to covered call writing, then directional call/put buying, and finally spread trading and other complex strategies. Interestingly, few traders will make it that far, though. It's a long and perilous path littered with paper losses, realized losses, and expired options contracts. Many become certificate of deposit holders, convinced that the whole market is nothing but a giant conspiracy to take their money. Most of those trying to win the big score end up as casualties of this path because they never factor in their strategy's probability of success.

GETTING TO KNOW THE STRATEGY

In trading and baseball, success depends on having a variety of strategies and using them in the right way at the right time. To illustrate that important concept, Shawn tells a true story from his Little League days.

I grew up in a family with a tradition of playing baseball. At a young age I, my older brother Erik, and my best friend Trevor joined the Little League team that my father coached. Just like every other boy on the team, my goal was to hit a home run each time I was at bat. Unfortunately, I was small for my age and possessed poor hand-eye coordination. Given my size (and lack of skill!) the chances of me ever hitting a home run were virtually nonexistent.

My buddy Trevor was even smaller than I, though he did have a little more skill. My brother Erik was very tall for his age but that meant he was gangly and clumsy. We all shared the same goal of wanting to win games by hitting homers. Dad's goals, on the other hand, were for us boys to have fun and win some games along the way, in that order. He knew that regardless of how much coaching he offered or how many hours we practiced, there was little chance that Erik, Trevor, and I would ever be home run hitters.

Dad had another strategy. Instead of working on our weaknesses, he focused on our strengths. Although I was small, I was quick. Dad figured that if he could teach me to bunt the ball, I was quick enough to get to first base. His strategy with Erik played to Erik's size. Erik was so tall that when he approached the plate, most of the kids thought he would crush the ball to the outfield, so they backed the outfield to the wall. Erik, however, also learned to bunt. Trevor was a leftie. If you've never seen what happens to left-handed kids in Little League, it's not pretty. Because most pitchers are right-handed, they tend to throw wide (the first base side of the plate, away from the batter). For a leftie, that meant the ball came flying in right where poor Trevor was standing. It seemed that two out of three times at bat, Trevor would take a ball to the rib cage, the thigh, or even the helmet. Tough for Trevor, but it gave our team another man on base.

Dad's strategy was to set up the batting order with me at leadoff followed by Erik and Trevor. I approached the plate with my high-probability, low-risk strategy. If the pitcher threw a strike, I got to bunt. If he threw a ball, I watched it go by and maybe got the walk. Either way, the chances of me getting to first base were very good, but the chances of me getting a home run were zero. How about the chances of a triple? Slim to none. The chances of a double? That might have happened if there had been a throwing error. The fact was I was sacrificing reward for a higher probability of success. That was the team strategy to win.

Next up, Erik would come out and the opposing outfield would back up to the wall while the infield moved to the outfield grass. With his long reach, Erik could just about bunt the ball out of the pitcher's glove so he would bunt anything and everything thrown in his direction. As the lead runner, the other team would try to get me while Erik loped his way to first base. But I had the jump and the speed so this strategy typically paid off, giving us runners on first and second.

Then it was Trevor's turn at bat. His strategy was to stand there and swing at anything that didn't hit him. Usually the first pitch nailed him and he would take the base. I advanced to third and Erik moved to second. Dad's strategy had successfully loaded all the bases with no outs.

Now the fourth kid up to bat was what I would describe as a 12-year-old gorilla. He was the overly developed kid with a deep voice and arms to match. His job was to crush the ball and try to drive in as many runs as possible. He usually had both the strength and the skill to hit a double, triple, or even a home run. He might not have had a very high batting average, but when he did connect with the ball, it often went over the fence. If he failed, the next batter up still had bases loaded and only one out.

Dad stacked the batting lineup, deliberately and strategically, to increase the team's probability of success versus any one individual's success. We won many baseball games and beat teams that we shouldn't have by using the right strategy at the right time while managing risk. Dad was working the probability of success into the game. Although neither Erik, Trevor, nor I ever hit a home run, we had more fun and consistently contributed to the team. Dad used each of our strengths and fit them together for overall success.

As a trader, you should approach your strategies with an eye toward overall success. Start by focusing on small, consistent winners using high-probability strategies while managing the downside risks. Too many times, traders want the glory of the home run and forget that those are usually few and far between. The most common home run strategy for beginners is long calls—unlimited profits and you can't lose more than the premium paid. So, new traders will load up on cheap, out-of-the-money, almost-expired options and try to hit home runs. They don't appreciate the fact that their chances of achieving profits are slim. Too many of these traders never learn to adjust their strategies for changing market conditions, nor do they factor in probability of success. They swing at every pitch thrown their way and, when they strike out, they rant and rave that the market is fixed or they're just unlucky. It's not a question of luck; they're matching the wrong strategy to their own level of skill and experience.

This is where the spread trade comes in. A skilled trader can adjust a spread based on market conditions for (1) a high probability of success with a limited return (a bunt), (2) a decent probability of success with a solid return (a double), or (3) a low probability of success but a high rate of return (a triple). However, a spread trader can never have unlimited profits (a home run). We prefer a trading strategy that consists mostly of base hits with an occasional double. That doesn't get anyone rich quickly—that only happens in the movies and on late-night infomercials.

Spread strategies give you the opportunity to make money in bullish, neutral, and bearish markets but, unlike most directional strategies, the maximum profit is limited versus unlimited. In the case of a vertical debit spread, the contracts will have the same expiration month but different strikes on the same underlying. You simultaneously buy the more expensive contract while selling a less expensive contract. This is true for both debit call spreads and debit put spreads. The less expensive contract gives you a credit to partially offset the cost of the spread. However, it's not enough to fully offset the cost, which leaves you with an overall debit for the position, giving this strategy its name.

Many new traders and investors first approach options by learning to sell a covered call on a long-term stock position within their account. Although this is a good way to get started, covered call writing can consume a great deal of an account's capital because the actual shares must first be purchased. Covered calls also do not protect the overall position from a dramatic downturn or gap in the price of the stock. Experienced traders recognize that a covered call strategy exposes a portfolio to large downside risk and limited upside potential.

A vertical debit spread removes much of the downside risk while keeping the upside potential. A vertical debit spread is similar to a covered call in a few respects. In a covered call the investor buys a least 100 shares and then sells a call option on the same underlying stock. The premium received from the sale of the covered call partially offsets the cost of buying the underlying stock. In a vertical debit spread using call options (also known as a bull call spread), you would purchase a call option instead of the underlying shares. This initial call option purchase may be in-the-money (ITM), at-the-money (ATM), or out-the-money (OTM), depending on your technical outlook over the time frame that you expect for the position to develop. Simultaneous to your call option purchase (long leg), you sell another call option (short leg) for the same expiration month but with a higher strike price. The sale of the higher strike option partially offsets the cost of the purchased option. Remember that with same-expiration calls, the higher the strike, the lower the premium. Just like with a covered call, you're giving up some of the potential profit later in return for the premium received immediately.

STRATEGY IN ACTION

Our model trader, Frank, had been watching an uptrending stock for six months. During that time, it set new highs each week, rising quickly from $39 to $51. At $51, Frank's candidate stood at a one-year high. Figure 9.1 shows the trend that Frank was looking at with his potential trade. Although there are many ways to trade this upward trend, it can be challenging to purchase shares or call options when a stock reaches long-term highs in a short time span. Frank was simply concerned that the stock was too high and he didn't want to be the last one holding it before

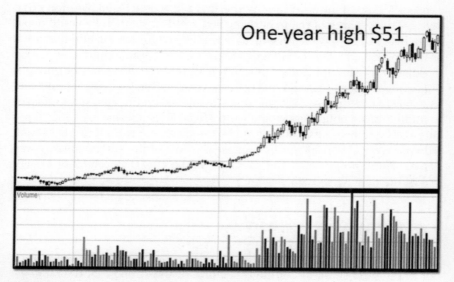

One-year high $51

FIGURE 9.1   Extended Uptrend for a Bull Call Spread

it dropped. Yet he still saw the bullish trend and wanted to trade the trend without all the downside risk. Therefore, to lower risk and to offset the cost of the position, Frank decided to open a bull call spread (vertical debit spread with calls).

Because the stock was at $51 and had shown a price growth rate of about $2 (4 percent) per month, Frank decided to build a spread around that rate of growth. After reviewing the option chain, he focused on options with six weeks to expiration in order to capture the next month's growth. He looked at the $50 call strike that was offered at $1.45. He then saw the $52.50 call strike that was bid at $0.60. Based on his analysis and the previous price behavior, he believed the stock had the potential to reach $52.50 within the next 42 days. However, he was doubtful it would surpass $52.50 by any significant amount. Frank set up the trade by entering the following order as a spread:

- Buy calls to open (BCO) September $50 @ $1.45
- Sell calls to open (SCO) September $52.50 @ $0.60

With 20 contracts and a net debit per share of $0.85, the total cost of this spread was $1,700 plus fees. This spread position gave him both a right and an obligation. Frank had the right to purchase 2,000 shares at $50 at any time for the next 42 days. At the same time he also had an obligation to deliver 2,000 shares at $52.50 at any time until expiration. With his obligation, Frank will only be at risk of assignment when the price of the stock exceeds $52.50. If the stock price exceeded $52.50 and Frank was forced to deliver 2,000 shares of the underlying stock at $52.50, then he could make the delivery by simply exercising his contracts to purchase 2,000 shares at a strike price of $50. This could happen via a same-day substitution, whereby the shares are simultaneously purchased and sold to close out the spread's obligation and right. Should this occur, executing the long calls would cost $100,000 (2,000 shares × $50 per share) while the credit from selling shares to fulfill Frank's obligation would yield $105,000 (2,000 shares × $52.50 per share). The remaining $5,000 would be the position profit. Note that Frank would not clear a $5,000 profit because the cost of the spread initially was $1,700. Therefore, Frank's net profit would be $3,300 ($5,000 less $1,700) or just under a 200 percent return.

STRATEGY MANAGEMENT

Although it's fun to run maximum profit scenarios on a strategy, that's often not a true representation of the real world or the strength of the strategy. The strength of the spread is realized when you compare it to the more basic strategy of just buying call contracts. We can illustrate the comparison with the same scenario we just discussed.

As we noted previously, the stock in Figure 9.1 rose from $39 to $51 in six months. Rather than creating a spread, suppose you simply buy long calls. For the same $1,700 you are able to purchase just 11 contracts at $1.45. Assume the stock continues to trend higher and upon expiration the stock is trading at $52.50. You could execute your right to the 1,100 shares at $50 and immediately sell them at the market price of $52.50, netting you $2,750. Subtract the $1,595 you paid for the calls and you would realize a profit of $1,155 (about 72 percent). The difference in returns is based on the fact that the spread allows for a larger position size (20 spread contracts versus 11 long call contracts).

Another important factor to consider is the break-even point, calculated as the long leg strike plus the net debit. For the example spread, the break-even is $50.85 ($50 strike of long leg + $0.85 net debit). The break-even for the directional long calls is $51.45 ($50 strike + $1.45 debit). The fact that the spread has a lower break-even point means that the stock has less price performance pressure. In the event that the stock does not continue to grow at a rate of 4 percent per month but rather slows to just 2 percent, the spread position would be profitable sooner than the straight calls. In fact, take note that the break-even point of the spread is $50.85, which is actually $0.15 less than the current price of the stock. This means that even if the stock failed to increase in value at all during the life of the spread, you would still make money ($300, to be exact). The price could actually drop down to $50.85 at expiration and you would only then be starting to experience losses.

This is a clear advantage over the long call strategy that has a break-even of $51.45. If the stock drifts sideways and remains at $51 at expiration, you would lose about one-third of your initial investment (with a $51 stock price, a $50 strike call has $1 of intrinsic value).

Never forget that each strategy comes with its own advantages and disadvantages. Now that we've discussed the advantages of the spread over the long calls, let's look at where the calls have the advantage. What if your analysis was too conservative and instead of the stock rising at the same 4 percent per month increase, it triples its rate and grows at 12 percent, achieving a price of $57 at expiration? One of the downsides of the spread is that the profit potential is limited by the obligation to deliver shares at the strike price of the short leg. In our example, the maximum profit is achieved at expiration when the stock trades at or above $52.50. If the stock reaches $57 at expiration, the maximum profit of the spread remains exactly the same as if the stock were at $52.50.

There is no profit cap on the long call strategy. At $57, the calls would be worth $700 per contract, giving the 11-contract position a value of

$7,700. If you purchased the 11 contracts for a net debit of $1,595, you would realize a $6,105 profit—about twice the return of the spread.

Bear in mind that the stock's price performance has to triple in order for the long call strategy to generate twice the return of the spread position, even though both strategies used the same $1,700 initial investment. The spread trade's profit was the result of the stock price continuing to grow at the six-month historical rate. Profitability did not require the stock to do something out of the ordinary in order to achieve the results. It is more reasonable to expect that the stock will continue to perform at its current rate than to expect it to accelerate its growth rate by 300 percent. For most traders, the advantages gained in the spread strategy outweigh the disadvantages of capping profit early. For this reason, spread trading and other multilegged strategies are popular choices among experienced option traders.

Calculations

Max profit	The difference between the short leg strike and the long leg strike minus the position cost (net debit plus fees).
Max loss	The net debit plus fees.
Break-even	The long leg strike plus the position cost (net debit plus fees).
Capital required	The amount of money required to create and hold a debit spread is simply the net debit of the overall position. You are not required to have the available funds to cover the purchase of the shares represented by the long leg. However, as expiration approaches and the underlying is trading between the long and short leg strikes, if you do not wish to exercise your right to purchase shares, you should close the spread by first buying back the short leg and then selling the long leg.

The calculations are based on the bull call spread (vertical debit spread using call options).

Expiring in No-Man's-Land A bull call spread is in no-man's-land when the price of the stock is above the long leg strike but below the short leg strike. Upon expiration, if you have not closed the spread and the stock is trading in this zone, the long call contract will automatically exercise and you will purchase shares at the lower strike. Because your short leg will expire out-the-money, you won't have a buyer for these shares. Therefore, you will be required to have the capital in your account to hold the shares long. At that point, you could sell the shares at market or create a new position such as a covered call to generate subsequent premium income.

Bear Put Spread

The previous example involved a bull call spread that is utilized in a bull market. The equivalent spread for a bear market is a bear put spread (vertical debit spread using put options). There is no difference in strategy, except that you are looking for downtrending stocks and ETFs, using puts and protecting against the upside risk. Otherwise, the strategy is exactly the same.

Six Steps to Creating a Bear Put Spread

1. Score the market trend for bearish (0 to −10) directions. Most stock screening tools allow you to scan for bearish technical and fundamental criteria.
2. Analyze the price chart to ensure that the trend is bearish. Confirm with price patterns and indicators. Be sure to identify key support (for price targets) and resistance (for risk management).
3. Choose your strike prices based on the likelihood of price movement as determined by recent price action. Execute your spread by purchasing the higher-priced put (higher strike) and selling the lower-priced put (lower strike).
4. Manage the position through frequent technical chart review, price alerts, and conditional orders.
5. If both legs move in-the-money you may close the position for a credit. If the stock is trading between the strikes and you are not holding shares of the underlying stock, you may choose to close the spread prior to expiration in order to avoid holding a short stock position. A short stock position would be due to the auto-exercise of your in-the-money long put.

Adjusting the Spread for Probability

Katie is an advanced technical options trader. She had been observing the market's ability to shrug off negative economic data and advance higher on positive economic data. Based on her technical analysis and the current economic conditions, Katie decided to create a vertical debit spread with call options (bull call spread) on the Nasdaq 100 tracking ETF (QQQ).

She began her analysis by constructing three bull call spread scenarios: (1) moderately bullish, (2) mildly bullish, and (3) neutral. If she were outright bullish on the market, she would use a long call strategy to capture as much of the expected upside movement as possible. At the time of her analysis, the index price was trading at $48.77. Her scenario analysis table follows:

Scenario	Max Gain	Max Loss	Break-Even	Price Move to Max Gain	Return at Max Gain
Moderately bullish (50/51)	$0.73 per share	$0.27 per share	$50.27	+$2.24 per share	270%
Mildly bullish (48/49)	$0.38 per share	$0.62 per share	$48.62	+$0.24 per share	61.2%
Neutral (46/47)	$0.16 per share	$0.84 per share	$46.84	−$1.76 per share	19%

First, in the case of the moderately bullish scenario, she selected strike prices that were both out-the-money. The long leg (lower strike) of the spread was the May $50 with an ask price of $0.48. The short leg (higher strike) of the spread was the May $51 with a bid price of $0.21. Katie could enter this trade at the natural market (buying at the ask and selling at the bid) for a net debit of $0.27 per share or $27 per contract. This is a one-point-wide spread. With a one-point-wide spread, the maximum profit would occur upon expiration (44 days) if QQQ closed above $51. This would require the price to move $2.24 or 4.6 percent in the next 44 days. If QQQ closed above $51 upon expiration, Katie would exercise the long leg by buying shares at $50 and simultaneously being assigned and selling the same shares for $51, netting her the $1 difference. From the $1 per share profit, she would subtract the position cost of $0.27 per share to yield a net profit of $0.73 (270 percent) in 44 days.

Second, with the mildly bullish scenario, Katie selected one strike price in-the-money for the long leg and an out-the-money strike price for the short leg. The long leg of the spread was the May $48 with an ask price of $1.52. The short leg of the spread was the May $49 with a bid price of $0.90. Trading at the natural market, she could buy the spread for a net debit of $0.62 per share or $62 per contract. Once again, this is a one-point-wide spread. With this one–point-wide spread the maximum profit would occur upon expiration (44 days) if QQQ closed above $49. This would require the price to move $0.24 or .047 percent in the next 44 days. If QQQ closed above $49 upon expiration, Katie would exercise the long leg by buying shares at $48 and simultaneously being assigned and selling the same shares for $49, netting her the $1 difference. From the $1 per share profit, she would subtract the position cost of $0.62 per share to yield a net profit of $0.38 (61.2 percent) in 44 days.

Finally, in the case of the neutral scenario, Katie selected strike prices that are both in-the-money. The long leg of the spread was the May $46 with an ask price of $3.08. The short leg of the spread was the May $47 with a bid price of $2.24. Trading at the natural market, she could buy the spread for a net debit of $0.84 per share or $84 per contract. Like the other two scenarios, this is a one-point-wide spread. With this one-point-wide spread the maximum profit would occur upon expiration (44 days) if QQQ closed above $47. This means that QQQ could actually drop by $1.76 (−3.6 percent) in the next 44 days and the spread would still reach maximum profitability. If QQQ closed above $47 upon expiration, Katie would exercise the long leg by buying shares at $46 and simultaneously being assigned and selling the same shares for $47, netting her the $1 difference. From the $1 per share profit she would subtract the position cost of $0.84 per share to yield a net profit of $0.16 (19 percent) in 44 days.

With the moderately bullish spread, Katie has very little capital at risk and a higher potential return. However, it requires a substantial upward move, decreasing the probability of success. With the neutral scenario, she risks more to make less, but the position has a built-in 3.6 percent downside cushion, greatly increasing her probability of success. With the mildly bullish spread, Katie achieves a nice balance between her risk and the price movement required for a successful trade. Katie's ultimate choice of strategy depends on her trading personality and appetite for risk. Those same factors will guide you when you must make the same decisions.

STRATEGY APPLICATION

The vertical debit spread may be created with calls (bull call spread) or puts (bear put spread). For either direction, the trade is best applied in neutral to slightly directional markets. For strongly directional markets, it would be generally better to use a straight directional trade (long call or long put) in order to capture more price movement. Nevertheless, the debit spread strategy has a broad range of market conditions in which it may be successfully employed. Figure 9.2 illustrates a recommended target range, with low-to-mid scoring values for both trend (positive or negative) and volatility.

Market Score Trade

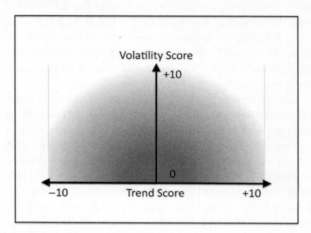

FIGURE 9.2 Market Score Application

Bearish Moving Average Crossover

The moving average is one of the most commonly used technical indicators in trading and investing. One reason is that most traders easily understand it. Moving averages are relatively simple to calculate and track price fairly closely. As a rule, the more complex the indicator, the more removed from price it becomes. Also, the concept of an average is common in everyday life. You talk about average income, batting average, and average fuel economy in a new vehicle. Second, moving averages serve as a support level when the price is above the average and as a resistance level when the price is trading below the average. They help make the identification of key price levels quick and easy. Third, moving averages may be calculated over multiple periods, which gives you greater flexibility because you can choose to use them as single indicators or in combination as multiple indicators.

Moving averages are known as trend-following indicators. This means that they are best applied when the stock price is in a trend—either up or down. Because a moving average is specifically intended to identify trends and reversals, it becomes much less reliable when the price is moving sideways. Even if the price has a wide trading range, indicating increased volatility, the moving average will go flat for a sideways (channeling) stock. When this happens, there will be numerous buy and sell signals, but they won't have much validity. Furthermore, the moving averages that served well as support and resistance during the trend lose their strength in a flat market as the price jumps above and below the lines. You need to be sure that the chart you're looking at has a trend in either direction before applying the moving average as a technical indicator.

In general, we recommend two primary moving average periods for option traders. The 50-day moving average is a good intermediate-term indicator because it approximates the number of trading days in a quarter. Companies post earnings and other reports quarterly, so it's good to have an indicator that smooths the quarter-to-quarter volatility that these events inevitably create. The second period is the 200-day moving average, widely recognized as the best long-term trend indicator. Many money managers, traders, and investors follow the 200-day moving average as a measure of the overall trend. Because so many others follow the 200-day moving average, it's important that you at least know where it is on your chart.

A common application of the moving averages is to select two different time periods and use both moving averages as crossover indicators. For the bearish moving average crossover, we use the 50-day simple moving average (SMA) and the 200-day SMA. The 50-day SMA is called the fast-moving average and the 200-day SMA is the slow-moving average. They are referred to as fast and slow due to their speed in responding to changes in price. If the 50-day SMA is above the 200-day SMA and the stock is trading above both, the stock is in an extended uptrend. This is illustrated at the left side of the chart in Figure 9.3. When the price trend starts to reverse, the

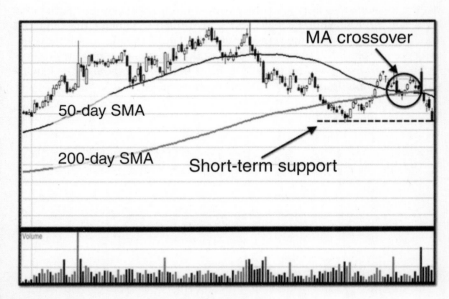

FIGURE 9.3 Bearish Moving Average Crossover

faster-moving average will respond to the price movement sooner. In this case, the 50-day SMA will begin to show the reversal before the 200-day SMA. Typically, the price will fall below the 50-day SMA and then down through the 200-day SMA, and then the 50-day SMA drifts lower until it reaches the 200-day SMA. The bearish moving average crossover is the point at which the 50-day SMA finally breaks below the 200-day SMA.

You can see the 50-day SMA (black line) crossing the 200-day SMA (gray line) at the right side of the chart in Figure 9.3. Notice how the price leads both moving averages at the far right side of the chart.

This example chart would be a good candidate for a vertical debit spread using puts (bear put spread). The chart does not indicate a strongly bearish trend because there is a short-term support level indicated by the dashed line in the illustration. It is quite possible that this stock may be moving into a channel rather than preparing to break to the downside. Of the three directions (up, down, or sideways), down and sideways are the most probable. Therefore, you would conclude that the most appropriate strategy would be one that profits in a neutral to slightly bearish market. Remember, if your analysis leads you to believe that the stock is strongly bearish (no support, high volume price drops), your best strategy is a directional position such as long puts. That would provide you with the greatest profit potential if your analysis is correct.

Your selection of strike prices for this example would follow the guidelines of profit, risk, and probability that we presented in the preceding strategy discussion. For this trade, you would identify the key resistance level and protect yourself against a move higher. Though the bear put spread strategy has a limited risk, you should still consider closing the entire spread position if the stock price breaks resistance and rallies to new highs. Otherwise, you can expect to have both legs expire OTM, leaving you with the maximum loss of the position net debit.

CHAPTER 10

Cash-Secured Puts

Novice traders tend to remember the basic option concepts by thinking of calls as the option to use when you're bullish on the market and puts as the option to use when you're bearish. In the simplest trade setup—buying a call or put as a directional strategy—that's not a bad way to become familiar with option trading. However, that approach oversimplifies the various choices you have as an option trader in constructing your trade for bull, bear, or sideways markets.

The put option may also be used when you're bullish on a stock or exchange-traded fund (ETF). The difference is that instead of buying the right to sell the stock (long put), you're selling that right to someone else. In doing so, you obligate yourself to purchase the stock because you must take the opposite side of the trade you sold. Remember, every buy matches with a sell and every right matches with an obligation. So if the person who buys a put has a right to sell stock, then selling a put places you into an obligation to buy stock. When would you want to buy stock? When you're at least somewhat bullish on the stock, of course. Cash-secured puts may be used to position yourself for buying stock that you would be willing to own based on your technical and fundamental analysis.

GETTING TO KNOW THE STRATEGY

Interestingly, we've observed that investors like to assign a fair value to a favorite stock when it comes time to buy that stock. This price is usually not established by any fundamental valuation. Instead, there seems to be a prevailing desire to buy stocks that appear to be on sale. Of course, we're trained as consumers to look for the deal and we extend that approach to our purchase of investment assets.

It's important to point out that, unlike buying a used car, the trader's objective is not to get the lowest possible price, but to purchase something that has the highest probability of price appreciation. A $5 stock is not inherently better than a $50 stock if the latter has greater price growth potential. The drive toward cheap stocks is one reason why companies have stock splits. When a company has a 2-for-1 stock split, the market capitalization doesn't go up one penny unless the stock price rises. And if you own shares in the company prior to the split, after the split you'll end up with twice as many shares but each share is worth half as much as before. The net effect to your equity is zero.

It might be prudent when negotiating for a used car to offer the seller 90 percent of his asking price in order to get the deal you want. However, buying a stock that has fallen in value by 10 percent over the past few days means you're buying into a stock that is controlled by sellers versus buyers. Although cash-secured puts may be used in slightly bearish markets as a way to buy stocks at a perceived sale price, you still need to recognize that you're buying against the trend. Many traders do the same thing when they place a limit buy order below the current trading price, thus ensuring that they will only make their purchase when the stock weakens. Do you really want to open a new position based on your stock price weakening and being controlled by sellers?

For that reason, we recommend cash-secured puts more as a bull market income strategy rather than as a stock accumulation strategy. Although you would be willing to own the stock, your primary goal is to collect premium, not to purchase the stock through assignment. The basic strategy involves selling a put option on a bullish stock, ETF, or index in order to receive a premium. Ideally, the underlying will continue to rise, the option will expire worthless, and the trader will get to keep the premium. It's not just about receiving the premium and then getting assigned to buy the stock.

There are three points to consider when you sell a put option. The first is that you are now obligated to buy shares of the underlying at a predetermined price (strike price) for a specified amount of time (until expiration). This isn't very different from placing a limit order. When you place a limit order, you also obligate yourself to buy a stock at a specific price, although you don't receive anything for entering into this obligation. One could argue that the limit order investor could cancel at any time. Although this is true, we've seldom observed cancelled limit orders for clients. Why don't investors ever cancel limit orders? Simply, they want the order to execute so they can pick up the shares at a discounted value from when they initially placed the order. With a limit buy order, the investor actually hopes the price will decline to his limit price, thereby allowing him to acquire shares.

This is a key difference between a cash-secured put seller and an investor placing a limit order. The put seller might be comfortable with an assignment of shares, but his real objective should be to continue selling cash-secured puts without getting assigned. If he does get assigned and has to purchase the shares, he was paid for the obligation through the premium received. In fact, if he truly wanted shares, he could increase his possibility of assignment by adjusting the strike price higher. The put seller receives a credit in his account in the form of the premium for his obligation.

The second point to consider is how time decay affects the position. For the cash-secured put seller, time decay is a good thing. For the buyer of any option, time decay works against the position. As each day passes, the portion of the option premium that represents time slowly melts away. That money doesn't just melt away and vanish into thin air, because the seller of that option is on the other end of the contract enjoying the benefit time decay. For each dollar your position lost in time decay, his value increased a dollar. Time decay, or theta, is negative for the option buyer and positive for the option seller. As a seller of cash-secured puts, your goal is to reach the expiration date without being assigned, at which point you realize the profit from complete time decay.

The third consideration you need to be aware of is that the cash-secured put will hold back or block a certain amount of cash to ensure that your account balance can cover the price of the shares that you're obligated to buy. This is money that cannot be withdrawn or used for other investments. It is the security for your transaction, hence, the name *cash-secured*.

STRATEGY IN ACTION

Let's take a look at a cash-secured put in action. Frank had been researching a company for several weeks and decided he wanted to purchase 1,000 shares for his portfolio. Figure 10.1 shows a chart of CS Put Co. with a support level of $27.60 clearly marked.

Frank considered two approaches through which he could acquire shares. The first was to simply buy shares on the open market. The current price at the time was $29.34. Although he didn't think that was a bad entry price, he was disappointed that he missed the pivot point around $27.60. Now he has trader's remorse because he thought about what he should have done. He could have placed a limit order at $27.60 and hoped the stock moved down to this level. Of course, then he would have to then hope that it would turn around and move higher. Notice that this is a strategy based on hope—which is not a strategy at all.

FIGURE 10.1   CS Put Co. Chart for a Cash-Secured Put

Pay attention to the capital requirements for the limit order trade. By placing a limit order at $27.60, he would need to have $27,600 in his account (assuming he doesn't wish to use any margin). However, if the stock were to continue its sideways trend or move higher, he would not acquire the 1,000 shares and, therefore, would have no possibility of capturing a profit.

Frank's second approach was to sell a cash-secured put option. He reviewed the CS Put Co. option chain and looked forward about nine months. Because he had a bullish bias on the stock, he focused his attention on the $30 strike price, which is just slightly in-the-money. He anticipated that in nine months' time CS Put Co. would be trading well above $30 and the contract would expire worthless, allowing him to keep the premium. In the event that the stock should be trading below $30 at expiration, he was comfortable with the notion of being assigned 1,000 shares. His only concern was the possibility of the stock falling below the major support level at $27.60.

When Frank checked the quote on the January CS Put Co. $30 put, it was $3.10 bid and $3.20 ask. Frank decided to place the following order: Sell to Open 10 CS Put Co. Jan 30 Put Limit 3.15. As a review, here are the parts of his order:

- Sell—The transaction is a sell.
- Open—Indicates that this is the first, or opening, transaction in the trade.

- 10—Frank sold 10 contracts representing 1,000 shares of CS Put Co.
- CS Put Co.—The underlying asset associated with the option.
- Jan—Expiration month.
- 30—Strike price for the selected option.
- Put—Put option rather than call option.
- Limit—Order type with a specified limit price—guarantees price but doesn't guarantee execution.
- 3.15—The price specified for the limit order.

If this order executed, Frank would receive a credit of $315 per contract (or $3,150 less commissions for 10 contracts) into his account. This money would be his and he could do with it as he chooses. In order for Frank's broker to ensure the funds remain available to fulfill his obligation to purchase 1,000 shares at $30, $30,000 will be blocked from being withdrawn or used to purchase other stock positions.

Consider for a moment that Frank would receive $3.15 for an obligation to buy shares at $30 at any time over the next nine months. If he does end up buying the shares at $30, his cost basis would be offset by $3.15. In other words, if he really did feel that $27.60 was the optimal buying point but he missed his chance, the cash-secured put, if assigned to him, would allow him to purchase shares with a cost basis of $26.85. That's a bargain in Frank's mind.

STRATEGY MANAGEMENT

Cash-secured puts are not a fire-and-forget type of trade. They still require management because you continue to have risk to the downside as long as your account is short the puts. As such, the minimum required trade management consists of protecting against loss when key support levels are broken.

Rate of Return

The numbers can be attractive on cash-secured puts. Many traders look at the cash in their money market accounts earning less than they would like—in some markets less than 1 percent annually. Selling puts gives you premium income while you hold cash in reserve for the possibility of buying the stock through assignment. The premium income you collect usually far exceeds interest income in a very low rate environment.

Actual rate of return = Premium received ÷ strike price

Annualized rate = (Actual rate ÷ number of days to expiration) × 365

Here's the calculation on Frank's trade: $3.15 \div 30 = 10.5$ percent, then $10.5 \div 290 = .0362 \times 365 = 13.22$ percent annualized rate of return.

Maximum Profit

Because the cash-secured put position obligates Frank to buy shares at $30 but affords him no right to buy shares at $30, his upside is limited at this time. A put seller should look at the maximum gain as the amount received in premium. In this case, Frank's maximum gain is $3.15 per share. If the stock rallies to $50 during the life of this put obligation, the put seller has no way to force the put buyer to execute and sell him shares at $30. It wouldn't make any sense that an owner of 1,000 shares worth $50 per share would have any interest in exercising his right to sell shares at $30.

Maximum Loss

The maximum Frank could lose on this strategy is calculated as the strike price minus the premium received. In this example, $30 - $3.15 = $26.85 per share, or $26,850 plus fees. This is one of the biggest disadvantages with this strategy. Frank has a relatively small reward for such a large risk. We often hear from people who consider this a free money strategy because uptrending stocks can deliver healthy returns over and over again using this strategy. These traders start to believe their stock will never come down and, if it did, they would just sell more puts because they want to buy this great company as cheaply as possible. We'll gently remind these folks that we heard the same thing about Enron, General Motors, Lehman Brothers, and Kmart. We know investors who are still holding on to shares of once high-flying stocks that fell out of favor and their cash-secured positions were assigned.

Break-Even

Break-even is calculated as the strike price less premium received—the same as the maximum loss. Frank will begin to lose money on his trade if CS Put Co. drops below $26.85 and stays there at expiration. Remember, the cash-secured put seller wants the price of the underlying to hold steady or rally so that the put reaches expiration out-the-money and expires worthless.

Exit Strategy

Frank's primary objective with this strategy was income. The secondary objective was to acquire shares of CS Put Co. at an attractive price point.

However, the trader's adage of "don't try to catch a falling knife" is appropriate here. If the stock is breaking down, it's best to close out the position. This is especially true because the risk-to-reward ratio is almost 9:1. Using a conditional order to execute a closing transaction (buy puts to close) if the price of CS Put Co. trades significantly below $27.60 will allow Frank to automate his exit. Exiting at this level will result in some loss, but because the position has positive theta, time is on his side. The more time that elapses between opening the position and closing it, the more the loss will be minimized. Time will not cure a trade that's gone bad, but in this case will help to lessen the damage.

There are three possible outcomes for Frank's position.

1. Put expires worthless. If Frank does not get assigned on his shares of CS Put Co., he does get to keep 100 percent of the premium from the sale of the put. This is the most positive outcome and even if CS Put Co. soared to new highs during this period, Frank met his primary income objective. Having a cash-secured put expire worthless is a positive outcome and should always be viewed as such.

2. Put is assigned. Assuming the price trended sideways and has not turned bearish, it's likely that the put will approach expiration in-the-money. When this happens, a trader should anticipate an assignment to buy shares at the strike. Shares will be delivered to the account over the weekend and cash will be withdrawn at the same time. Because many investors use this strategy as a way to acquire shares of what they feel are good-quality, long-term investments, investors are often delighted when they are assigned shares at the strike price. Now that they own shares, some investor will immediately move to a covered call strategy and start selling out-the-money covered calls with a near-term expiration. This allows the investor to continue to produce income with the position through call writing.

3. Close the trade early. If a profit target is reached, a loss threshold violated, or the market in general begins to turn against you, your best recourse is to buy the put back to salvage the profit or remaining equity.

Dividends and the Put Seller

Assume CS Put Co. pays an annual cash dividend of 3.4 percent. Because Frank is a put seller, he is not entitled to nor will he receive any dividend unless and until he becomes an actual shareholder. If he had placed a limit order at $27.60, he would also not receive the dividend unless and until he acquired the shares. Another important item to note is that on the day the stock trades ex-dividend, the share price will open lower by the amount of the dividend. If CS Put Co. pays a $0.25 quarterly dividend, then on the date the stock trades ex-dividend, the price will open $0.25 lower than the previous day's close. Therefore, the price of the put option will increase slightly due to the drop in the value of the underlying shares.

Capital Requirements

Selling cash-secured puts is a capital-intensive strategy. In a retirement account or a nonmargin account, the capital requirement is equal to the cost to purchase the shares minus the premium received. As a result of this substantial capital requirement, many put sellers prefer credit put spreads. Using a credit spread is far less capital-intensive and will substantially reduce overall risk.

A Hard Lesson Learned

We once worked with a client who had amassed several million dollars worth of Dell stock after working for the company from its earliest days. He had retired in his early forties after learning a little about option trading from a coworker. His position at the time was worth around $3 million. Because he had retired early, he was selling puts as a way to produce monthly income. Besides the shares of Dell, he had very little cash in the account. He was using the equity from his Dell shares as collateral to sell out-the-money puts on Dell and was living off the cash generated each month. He was selling so many contracts that his obligation would be upwards of $1 million if he were to be assigned.

We began to work with him on risk management strategies for his benefit as well as his brokerage firm's benefit. Because he didn't have enough cash available to cover his obligation, he would need to borrow against his large position of Dell should he be assigned. The firm was asking him to hedge this large position with protective puts or switch to credit spreads that would better define and limit his risk. We explained that the risk to him and the firm was increased due to his concentrated position in Dell and the fact that he was using his shares in Dell as collateral to fulfill his obligation to buy shares on margin (margin is a loan the brokerage makes to the investor based on the value of his stock or bond positions). If Dell were to drop, the equity from his shares would also decline and he would start to get assigned on his naked puts. As opposed to cash-secured puts that are collateralized by cash, naked puts don't have cash set aside to cover the obligation. Instead, he would use borrowed money to purchase the shares and pay the firm margin interest until the position was paid off.

A 33 percent drop in Dell's value would then put his equity at $2 million. Because his obligation to purchase shares was around $1 million, he would be forced to liquidate shares of Dell at lower prices in order to buy shares of Dell at higher prices. Alternatively, he would start to accrue considerable interest each month if he opened a margin loan. It was a problem because we knew he was living off the monthly premiums and the potential downward spiral placed both the client and the firm at risk.

He was opposed to the idea of hedging the position because a hedge would cut into his income. He also disliked covered calls because he didn't want to cap the value of his Dell shares or be forced to sell them if his calls were assigned.

As a result of our consultations, the client sent in a comprehensive historical price analysis that indicated that the price of Dell had never fallen to a level that would put him or the firm at risk during the period in which he was selling puts. In his opinion, we were acting irrationally and had no data to justify our concerns. Our irrational behavior was preventing him from making even more money using his foolproof strategy. His analysis failed to persuade the firm's risk department, and he was held to a special maintenance. This prevented him from assuming any more risk than he already had unless he hedged the overall position or diversified the portfolio.

You've probably already figured out how this story ends. This story took place in the late 1990s when Dell was trading well above $40. The event that couldn't possibly happen according to the client's calculations did, in fact, happen. The client suffered massive losses as more and more shares of Dell were liquidated at progressively lower prices in order to meet his obligation to purchase Dell at higher prices. Along with the losses, margin interest, and commissions, the client also had taxes due.

Surprisingly, he didn't go broke but he did go back to work. As you learn credit spreads in other chapters, think back to this example and ask yourself, "Why didn't he just do a credit spread?" Each time we think back to this client we recall that he was fully aware of other strategies that would have better defined his risk. Despite our many attempts to educate him on hedging, risk management, position management, and defined risk trading, he was convinced that a strategy that had worked so well for so long was infallible. He was willing to take the risk and was not willing to give up any of the income. Just because a strategy makes money for a time doesn't mean that strategy is necessarily sound.

STRATEGY APPLICATION

The cash-secured put may be used in a neutral to slightly bullish market as an income strategy with a secondary objective of a stock accumulation strategy. Alternatively, the strategy may be more focused as an income-only strategy in a stronger bullish market. The stronger the uptrend, the less likely you'll see an assignment. That means the primary objective in a strong uptrend is income. As you can see in Figure 10.2, any volatility level (0 to +10) with an up-trending score (0 to +10) is appropriate for the cash-secured put.

Market Score Trade

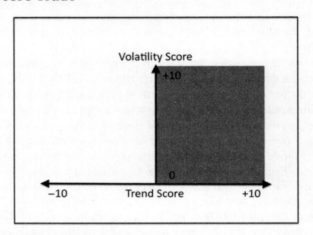

FIGURE 10.2   Market Score Application

Base after Pullback

You know from observation that uptrends and downtrends don't last forever, however unlikely that seems when you're on the wrong side of one! It is common to see a stock move sideways after an extended uptrend, only to break the sideways channel and experience a significant drop in price. This is illustrated in Figure 10.3.

Notice how the price drifts lower at a relatively shallow angle for the first half of the chart. At the right side, you can see how the price drop accelerates and volume increases. Think about the story that is being told by the chart. Price is dropping quickly and volume is rising at the same time, telling you that the sellers are becoming increasingly aggressive. At some point, the sellers will run out of steam and that's what you want to watch for in the chart. That point is indicated buy a drop in volume and a stabilization of the price.

In the example shown, you can see that the highest volume occurs with the trading that leads to the support level indicated by the dashed line. Although volume stays slightly higher after the drop than before, the chart reveals a clear decline from the spike you see during the price fall. What you can take from this picture is that the selling pressure is leaving the market in favor of a balance between buyers and sellers.

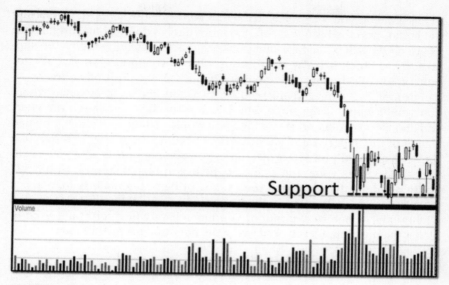

FIGURE 10.3 Base after Pullback Chart

Notice, also, that the candles are typically longer after the price drop. Compare the candles that occur around the drawn support level with the candles at the left side of the chart. You see longer bodies and shadows at the right side of the chart, indicating more volatility in the price. Although the price doesn't have an established direction, telling you that the buyers and sellers are holding it at relatively steady levels, there is a lot of back-and-forth. For the cash-secured put seller, that volatility translates into higher premium income.

The strategy for the cash-secured put seller in this scenario begins with making sure you have a well-established base. This is not a strategy that should be used at the first sign of support following a sharp drop. Without a clear base of support, the risk of selling puts into a short-term breather is too great. A sharp decline in price will often see one or two candles that slow or stop the decline. They may appear as green candles and may even have high associated volume. These do not necessarily indicate that the sellers are finished, but rather that they're regrouping for the next leg of the fall! As you can see in the example illustration, the support level has been confirmed by three separate tests of support. Remember that your goal is income, not buying stock as the price falls past your strike.

Your selection of the strike price should be based on the trading behavior of the stock during the base. Generally, you want to sell a strike that is close to the base support level. If you want to decrease the likelihood of assignment, you may sell a strike that is just below support. Obviously, the higher into the base you sell, the more likely you'll see an assignment. There really isn't a need to sell a strike that is significantly below the support. If the stock price were to drop well below support, you would not hold on to collect your premium; you should exit the position entirely.

Proper risk management requires that you decide in advance where you would stop out the trade. The best approach is to analyze the chart and choose a specific price at which you would sell the stock if you owned shares of the underlying. That price then becomes your trigger for exiting the cash-secured put. If, for example, you see support at $38 you might choose $36.85 as your stop price. Suppose you then sold puts with a $37 strike price. At the point that the trading price of the underlying reaches $36.85, you don't hold your puts open and hope that the price moves slightly higher before expiration. You immediately buy your puts back to closet the position, thereby removing the potential for further loss.

Role Reversal Support

Key price levels tend to shift back and forth between acting as support and acting as resistance. It would almost appear as a battleground between the buyers and sellers as they struggle for control of the trading direction. When a price level starts as support and then becomes resistance, or vice versa, that is known as a role reversal. Role reversals occur in all time frames, from intraday to monthly charts. These often serve as solid guidelines for entering and exiting trades because, by definition, a role reversal has at least two points to confirm the level.

Figure 10.4 shows a stock that begins with an established resistance level, noted by the "R". In fact, you could extend the dashed line to the far left side of the chart and see that the resistance level was confirmed earlier. You can then see how the price enters a series of green (white) candles that results in a break above resistance. At the same time, volume sharply increases, lending strength to the significance of the breakout. Following the breakout, the price swings wildly but still holds above the former resistance. At the point that price falls to the previous resistance level ("S" on the chart), it bounces higher, thereby confirming the role reversal. Resistance broken has become support.

A cash-secured put may be used effectively following the confirmation of a role reversal support. As you can see in our example, volatility is often higher after a breakout, which adds to the premium you'll be able to collect from selling the puts. Because this strategy is built on a breakout setup, you often have the ability to manage your position as the price moves higher. You would initially sell a put with a strike at or near the role reversal. As the stock price moves higher and sets new support levels, you can adjust your

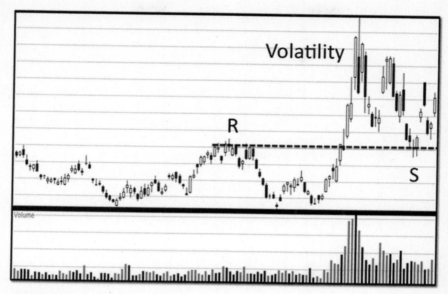

FIGURE 10.4 Role Reversal

position by buying back your first puts and selling higher strikes. When you buy to close your initial puts, you can expect pay less than what you collected from the initial sale. You then sell puts at a higher strike, once again keeping the strike at or near the new support level. Both trades result in credits to your account.

Risk management in this setup is fairly straightforward. As with the base after pullback trade, you must first decide on a price at which you would exit the trade if you owned the underlying shares. For the role reversal, your stop price should be just below the role reversal level. Again, be sure to have a specific price targeted. It does you no good to generally agree to exit the trade somewhere below the role reversal support. Without a clear price in mind, when the time comes for you to properly close the position, you'll have a remarkable gift for creating reasons why you should hold the trade open just a little longer. Also, if you observe that the price is starting to get heavy—that is, the highs are getting lower and the support is being tested more frequently—it may be best to exit the trade even if the role reversal support isn't broken. Because the cash-secured put gains from time decay, you may be able to buy your puts back for pennies as you get closer to expiration. If the price appears to be weakening and you're nearing expiration, don't wait for support to be broken.

CHAPTER 11

Credit Spreads

C onceptually, credit spreads are relatively simple and that makes them a favorite of many traders. Although credit spreads are a bit more complex for novice traders than a directional option, they are simpler to manage than debit spreads. Nevertheless, novice traders think in terms of buying first and selling later, so the debit spread is one of the first complex option strategies they gravitate toward. This is one of the reasons you will find more debit spread traders at the novice levels and more credit spread traders at the more advanced end of the learning curve.

It may take a little longer to get accustomed to the way the various parts work together. It's a little bit like driving a car in the United Kingdom versus the United States. They are practically identical, with a few important differences that most drivers will quickly accommodate. When driving in both regions, the brake, accelerator, and steering all work in the same fashion. The big difference is that the driving position is reversed, and, therefore, the side of the road for traffic flow is reversed. In time, a person makes adjustments and should be able to readily move back and forth between the two styles. (If not, the process tends to be somewhat Darwinian!) The same is true for trading debit and credit spreads. There are differences in the direction of the trade (buy versus sell) that dictate how profits are ultimately captured. Those will be evident when we re-cast the identical trade from the debit spread chapter as a credit spread position.

GETTING TO KNOW THE STRATEGY

In a bull put spread (another name for a vertical credit spread using put options), you sell a higher-priced put option (higher strike) and use some of the proceeds to buy a lower-priced put option (lower strike). Notice the difference from the bull call spread (which is a debit spread) where you buy a higher-priced call option (lower strike) and sell a lower-priced call option (higher strike) to partially offset the price.

Let's look at a basic example. Will, another model trader, had been using debit spreads to trade both bull and bear markets over the past few years. As much as he had been enjoying a successful streak of trades, he wished he could avoid the commissions associated with entering and exiting his profitable debit spreads. He always figured that commissions were the cost of doing business in complex option strategies. Then he attended a workshop on credit spreads where he saw the commission advantages of the credit spread over the debit spread. He decided to create side-by-side debit and credit spreads on his next position. We'll take a look at that next.

STRATEGY IN ACTION

Will was moderately bullish on a $21 stock. Based on his chart analysis, he believed it would move higher than $22 within the next month. Typically, he would use a debit spread, buying a $21 call and selling a $22 call with the same expiration. That debit spread is known as a bull call spread. In summary, here was Will's position with the bull call spread:

- He's moderately bullish.
- He's long the $21 call, giving him the right to buy shares at $21.
- He's short the $22 call, placing him in the obligation to sell shares at $22.
- He pays a net debit of $0.45 per share for the spread.

If Will executed a 10-contract position he would have a total debit of $450 plus fees. Because the spread was one dollar wide, the most he could make by buying shares at $21 and selling shares at $22 would be one dollar per share minus the $0.45 per share cost of the spread, yielding a maximum profit of $0.55 per share. His maximum possible loss is what he paid for the spread. This was a bullish position, so he needed the position to move higher to be profitable. Will's break-even of $21.45 (excluding fees) was calculated by taking the long leg strike of $21 and adding the position net debit of $0.45.

After he had set up the debit spread, he began to calculate the credit spread. Because his analysis and opinion of the stock remained the same, he chose to use the same $21 and $22 strike prices to create his credit spread. The difference is that instead of using calls in a bull call spread (debit call spread), he used puts to build a bull put spread (credit put spread). He considered selling the same month's $22 put at the bid price of $1.35 and using some of the proceeds to buy the $21 put at the ask price of $0.80. This transaction would provide a credit of $0.55 per share or $550 for a 10-contract position.

Notice that the credit Will would receive through the credit spread was equal to the maximum profit of the debit spread. Also take note that the maximum loss for the credit spread was the difference between the width of the spread ($1 per share) and the position net credit ($0.55 per share), or $0.45 per share. The maximum loss and maximum gain for the debit spread was the same as he calculated for the credit spread. He calculated the break-even price by taking the short leg strike ($22) and subtracting the position net credit ($0.55) for a break-even price of $21.45. This was the same as the break-even for the debit spread. Up to this point the two trades were essentially the same.

Because Will had been consistently successful with his debit spread trades, let's see what happened when he was successful with his credit spread trade. The day prior to expiration and an hour before the market was to close, the stock was trading at $22.15. Both legs of his debit spread were in-the-money. If Will failed to close the trade in that final hour, he would be auto-assigned and auto-exercised over the weekend.

Will didn't want to go through the exercise and assignment process, so he prepared to close the position. He needed to buy back the $22 call (BCC, or buy call to close) and sell the $21 call (SCC, or sell call to close) to close the spread. The $22 call had an ask price of $0.18 and the $21 call had a bid price of $1.16. That would allow Will to close the position with a credit of $0.98 per share. Because he wanted to avoid the exercise and assignment process (also known as a same-day substitution), his spread suffered some slippage due to the bid/ask spread. This slippage, along with the fact that he had commissions to close the spread, took a few percentage points off his maximum profit. If he did go through the same-day substitution, he would typically be charged two stock transaction fees but would not suffer the slippage.

Let's look at what would happen in this same situation if Will had a credit spread instead of a debit spread. Because the stock was about to close at $22.15, both the $21 strike put and the $22 strike put would go into expiration out-the-money, and thus, expire worthless. Will need not do anything and the credit spread would have reached the point of maximum profit. The $0.55 per share credit that he received 37 days prior would remain in his account. Will wouldn't experience any slippage, commissions, or the hassle of closing the position.

To keep this example balanced, let's look at what happens when the trade goes the other direction. Suppose the stock declined and was trading at $20.85 one hour prior to close the day before expiration. The debit spread would be out-the-money and Will could just let it expire worthless. In doing so, he would experience the maximum loss of $0.45 per share but would not be required to take any action. The credit spread, however, would be in-the-money and Will would need to either close the trade (in which case he would suffer some bid/ask slippage in addition to fees) or he could go through the exercise and assignment process over the weekend and incur stock commissions. If he were to allow the position to move to expiration, he would also experience maximum loss of $0.45 per share plus fees.

As Will discovered, credit spreads instead of debit spreads help to reduce trade maintenance and commissions. In theory, skilled and disciplined option traders should experience more successful than unsuccessful trades. Therefore, it stands to reason that using a strategy with less maintenance and associated costs is superior to a strategy that has more maintenance and higher associated costs. Even though the maintenance and fees for profitable trades are lower, many traders start with debit spreads as a natural evolution from covered calls and other beginner-type strategies.

STRATEGY MANAGEMENT

We've already mentioned that the credit spread allows you to profit without additional steps when the market moves in the direction of the spread, but that doesn't make the credit spread an entirely hands-off strategy.

Calculations

Max profit	The position net credit less fees.
Max loss	The width of the spread minus the position net credit received. For example, a $20/$21 credit spread with a $0.55 credit is calculated as $1.00 − $0.55 = $0.45 (plus fees).

Break-even	The short leg strike minus the position net credit plus fees.
Capital required	The amount of money required to initiate and hold a credit spread is equivalent to the maximum loss of the overall position. You are not required to have the available funds to cover the purchase of the shares represented by the short leg. However, as expiration approaches and the underlying is situated between the long and short leg strikes, if you do not wish to be assigned on your obligation to purchase shares, you should close the spread by first buying back the short leg and then selling the long leg.

The calculations table is based on the bull put spread (vertical credit spread using put options).

Expiring in No-Man's-Land A bull put spread is in no-man's-land when the price of the stock is below the short leg strike but above the long leg strike. If expiration approaches and the spread is in this zone, you risk being assigned. You would be required to purchase shares at the higher strike. Because your long leg is still out-the-money, you are faced with a position maintenance decision.

One choice is to hold the shares assigned to you as a long position. You could then sell calls against the long position to generate additional premium income. Another choice would be to subsequently sell the shares on the open market at the current price. It's important that you recognize that holding shares beyond the expiration of the long leg of the option exposes you to a maximum loss greater than the initial spread. Think of the long leg as an insurance policy on your car and your shares represent your car. Once the policy expires, you are no longer insured. You need to ask yourself the question, "Can I afford the risk of driving an uninsured car after the insurance has expired?" If your answer is no then you need to sell the shares prior to the option expiration date.

Trading in 3-D

Too often traders take a two-dimensional view of trade opportunities. If you had to choose from among the following three trades, which would you pick?

Trade	Risk	Reward
A	0.35	0.65
B	0.50	0.50
C	0.65	0.35

Typically, there is little hesitation when we ask traders this question. The clear choice is Trade A, in which there is the least risk and the most reward. You look at Trade B and think that it is no better than a coin flip. Even more so, Trade C seems to make no sense whatsoever. It would seem foolish to take a trade in which you'd lose twice as much as you could gain.

As we've pointed out several times, the market is an efficient machine that maintains a constant balance between variables. There is no free money out there. Choosing a trade setup based only on risk versus reward misses a key component that the professionals never miss: probability. A former colleague who spent 25 years on the floor of the Chicago Board Options Exchange explained his strategy as "spending each and every day picking up nickels and dimes in front of a steam roller. It's easy money but if I ever slipped I'd be crushed."

In simple terms, professional traders take high-probability trades with small returns and large dollar risks. They manage the risks with hedge strategies and quickly exit a trade before much of the risk is realized. The professionals take Trade C. Retail traders, on the other hand, tend to take low dollar risk trades with high returns but low probabilities of success. They take Trade A. The retail trader selects trades based on two dimensions: (1) how much can be made (reward) and (2) how much can be lost (risk). The greater the difference between these two, the more they like it. The professional trader selects trades based on risk, reward, and the additional dimension of probability of success. The higher the likelihood of receiving the reward, the more desirable the trade is.

Let's revisit the table and add a third column in order to better understand how to trade in three dimensions: risk, reward, and probability.

Trade	Risk	Reward	Probability of Success
A	0.35	0.65	Low
B	0.50	0.50	Medium
C	0.65	0.35	High

The trade in which the greatest amount of money is at risk also has the highest probability of generating the smallest profit. The trade that has greatest amount of potential reward has the lowest probability of success. It's this balance that becomes so important for you to consider. Because it is balanced, there is not a right or wrong answer. Instead, you must assess your appetite for risk in determining which trade is appropriate for your portfolio.

Nobel laureate William F. Sharpe devised a formula for calculating whether a portfolio's returns were a result of successful strategy application and management or the result of excess risk. This formula is the Sharpe ratio. Although we are not going to take a deep dive into the theory behind the Sharpe ratio, it's important to understand that measuring a strategy's worth, a trader's success, or a hedge fund's performance is meaningless in the absence of an analysis of the risks. This analysis must include probability.

Let's illustrate the risk, reward, and probability balance with a parallel scenario in the real estate world. Suppose an investor has $150,000 with which to purchase a residential rental property. In the same county he finds three very different types of properties. His first potential market is the valley, where he could purchase a three-bedroom, two-bath home for $150,000 (Property A). These homes are basic tract homes that are fairly easy to rent out for $1,500 per month. Because the home could be purchased with cash, the majority of the $1,500 is income to the investor. At the peak of the recent real estate market, properties in these neighborhoods were selling for $250,000.

The second market is closer to the coast in a small, picturesque community. The same style tract homes are selling there for $350,000 (Property B) with monthly rents of about $1,750. To purchase one of these, the investor would need to borrow $200,000. The rent would then go toward the monthly mortgage, consuming most of the monthly income. However, at the peak of the market, these homes were selling for $650,000.

The third market is along the scenic coast with small, older, two-bedroom, one-bath bungalows that are selling for $450,000 (Property C). Due to the bungalows' age and small size, the rent would be only $1,400. To purchase one of these properties, the investor would need to borrow $300,000. The $1,400 rent wouldn't cover the mortgage and, therefore, each month he would need to contribute additional funds for the mortgage payment. At the peak of the real estate market these homes were selling for $1,000,000.

By now you should begin to see how these three properties are balanced against each other. Property A is inexpensive and produces a healthy 12 percent return on investment through the monthly rent, but has limited upside appreciation (66 percent). Property C has a terrible return on investment because the rent will not even cover the mortgage payment, but the potential price appreciation is tremendous (144 percent). Property B fits somewhere in between the first two when comparing return on investment and appreciation. Property C has the greatest potential for price appreciation but also the lowest probability of a return on investment because it produces no net income. If the market does not show a recovery, then Property C will actually be an investment loss. Property C is entirely dependent on a future, uncertain event. Property A, on the other hand, would produce a consistent monthly return even if the real estate market were to remain flat without any price appreciation.

In order to make the best decision, the investor needs to assess his appetite for risk. If the investor were to choose Property C and the market increased dramatically, he could sell the property for $1,000,000. That doesn't necessarily mean he was a "good" investor or better than another investor who might have selected Property A. It simply means the investor's highly risky investment paid off.

There is no right answer in this example, just as there is often not a right answer when determining which strike prices to use when building a credit spread. Technical analysis is beneficial to help you estimate the likelihood of a price move of varying magnitudes. In doing so, you can vary the legs of a spread up or down one or more points to change your risk, reward, and probability of success. Each spread must be evaluated on the three levels: (1) risk, (2) reward, and (3) probability.

Bear Call Spread

Our model trader, Frank, had been seeing more signs of bearishness in the market when the indexes fell below both the 200-day SMA and the 50-day SMA. He had also been watching a technology stock that had been in a sustained downtrend with recent acceleration downward. Frank believed those bearish trends would continue so he chose to set up a bear call spread (vertical credit spread with call options). He was bearish but he wasn't quite sure how bearish.

He began his analysis by constructing three bear call spread scenarios: (1) moderately bearish, (2) mildly bearish, and (3) neutral. Following is a table that represents the three scenarios when the stock is trading at $22.93.

Scenario	Max Gain	Break-Even	Max Loss	Price Move to Max Profit	Return on Risk
Moderately Bearish 21/22	$0.70	$21.70	$0.30	−$1.93 (−8.4%)	233%
Mildly Bearish 22/23	$0.55	$22.55	$0.45	−$0.93 (−4.1%)	122%
Neutral 23/24	$0.40	$23.40	$0.60	+$0.11 (+0.47%)	66%

In the case of the moderately bearish scenario, Frank had selected strike prices that were both in-the-money. Because Frank was bearish on the market, and specifically on this stock, he was obligating himself to sell shares at $21. Even though Frank did not have shares to sell, he didn't think he would have to fulfill this obligation. The stock would need to stay below $21 at expiration for Frank to avoid his obligation to sell at $21. However, even if Frank's analysis was to prove incorrect, he had still bought the $22 strike price call, which gave him the right to purchase shares at $22 in the event he would be assigned to deliver shares at $21. By buying the $22 call, he had a way to meet his obligation in the event that the stock traded above $21 by expiration.

Note that with the stock trading at $22.93, $21 was a full $1.93 below the trading price at the time of analysis. That meant the stock would have to drop 8.4 percent in 37 days in order to reach maximum profitability. Break-even for that scenario was $21.70, which was 5.4 percent below the current price. This was the most aggressive of the three trades. It had the lowest probability of success, but also risked the lowest amount ($0.30) and provided the greatest potential for reward (233 percent ROR). Here's where technical analysis plays a key role. Frank would need to review the charts and see if it was reasonable to establish a trade that must drop 5.4 percent to break even and 8.4 percent in 37 days to achieve maximum profit. The trend, volatility, and past price performance help serve as a guide to what would be a reasonable expectation.

On the other end of the analysis was the 23/24 spread. That scenario was considered neutral because it was not dependent on the stock moving up or down in the 37 days leading up to expiration. That spread had the lowest return on risk at 66 percent, but the highest probability of success along with the greatest dollar amount at risk ($0.60). The break-even of the 23/24 spread was $23.40 and the maximum potential profit would be reached with the underlying at $23. Therefore, if the stock were to stay at the same level ($22.93), drop, or even increase by a few cents, Frank would still achieve maximum profit. In fact, this spread could go against Frank (stock price moves higher) a full 2 percent before he would start to lose money upon expiration. However, because of the low ROR and increased dollar amount at risk, any technical move higher should prompt quick action to close the spread.

In the case of the mildly bearish scenario, Frank selected a strike price that was in-the-money for the short leg and a strike price that was out-the-money for the long leg. The lower strike (short leg) of the spread was the $22 call. The higher strike (long leg) of the spread was the $23 call. Because this was the mildly bearish position, it stands to reason that this spread would achieve maximum gain if the stock were to decrease in value. This was evident in the value for maximum gain that would occur at $22 (−4.1 percent) and the break-even price of $22.55 (−1.7 percent).

One hallmark of a successful trader is the ability to manage risk while utilizing high-probability strategies. Too often, traders evaluate themselves based on how much they made or lost relative to others. This metric is useless without a consideration of the risks assumed, how the risks were managed, position sizing, and strategies utilized. Just because you made money, that doesn't mean you did something right. Just because you lost money, that doesn't mean you did something wrong. Spreads allow you to modulate risk, reward, and probability better than any other strategy.

STRATEGY APPLICATION

The vertical credit spread may be created with calls (bear call spread) or puts (bull put spread). For either direction, the trade is best applied in neutral to slightly directional markets. For strongly directional markets, it would be generally better to use a straight directional trade (long call or long put) in order to capture more price movement. Nevertheless, the credit spread strategy has a broad range of market conditions in which it may be successfully employed. Figure 11.1 illustrates a recommended target range, with low-to-mid scoring values for both trend (positive or negative) and volatility.

Market Score Trade

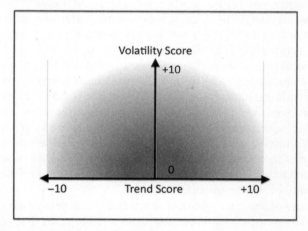

FIGURE 11.1 Market Score Application

Gaps with Follow-Through

Gaps are considered the bane of traders when they inconveniently and unexpectedly show up in the middle of an otherwise well-behaved trade.

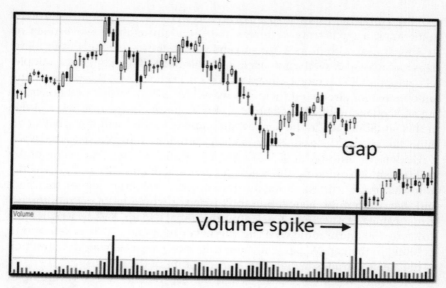

FIGURE 11.2 Price Gap with Follow-Through

Nevertheless, they may sometimes be put to use when you understand the driving force behind them.

A gap occurs when there is a significant difference between the closing price of one day and the opening price of the following day. That price difference shows up as "air" or space between the candles on a candlestick chart. This is illustrated in Figure 11.2.

You can see the gap down that occurred as noted on the chart. Notice that on the actual day of the gap, the candle was a long black (red) candle, indicating that the sellers were strongly in control of the trading. Furthermore, you can see solid confirmation by the volume spike that accompanied the gap. The basic story behind the gap-down trading day is that the sellers were aggressive in their selling, there was considerable activity surrounding the move, and the buyers simply refused to step in and support the price.

The gap itself is the result of changing market dynamics during the period that the markets are closed for trading. It may be the result of any number of catalysts: earnings, a filed lawsuit, drug approval, executive departure, merger announcement, and so on. At the close of the previous day, the market traded the stock at a particular price that reflected the perceived value for that stock. When the news or event gets out to the traders and investors while the market is closed, there is a collective repricing and that drives the following session's open. The greater the impact of the catalyst, the greater will be the size of the gap.

Typically, the response to a gap is either a reversal or a follow-through. Sometimes, a gap is truly an unreasonable and unsustainable overreaction to the catalyst. Oftentimes, those gaps will begin to reverse within a few days and may very well trade back up to the start of the gap. For example, let's suppose XYZ's stock closed at $50 on Friday. Over the weekend, an announcement circulated the news wires that a competitor was considering an acquisition of XYZ. Generally, the acquired company stock will rise in this situation, while the acquiring company's stock will fall. That's certainly not always the case, but it is fairly common. In response to the news, XYZ opens on Monday at $55. The $5 price difference was the result of the enthusiasm surrounding the weekend announcement. However, over the following days, it became apparent that there was more rumor than fact and that, even if the acquisition took place, it would be many months before it came together. One week after the initial gap up, XYZ was right back down to $50 and trading as if the gap never happened. This is referred to as filling in the gap. A gap fills when the price reverses from the direction of the gap and trades back at the starting point of the gap.

Another possible scenario is that the gap reflects a true revaluing of the stock and not an overreaction. In that instance, the gap is more like a new benchmark and will continue to trade in the direction of the gap. At the least, it will move sideways as it stabilizes around the new price benchmark. When that happens, the price follows through and doesn't reverse back to fill the gap.

It is in this scenario that you could consider a credit spread. Figure 11.2 shows a gap down with follow-through. Notice how there was a slight continuation of the downward trend immediately following the gap. Then the price moved slightly higher but found resistance very near the price to which it gapped when it made the initial move down. At the far right side of the chart, there is yet another attempt to move higher with resistance again holding the price down. You would reasonably conclude that the gap accurately reflects where the market thinks this stock should be trading. With this information, the most likely direction for the stock over the short term would be sideways to slightly lower.

If you were bearish on a stock such as this, the appropriate credit spread would be a bear call spread similar to the one we presented with our model trader, Frank. You could run though the same risk/reward/ probability sensitivity analysis to determine the best choice of strikes for your objectives and trading style. Just keep in mind that you'll buy the high strike and sell the low strike to create the credit. Your goal is for the stock to trade lower, leaving both options out-the-money and the premium in your account.

CHAPTER 12

Horizontal Spreads

T he horizontal spread is a member of the calendar spread or time spread family. In order to draw a real-life analogy to illustrate the concept, Shawn relates a story about his family's approach toward hands-on investing:

I grew up on the central coast of California in the 1970s. This period was characterized by high inflation, high interest rates, and lackluster stock market returns (not to mention questionable fashion taste!). The one bright spot for the central coast was the rapid and dramatic increase in residential real estate values and rents.

My parents were interested in acquiring real estate assets as a way to stay ahead of inflation and position themselves for retirement, still decades away, with income-producing investments. As a family, we set out to acquire several properties over the next few years with a strategy that was similar to the way an options investor would use a horizontal spread.

Every few summers, my parents would go looking for a single-family residence in need of repairs and some updates. They could usually purchase the property with a minimum down payment and then finance the balance, keeping enough money aside to repair and renovate their new investment. As new investment properties were purchased, they would be added to an existing portfolio of residential rental properties. Because both my parents were in education for the local school district and my brother and I were both students, the four of us had the entire summer off to refurbish a new investment. Some summers we would go on a long family vacation, but other summers we would purchase a property and go to work ripping out carpet, replacing shingle roofs, repairing plumbing, and spending hours painting and cleaning. It was mostly sweat equity because we had more time than money.

By the end of the summer, the house would be finished, but my parents wouldn't sell it, even though they could almost certainly realize a small profit from the sale. Instead, they made it available as a rental. I remember my parents always seemed quite relieved to have the house rented as we started back at school. I assumed it was because there was a decent return on our investment. I supposed that renting the house generated a steady profit that provided additional income to our household.

As I got a little older, I asked my parents how much profit we were making on these houses. I was shocked to learn that we weren't making any profit at all. In most cases, the rent was just enough to cover the mortgage payment. In one instance, we were paying $550 for the mortgage and only getting $500 from the rent. Why in the world were we giving up our summers, spending hours each day fixing up a smelly old house, just to go and lose money month after month? I knew what charity was and this was not a charitable effort. This was supposed to be an investment, and investments were supposed to make the investor money, but these properties didn't appear to be making us any money and in one case appeared to be losing money each month!

My father explained that we were making money on the property but it wasn't in a way that was obvious or immediate, as I had assumed. Dad explained to me the three ways we were profiting, although none of them made much sense to me at that time. However, I now realize just how prudent the strategy was. First, there was a tax advantage to the mortgage payment that saved us money. Second, the value of the property was increasing each month (price appreciation). Third, the renters were paying down the principal on the property (cost basis reduction). Eventually, the rent would become income and the value of the property would have far outpaced inflation.

Fast-forward three decades and Mom and Dad's foresight, hard work, and diligence have worked out well. The three advantages that Dad described to me have borne fruit because most of the properties in their portfolio are mortgage-free and provide a solid equity base with steady income for my parents in their retirement years.

Through horizontal spreads, we will introduce the use of a similar strategy in the options market to sacrifice short-term profits for longer-term gains. We will look at a spread that pays down the overall premium of a longer-term position and ultimately provides income, price appreciation, or both.

GETTING TO KNOW THE STRATEGY

Calendar spreads come in two varieties, horizontal and diagonal. To introduce the concepts of calendar spreads, we will start with the most basic type, the horizontal spread.

A horizontal spread is the simultaneous purchase of a long-term call or put contract along with the sale of a shorter-term call or put contract with the same strike price. This action creates a net debit for the overall position because the longer expiration option will cost more, all else being equal. The short-term contract has a much greater rate of theta (time decay) versus the longer-term contract. Because time only moves in one direction, the position benefits from the time decay. Time will actually erode both sides of the spread, but the difference between the rates of decay is how you capture your profit from the spread.

In the following table, we have pulled data from the S&P 500 index ETF (SPY) call option chain when the current price of SPY was $113.55. All three of the reference quotes are at-the-money calls, the only difference being time to expiration.

Strike	Days to Expiration	Time Value	Theta	Delta
$114	29	$4.50	−0.072	0.499
$114	85	$7.20	−0.036	0.512
$114	267	$10.86	−0.015	0.520

You can readily see from the theta values in the table option chain that the more time an option has before expiration, the lower the cost of time per day. Notice that if you purchase a call with 29 days, it will cost $7.20 per contract per day. Purchasing a call with 85 days will reduce the time cost by half to $3.60 per day and buying the call with 267 days will further reduce the time cost to $1.50 per day. Although the options with more time will cost more, they are a better value because they cost less per day.

Remember that in each of the three references above, the strike price remains at $114 in order to perform this side-by-side comparison. Now that we've pointed out the substantial differences in the cost of time, is there much of a difference in the expected change in value based on the movement of the underlying instrument? To answer this, we need look at the delta values of the three examples. As the numbers illustrate, there is a meager 0.021 difference in delta values between the high and low deltas. That means these three contracts will gain or lose value at almost the same rate at this time. The gamma (rate of change of the delta) values for the three options are different, so the 0.021 difference would not remain constant as the price of SPY moves up and down and these contracts move in-the-money or out-the-money.

The horizontal spread trader is primarily looking to exploit the differences in time decay values to pay down the cost of the longer-term contract. In our example, a horizontal spread could be constructed by buying the SPY $114 with 85 days to expiration for around $7.02 while simultaneously selling the SPY $114 with 29 days to expiration for around $4.50, for a net debit of $2.52. Essentially, you would be selling 34 percent of the remaining time of the long leg and offsetting your cost by 64 percent. Assuming that SPY stays at the same price ($113.55) over the next 29 days, the short leg would expire worthless. You could then sell another short leg in a new horizontal spread to further offset the cost of the long leg and produce some income or you could keep the long leg as a bullish directional position for the remaining 56 days. If you did elect to keep the long leg by itself, your position would shift from being almost delta neutral to delta positive and theta negative.

Although our example horizontal spread is theta positive and delta neutral for the next 29 days, the overall trade is bullish based on the fact that after the short leg of the horizontal spread expires, the position becomes a long call unless the first short leg is replaced with another short leg. Therefore, this would be a good strategy if you have a short-term neutral outlook but a longer-term bullish outlook. This makes the horizontal spread a strategy best initiated in flat or range-bound markets with a directional opinion over the longer term.

Horizontal spreads are more attractive in high-interest-rate environments because the time value of money is greater when interest rates are high versus low. The horizontal spread works best in an environment in which interest rates are increasing. This is ideal because when the long-term leg of the spread is purchased, the option is priced based on interest rates at that time. If interest rates do increase, then each time the short leg is sold in future spreads, you benefit from the higher interest rate valuations of the short-term options relative to the long-term leg that you own. An increase or decrease in interest rates will affect the long leg more than the short leg in a horizontal spread.

STRATEGY IN ACTION

In a flat market, our model trader, Frank, is more limited in his choice of strategies. Most mainstream strategies are at least somewhat directional in nature and profit is therefore dependent on being on the right side of the trend at the right time. Because he was seeing a nontrending market, Frank decided to utilize a horizontal spread. After an initial screen for uptrending moving averages, he found a stock that had a slight bullish trend. Although the rate of ascent was minimal, it did exceed the rate of the overall markets.

Frank first took a look at the news to determine the date for the next earnings announcement. He saw that the most recent announcement just occurred two weeks earlier. He estimated that he had over two and a half months before the next earnings announcement. Based on his technical analysis and review of the stock's fundamentals, Frank believed there was still more upside to the stock's price, although that could be many months off.

The stock was trading at $30.34 per share at the time of Frank's analysis. He wanted to buy a longer-term at-the-money call and considered the October $31 strike with 187 days remaining before expiration. The October $31 call was quoted $1.70 bid and $1.73 ask. He was able to purchase 10 contracts between the spread at $1.72. Excluding fees, he paid $1,720 for the contracts. Because his contracts controlled 1,000 shares and the entire premium was extrinsic value (time value only), his cost per day for the position was simple to calculate. The $1,720 total premium divided by 187 days yielded a cost of $9.20 per day to hold the position. The delta of the long leg was 0.47.

Once the long leg of the transaction was opened, Frank focused his attention on the short leg. He looked out to an expiration that was six weeks away, knowing that theta decay would begin to accelerate about six weeks out from expiration. He considered the May $31 call with 40 days to expiration. It was quoted $0.69 × $0.70 with a delta of 0.41. He decided to sell 10 contracts at $0.69 and brought in a credit of $690. Because this position was also out-the-money, the entire premium credit he received was extrinsic value. Because the contracts had just 40 days left until expiration, he calculated the daily theta decay to be $17.25 per day ($690 credit divided by 40 days). The short leg had a delta of 0.41.

STRATEGY MANAGEMENT

Once Frank built each leg of his position, he could analyze the spread as a whole. This was his horizontal spread:

Action	Quantity	Type	Days to Expiration	Delta	Theta
Buy to Open	10	$31 call	187	0.47	−0.0092
Sell to Open	10	$31 call	40	−0.41	0.0172

Theta Analysis

Because Frank's plan was to take advantage of the difference in time decay rates through the use of a horizontal spread, it's important to understand his theta strategy. The cost to carry the position was $9.20 per day and the credit to carry the position was $17.25. Frank's horizontal spread was positive $8.05 per day, making it theta positive. Assuming the underlying didn't move up or down, this position would produce a profit of $8.05 per day from time decay alone.

Delta Analysis

Because this was a debit spread (overall position results in a net debit) and the market was flat, Frank looked at a slightly bullish stock in order to have a position that was somewhat delta positive. The delta of the October $31 call (long leg) was +0.47 and the delta of the May $31 call (short leg) was −0.41. That made the horizontal spread net positive 0.06 deltas. If the underlying were to move up (as Frank anticipated) one dollar, he would theoretically experience a $60 change in the net value of the spread ($0.06 per share or $6 per contract or $60 for the total position).

As mentioned earlier, the gamma values of the two legs were different. The delta of the short leg, having less time to expiration, would be more sensitive to price changes than the long leg. This could change Frank's horizontal spread from being delta positive to delta negative, depending on the movement of the underlying. If the underlying were to drop, Frank's position would become more delta positive as the long leg began to participate in more of the downside movement. Therefore, much like a covered call, although the downside risks were cushioned, any significant move in the underlying below support should trigger a protective order to close the horizontal spread. In a bearish-biased horizontal spread, the opposite is true; you should close the spread on a significant move to the upside through resistance.

Trading Plan

Because the trade was planned to take advantage of short-term time decay and lack of directionality, ideally the short leg would expire in 40 days with the underlying right at $31. If this were to happen, the 40 days that made up the short leg duration would account for just 21.3 percent (40 days divided by 187 days) of the time of the long contract. However, the time decay paid for just over 40 percent of the net cost of the trade ($690 collected from the short leg divided by $1,720 paid for the long leg).

This efficient use of time and principal was exactly the premise for Shawn's parents' real estate investing. Allow other people to pay down the value of the underlying. Assuming the analysis was correct and Frank's short leg expires (or he buys it back), when the next earnings approached he would no longer be in a spread position but would own 10 call contracts. He would have a long call position for over 100 days with a delta around 0.5. His net cost to acquire those contracts would be 40 percent less due to his use of the horizontal spread. If, after earnings, the stock were to move sideways or up and then begin to consolidate again, he could move into another horizontal spread or a diagonal spread to continue to pay down the principal.

Rolling Out

Let's suppose that Frank's stock moved up just a little in 37 days and was trading at $31.15. With three days to go until expiration and the market showing signs of bullishness, Frank decided to roll out the spread. Rolling out consists of buying back the short leg while simultaneously selling the same strike for the next month (or more) for a net credit. For example, Frank initially sold the May $31 calls for $0.69. With just three trading days left and the price of the stock at $31.15, the May $31 calls could be purchased back for $0.25 per share or $250. Frank would simultaneously sell the June $31 strike price for $1.10 per share or $1,100. The $1.10 per share credit would offset the $0.25 per share debit by $0.85, thereby placing another $850 into Frank's account. This is the one maintenance strategy with a horizontal spread and is best done in a flat to slightly bullish market.

Calculations

Max profit	Maximum profit occurs at expiration when the price of the underlying settles right at the strike price of the short leg. Unlike many strategies that profit from a change in value due to price movement, profit with a horizontal spread is the result of time decay alone.
Max loss	Because the horizontal spread is a debit spread, the most that can be lost on the spread is the value of the debit plus fees. If the spread is constructed with calls, then the risk is to the downside. If puts are used, then the risk is to the upside. Maximum loss is reached when the long leg expires out-the-money.
Break-even	Break-even can be a bit tricky with a horizontal spread due to the staggering of the expirations between the long and short position and the value of the remaining time in each contract. Generally speaking, break-even is calculated the same as a debit spread: the long strike price plus the debit in the case of a horizontal call spread or the long strike price minus the debit in the case of a horizontal put spread.
Capital required	Because horizontal spreads are essentially debit spreads, the capital requirement is the same: the position debit plus fees.

Candidates

Some of the best candidates are stocks that have recently released earnings and appear to be going into a period of market complacency. Because earnings are released approximately every three months, buying a horizontal spread with the long leg out six to nine months and the short leg less than three months is a good starting point. This trade setup has the benefit of an anticipated quiet period in which time decay can work in favor of the overall strategy.

Stocks and ETFs that pay dividends may also help to define a candidate list. A word to the wise: In a bull or bear market, it is unadvisable to search for stocks that are trading flat. Neutral market strategies like horizontal spreads should be backup strategies only used in flat markets. There are far better and more profitable trading opportunities to be found in trending markets than flat markets. Therefore, horizontal spreads should be an alternative strategy for flat markets versus a primary strategy. Historically, the markets do not stay quiet for very long. Nevertheless, as a skilled trader you will need to have a strategy to turn to when the markets stop trending and move sideways for a period.

Horizontal Spreads as a Backup Plan

We have often looked at the horizontal spread as a backup option strategy behind a directional position. For example, if you are bullish or bearish on a stock or ETF and you position with log calls or long puts, you are dependent on the market to move in your direction. If the underlying moves into a consolidation period and starts to trend sideways, time erosion slowly but surely begins to eat away at your capital. To slow down the time decay on your longer-term contracts, you can use a horizontal spread to offset the effect of time decay and maybe even come out with a little profit. Perhaps you look at when the next earnings release is scheduled and then sell a near-term option with the same strike as your longer-term option. This creates a horizontal spread in which time decay works to your advantage. This morphing of a trade is just one of many advantages of having a thorough understanding of all option strategies.

STRATEGY APPLICATION

The horizontal spread is best suited for a neutral market where the time decay represents the primary profit motive. Directional moves are welcome after the short leg expires and you continue holding the long leg. Therefore, the initial spread setup is best applied in markets with very low trend scores. Volatility scores may range from low to high depending on your appetite for risk because volatility may yield to a directional breakout (see Figure 12.1).

Market Score Trade

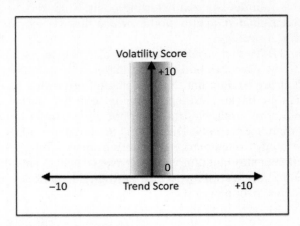

FIGURE 12.1   Market Score Application

Post-Earnings Lull

Admittedly, the term *post-earnings lull* is not a pure technical pattern, but rather an observation in trading behavior. The fact is a lull can follow any period of high market activity. Sometimes it may be referred to as traders taking a break, regrouping, or consolidating. The truth is the name is secondary to the observation that a slow and steady drift sometimes follows frenetic market activity. It is this drifting time, assuming that any trend is negligible, that makes for a good horizontal spread setup.

Figure 12.2 shows the price chart for a stock that entered into earnings with an extended channel. Notice the sideways trading leading up to the rally. When the earnings announcement hit the news, the traders and investors rallied the stock price with both a gap up as well as some follow-through. This created a quick, sharp rally that was confirmed by a spike in volume. This stock had a historical tendency to react sharply on earnings and then settle into a sideways trading range. It appeared to be doing the same on the illustration chart. Notice how the stock quickly begins to trade sideways after the sharp move higher. With only a couple exceptions, volume also dropped back into the pre-earnings range. Pay attention to the size of the candle bodies after the rally. Compare the long bodies evident during the rally with the very small bodies as the stock moves into the channel. Without delving into hard calculations on volatility, it's easy to see that volatility has decreased. The open and close for the subsequent days are very near each other, telling you that neither the buyers nor the sellers are willing to drive the stock higher or lower.

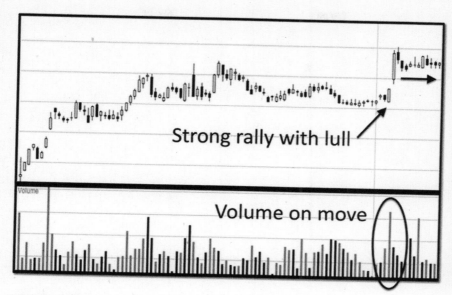

FIGURE 12.2 Earnings Rally with Post-Earnings Lull

The trade for this example would be a horizontal spread with the short leg expiring prior to the next earnings announcement and the long leg extending at least several months beyond. You want to be sure that you have plenty of time left past the next earnings in the long leg so that you can benefit from a directional move if the stock fails to repeat its pattern of drifting sideways. Of course, you will be expected to choose a direction and that is a tenuous decision when you're dealing with an earnings announcement that is several months away. However, you can choose a direction and if, as earnings approaches, you decide that your direction was in error, simply close the long leg prior to earnings. If you choose to hold the long leg into earnings, you can keep the long leg by itself or change the trade into another type of spread to suit your analysis. That's the beauty of options; you can dance to the music by arranging the legs for your objectives and analyses.

CHAPTER 13

Diagonal Spreads

We introduced the concepts behind horizontal spreads with a real estate investing story from Shawn's family. We'll continue this theme to explain the premise for the diagonal spread and how it can become one of the primary strategies in your trading portfolio.

By the time I was a teenager, we had several houses in the family portfolio. They were all rental properties and that meant any time there was a problem, like a leaky roof or floor that needed to be retiled, my brother and I were helping Dad fix things. When the house wasn't rented, we were financially under pressure because the properties were not paying for themselves while they were vacant (lots of meatloaf and leftovers for dinner).

One day Mom and Dad told us we were going to the mountains for a summer trip and staying at a cabin. As teenagers, we didn't ask whose it was or where it was, we were just happy to be going on vacation. We stayed at a nice two-story cabin that we had assumed our parents had rented for a few days. Over dinner Mom and Dad surprised us and announced that we were going to buy the cabin if we all liked it. Erik and I were very excited to know that this cabin would soon be ours. We dreamed of having our own cabin—skiing in the winter and hiking and fishing all summer!

My parents then explained to us that we wouldn't have the use of it all the time. The plan was to buy the cabin and then rent it out during the high season and on holidays to pay for the monthly *mortgage. Although we would not have access to it all the time, we would have access to it much of the time. Because the cabin would rent for as much as $300 per night during the high season and holidays, we could easily rent it for a weekend or two to pay for the mortgage, taxes, insurance, and even the utilities. Some months we couldn't rent it and we would run a deficit, and other months we would run a surplus. This cabin appeared to have the financial benefits of the other rental properties but the added advantage that we would get to use it ourselves.*

GETTING TO KNOW THE STRATEGY

The idea of renting a cabin that provides other benefits is the same idea behind the diagonal spread. The diagonal spread can pay for itself over time while allowing you to enjoy some of the position upside. The diagonal spread is a debit spread in which you purchase a higher-priced option (call or put) with more time to expiration and then sell a lower-priced option (same type as the long leg) with a different strike price and less time to expiration. By doing this, you create a position that is both delta and theta positive, meaning you will benefit from both time decay as well as a positive move in the direction of the trade (bullish or bearish).

Consider the following call option chain for an underlying that is trading at $113.55. Notice how the in-the-money far-term calls have lower theta and higher delta as compared to the out-the-money near-term calls.

Strike	Days to Expiration	Bid	Ask	Theta	Delta
$115	29	$3.90	$3.98	−0.071	0.462
$103	365	$18.63	$19.25	−0.011	0.703

Because a diagonal spread is a directional position, it's important to determine the overall market sentiment prior to building the spread. In the case of a bull market, you might decide on a bull call spread (Chapter 9). A bull call spread is a directional spread with negative time decay and positive delta. The primary difference between a bull call spread and a diagonal spread is the purchase of a longer-term contract and the sale of the shorter-term contract to take advantage of the difference in time decay. Diagonal spreads enjoy positive time decay. It's important to recognize that with the bull call spread, time works against the trade, whereas with a bullish diagonal spread, both time and directional movement can work in your favor.

A covered call in which the short leg is out-the-money is very close in strategy to the diagonal bull spread. As with the diagonal bull spread, the covered call also profits from time decay and directional movement (assuming the underlying direction is upward). The downside to a covered call is the amount of capital required in order to cover the position. The first step to writing a covered call is to buy shares; requiring that significant capital be placed at risk (the entire amount of the underlying share purchase).

In the case of the diagonal bull spread, the long call option leg replaces shares of the underlying. Instead of having shares to cover the short leg, the long-term option represents the right to acquire shares at any time at a lower strike price. This right to purchase means the short leg is covered. However, in a diagonal spread the long leg is seldom, if ever, exercised. You would generally unwind the position (buy the short leg and sell the long leg) for profit or loss, based on the movement of the underlying.

An advantage to this type of spread goes beyond the efficient use of capital. This spread also defines risk better than a covered call. For example, suppose you buy 1,000 shares of a $25.50 stock. You then sell a covered call against your long shares by selling the $26 strike price for $0.75 per share with 25 days left to expiration. This reduces your risk exposure from $25,500 to $24,750. Although unlikely, the stock could drop to zero and produce a loss of $24,750.

Let's look at the same scenario using a diagonal bull spread. You would first buy a long-term in-the-money call option to replace the underlying share purchase. Suppose you buy a call option with a $23 strike and 287 days to expiration for $4.15 per share. You would control 1,000 shares of the stock for 287 days with a delta of 0.72 for a cash outlay of $4,150. Then you could sell the $26 strike price call for $0.75, bringing in $750. This $750 offsets the $4,150 cost of the long-term contract, lowering your cost basis to $3,400. The $3,400 is now your maximum risk, even if the stock drops to zero. Of course, there are differences between the stock delta and the long-term call option delta as well as dividend considerations, but to most experienced traders these differences often do not justify the risks.

Based on the comparison to a covered call we just introduced, here's what the diagonal spread looks like with the stock trading at $25.50:

Action	Quantity	Type	Days to Expiration	Delta	Theta
Buy to Open	10	$23 call	287	0.73	−0.003
Sell to Open	10	$26 call	25	0.43	−0.016

Delta Analysis

Recall that the delta on Frank's horizontal spread in Chapter 12 was just slightly positive at 0.06, whereas the net delta on this diagonal spread is 0.30 (0.73 minus 0.43). Being positive delta means this position will increase or decrease $0.30 per share for each one-dollar gain or loss. This diagonal spread is a 10-contract position so it will theoretically gain or lose $300 if the underlying moves up or down one dollar. Therefore, it is important that you create spreads that are in line with the overall trends of the market, sector, and the stock, ETF, or index you are trading.

Theta Analysis

Theta for this spread is positive, based on the fact that it has a long-term, deep in-the-money leg that will have a high delta and low theta. The long leg is somewhat offset by the short option, which is near-term and slightly out-the-money, giving it a lower delta and higher theta. In our example, theta is 0.013 positive (0.016 minus 0.003). Because the 10-contract position represents 1,000 shares, you can then calculate the per-day value of theta for the entire position. This would be 0.013 per share multiplied by 1,000 shares or $13 per day on the total spread position. Clearly, time is worth something ($13 per day), but that hardly compares to the delta ($300 for a one-dollar move).

Closing the Spread Prior to Expiration

You can appreciate how the family cabin required more maintenance and attention than a long-term residential rental property because vacation renters were constantly coming and going. The diagonal spread also requires a higher level of maintenance because you will likely be selling the near-term options multiple times. Following are a few scenarios in which you would need to take action.

Taking a Profit   If an acceptable profit target has been reached or the market conditions are starting to degrade, it may be time to close the spread and capture whatever profit you have in hand. Just like any spread trade, you must first close the short leg of the trade by buying to close the call or put. Once the short leg is closed, you may then sell the long leg to complete the liquidation of the spread.

Taking a Loss   Prior to entering any trade, you must determine where you would get out if you were wrong. At that precise point, you must take action to salvage and protect the remaining capital by closing the trade.

This is typically accomplished by identifying where the support or resistance is for the underlying and placing a conditional order that will trigger a series of trades if the support or resistance level is penetrated. With some brokers, you are able to create a conditional order that will program a series of orders to sequentially buy back the short leg first and then sell the long leg last. Alternatively, you may elect to have the condition on the underlying trigger an alert rather than an actual order. This would allow you to manually close the spread, perhaps improving your prices by trading within the bid/ask spread.

Rolling the Spread

Rolling a spread happens prior to the expiration of the short leg. A roll involves buying the short option to close the short leg while simultaneously selling another short option in its place. Because the long leg of the diagonal spread will always contain more time than the short leg of the spread, as the short leg nears expiration you need to determine how and when you are going to roll the trade.

If the spread enters expiration week in-the-money, then it is advisable to roll the spread on Monday or Tuesday of that week. Rolling early in the week will help lower the probability of an early assignment. If the short leg strike is close to the trading price, then you have some more time to make the decision and may decide to wait right up to expiration. If it is clear the short leg is going to expire out-the-money, then you should simply allow the short option to expire worthless and open a new short leg the Monday following expiration.

Rolling Out Perhaps the simplest type of roll is the roll out. In our example, let's assume that the stock moved up a small amount over 22 days and reached $25.95 with three days to go until expiration. With the market showing signs of bullishness, you decided to roll out the spread to avoid an early assignment. This would be a good time to consider rolling out.

You roll out a Diagonal Spread by buying back the short leg and then immediately selling the same strike for the following week or month (or more) at a higher price than your cost to buy back the initial short leg. For example, suppose you initially sold the October $26 calls for $0.75. Then, with just two trading days left and the price of the stock at $25.95, the October $26 could be purchased back for $0.10, or $100. You would then sell the November $26 strike price calls for $1.35. The $1.35 credit offsets the $0.10 debit by $1.25, placing another $1,250 into your account. The $1,250 reduces the cost of the long leg from $3,400 to $2,150. This strategy for maintaining the diagonal bull spread is best done in a flat to slight bull market.

Rolling Up and Out   A roll up and out for a diagonal bull spread is almost identical to a roll out, except that you would sell a higher strike price call for the new short leg. This is the preferred roll when the stock price has moved up enough to make the short leg in-the-money, thereby creating a higher risk of an early assignment.

Let's suppose there were four trading days to go until expiration and the stock was trading at $26.35. Because $26.35 is $0.35 above the short leg strike (in-the-money by $0.35), you would be at risk for an early assignment. You decide to roll the spread by buying back the October $26 strike and then selling the November $27 strike. In this case, the October $26 was quoted with an ask price of $0.45 and the November $27 had a bid price of $1.35. Rolling the trade would provide a net credit of $900 ($1.35 per share minus $0.45 per share, multiplied by 1,000 shares). You would also increase the width of your spread from $3 (long July $23 and short October $26) to $4 (long July $23 and short November $27). This would increase your ability to profit from price appreciation down the road. Rolling up would also increase the net delta of the spread because the long leg has gone even further in-the-money and the new short leg would be further out-the-money than the initial short leg.

Rolling Down   Rolling down in a diagonal bull spread is a defensive strategy for a trade that starts to show some signs of moving against you. If you see clear signs of a breakdown, then it is always best to just close the trade. Rolling down involves first allowing the short leg of the spread to expire worthless. The following Monday you would then sell a new short leg with a lower strike price.

Changing our example a little will illustrate this point. Instead of the stock trending up over 25 days, suppose the stock had been mostly flat with a slight loss of value and reached expiration trading at $25. The November $26 strike was only valued at $0.35 and the November $25 strike was valued at $0.80. You could roll down the spread and sell the November $25 strike price the Monday following expiration, netting you $800. Rolling down will decrease the net delta of the position because the new short leg has a higher delta than the initial short leg and the long leg is now less in-the-money.

Early Assignment

The diagonal spread is a first cousin to an out-the-money covered call. When an out-the-money covered call is first written, there is very little chance of an early assignment. Why would anyone want to buy stock at a higher price than the current market price? In fact, they wouldn't and they don't. However, if that out-the-money (OTM) covered call becomes an in-the-money (ITM) call, the situation changes. When an OTM call becomes an ITM call due to price appreciation, the delta that was initially low (0.3 in this example) becomes much higher (0.8). We know that ITM options have higher deltas and lower thetas, thereby making the time value less of a driving component of the valuation. This loss of time value increases the possibility of an early assignment, especially for a stock in which a dividend is coming due.

For example, suppose you owned 500 shares of a $30 stock and you decide to sell a covered call with four weeks remaining until expiration. You could sell the $31 strike with a 0.45 delta and receive $0.60 per share. Further, assume the stock paid a 4 percent annual dividend and was scheduled to release the quarterly dividend of $0.35 to shareholders in two weeks. With the stock trading at $30, there would be a very low chance that the buyer of the $31 call would want to exercise early just to get a $0.35 dividend. Remember, the buyer of the $31 call paid $0.60 so his break-even point was $31.60.

However, as the ex-date (ex-dividend date) draws closer, the stock's price rises. Two days prior to the ex-date the stock is at $32. You would very likely experience an early assignment and would be required to sell your 500 shares at $31. Because this would happen prior to the ex-date, you would miss the $0.35 dividend. Instead, the new shareholder would receive the dividend on the pay date (usually a few weeks after the ex-date).

Although you are disappointed that you were assigned early, this is not a problem for you because you were covered by the shares you owned. Your broker would assign you on 500 shares and make electronic delivery by removing the 500 shares from your account and depositing $15,500.

Let's shift gears here and look at the exact same scenario using a diagonal bull spread. The long leg was five contracts of the $25 call long-term equity anticipation security (LEAPS) and the short leg was the same $31 call we discussed in the preceding covered call example. As a diagonal bull spread trader, you are also covered by your long leg, but you can't make delivery quite so easily because you don't have actual shares to deliver. If you were to be assigned early, you would be short 500 shares in your account. You would need to quickly flatten your short position by purchasing shares in the open market at current prices.

Under our scenario, those shares would cost you $32. You received $31 per share and would be buying shares at $32, so your loss would be $1 per share or $500 for the position. Technically, this loss would be an offset loss because the long leg would have increased in value when the shares moved higher, offsetting the loss of the early assignment. Remember, the increase in the value of the long leg is an unrealized gain that could vanish if the price were to move lower. The $500 is a realized loss that will not vanish regardless of the stock's movement.

When we teach diagonal spreads to novice option traders, we often point out that this is a strategy that is easy to put on, but a challenge to maintain. Early assignment is just one of the variables that needs to be considered when using a strategy like this. A clearly defined trading plan makes the management much easier. Understanding when the conditions exist that could trigger an early assignment are critical. Once the circumstances are present and the likelihood of an early assignment becomes high, the logical step is the roll the spread as outlined previously.

STRATEGY IN ACTION

Frank had been watching the market closely over the past few weeks and made several observations that he believed would feed into a shorter-term diagonal bear spread. Although the indexes were all trading down, there had been periods in which the market made short-term bullish crawls higher. Recently, those bullish runs had failed and quickly pulled back to support levels. Frank also noticed that on the bullish days the volume was lackluster but on the bearish drops the volume was much higher. Frank considered buying puts with longer expirations because he believed the bears would control the market for several months. However, the put options had inflated premiums and he couldn't justify the risk for the reward.

Frank thought about alternatives to the direction long put strategy and thought a shorter-term diagonal bear spread might be a good solution. Although Frank was confident that the bears would prevail in time, he was not certain about how much time the markets would remain in the oscillating channel. Frank had familiarized himself with the Weekly options that were trading on several exchanges. Because Frank wanted to build a diagonal spread but he didn't want to sell the short leg with more than a week or two, he decided to utilize a weekly option for his short leg.

Frank chose to use options on a small-cap index exchange-traded fund (ETF) that was showing more weakness than the mid-cap and large-cap indexes. This index ETF (XYZ) was trading at $65.43 with near-term support at $64 and long-term support at $59. Frank decided to build the diagonal bear spread by buying an in-the-money put with 115 days remaining until expiration. His intent was to close the long leg before time decay began to accelerate (about four weeks out from expiration). By buying the $68 strike put expiring in 115 days, he would have ample time (over 90 days) to either sell short-term options to collect the time premium or profit from the anticipated move while avoiding the steepest part of the time decay curve. However, if he approached expiration and XYZ was still trending downward, the increase in value due the price move would easily overshadow the much smaller loss in time decay and he would hold the position to expiration.

For the short leg Frank decided to sell the weekly option that was very close to expiration. He decided to sell the $64 put that had three days left until expiration because that contract had the highest time decay with a strike at support. Although Frank believed XYZ could approach $64 in the next two trading days, he did not believe $64 would be broken. The following table illustrates the diagonal bear spread Frank created.

Order	Strike	Days to Expiration	Delta	Theta	Price
Buy Puts to Open	$68	115	−0.56	0.02	$7.75
Sell Puts to Open	$64	3	−0.32	0.17	$0.66

Because calls have positive delta and puts have negative delta, a diagonal bear spread is strictly considered to be delta negative. For the sake of this text, any position referred to as being delta positive will profit from a move in a direction favorable to the trade, regardless of whether the position is built with calls or puts. Therefore, Frank's diagonal bear spread is *directionally* positive 0.34 deltas and will theoretically increase in value $0.34 for a one-dollar drop in XYZ.

(Our goal is for this text to be practically intuitive and easily applied. For a more rigorous treatment of the nuances of Greek signs, pricing models, etc., the reader will find many good references within Wiley's published library.)

STRATEGY MANAGEMENT

Frank has always worked off the trader's adage of "it's better to have and not need than need and not have." As such, he outlined a detailed trading plan that would allow him to (1) maximize profits, (2) minimize losses, and (3) remain unemotional by automating his decisions based on several scenarios as follows.

Frank had already defined the trend as being bearish, as evidenced by the fact that all the major market indexes were trading below their 50-day SMA and 200-day SMA and the 50-day SMA had crossed below the 200-day SMA. Because this was Frank's reason for getting into the trade, it would also serve as his reason for getting out of the trade in the event that XYZ were to rally and the spread were to move against him. If XYZ were to move higher and trade above the 50-day SMA, Frank would close the spread. Closing the spread would not necessarily mean that the trade was a loser. In fact, with the current 50-day SMA trending lower, a cross to the upside might mean the trade could close profitably, assuming an exit point at or lower than the entry point. A close above the 50-day SMA would be enough proof to Frank that the bulls were back in control of the major market and with enough momentum to potentially reverse the existing bearish trend. Such nonemotional, pragmatic risk management (either XYZ is above the 50-day SMA or XYZ is below the 50-day SMA) helps Frank decide if he should stay in the position or close the trade.

With his risk management strategy already defined by the movement of the underlying price, Frank considered how he could manage the trade's moving in a profitable manner. Keep in mind, with a diagonal bear spread, a sideways move would be profitable due to time decay. Furthermore, a downward move would be profitable due to time decay and the overall delta of the position. Recall that Frank identified $64 as the short-term support. His trading plan consisted of selling the $64 weekly put option against the $68 long leg each week that XYZ remained above $64. If XYZ were to break down through the $64 support level, Frank expected that XYZ would then fall to the secondary support at $59. If that were to happen, Frank would not want to be spread. Instead, he wanted to be positioned as bearish as possible. To accomplish that, Frank would need to buy back the weekly $64 strike to close the short leg. Closing the short leg would change the position from a spread to a long put trade. The puts would have a delta greater than 0.56 because XYZ would have declined, placing Frank's $68 strike puts further in-the-money.

Because Frank wasn't excited about the prospect of having to watch the market all day, he decided to utilize conditional orders to manage the position. Frank created a conditional order such that if XYZ traded at or below $63.99, a buy to close order would automatically close the short leg at market. That automated order function would lift the short leg upon a move below $64, morphing Frank's position from a diagonal bear spread to a long put.

He could also use a conditional order to manage a move against him. To do that, Frank first analyzed the chart to determine that the exact level of the 50-day SMA was $71.88. Frank set up another conditional order at $71.89 such that if XYZ traded at or above $71.89, he would close the entire spread. This consisted of a buy to close for the short leg and then a sell to close for the long leg, both trades executing at the current market prices. Each night when Frank wrapped his day, he could adjust his exit point based on the most recent price of the 50-day SMA. This would effectively act as a technical trailing stop order that only moves in the direction of profit.

Frank prudently established the trade based on his factual analysis of the charts and not on emotion. He used his broker's automated order functionality to avoid being distracted throughout the day with unnecessary and disruptive quote checking. Using this automation also allowed Frank to concentrate on his work and know that the automation will better position his trade in the event XYZ were to drop aggressively.

He anticipated that in an ideal situation, XYZ would move sideways to slightly lower over the next few weeks, allowing him to sell short-term premium to pay down the $7.09 debit for his spread. If XYZ were to trade sideways, then he would be able to pay down the net debit rather quickly. After all, selling the three days that remained with the out-the-money $64 weekly option reduced the cost of his long puts by 8.5 percent for just 2.6 percent of the remaining time. At the same time, he was still 0.34 delta positive. After he had sold a few weeks of the $64 weekly puts, he would have liked to have seen a decline through $64. That decline would trigger an order to close the short leg, leaving him with long puts. After a breakdown through $64, Frank expected a continuation down to at least $59, at which point his $68 puts would have an intrinsic value no less than $9.

STRATEGY APPLICATION

The diagonal spread may be created with calls (diagonal bull spread) or puts (diagonal bear spread). For either direction, the trade is best applied in neutral to slightly directional markets. For strongly directional markets, it would be generally better to use a straight directional trade (long call or long put) in order to capture more price movement. Nevertheless, the diagonal spread strategy has a broad range of market conditions in which it may be successfully employed. Figure 13.1 illustrates a recommended target range, with low-to-mid scoring values for both trend (positive or negative) and volatility.

Market Score Trade

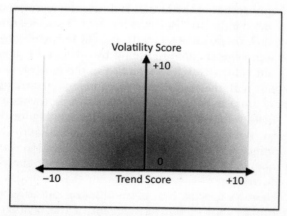

FIGURE 13.1 Market Score Application

Moving Average Convergence/Divergence (MACD)

The moving average convergence/divergence (MACD) indicator is a composite indicator that combines two exponential moving averages into a single MACD line. It is often used with a second line, known as the signal line, that smoothes the MACD line by a specified period. The smoothing is accomplished by calculating an exponential moving average (EMA) of the MACD line. Buy and sell signals are generated based on the relationship of the MACD line to the signal line.

The most common EMAs used in constructing the MACD line are the 12-day EMA and the 26-day EMA, also referred to as the 15 percent EMA and the 7 percent EMA. The MACD is calculated as the difference between the two selected EMAs:

$$MACD = 12\text{-day EMA} - 26\text{-day EMA}$$

As mentioned, the second line used in the MACD indicator is the signal line. The default smoothing for the signal line is often nine days. When you smooth data through a moving average calculation, the new line is slower to respond to price changes than the original line. For that reason, the MACD is considered the fast line and the signal line is considered the slow line. Keep in mind that we're discussing common default values for the MACD calculation (12, 26, and 9); however, these values may be adjusted to create more or less sensitivity in the indicator.

The MACD is often shown as a histogram that plots the difference between the MACD line and the signal line. The histogram may assume a positive or negative value, depending on whether the MACD is above or below the signal line.

A popular application of the MACD is to use the histogram as an overbought and oversold indicator. Because the MACD may assume any range of values, you can't assign an absolute threshold for overbought and oversold. With some indicators that are bound by −1 and +1, it's common to look at a constant value (0.80, for example) as the indication of the stock being overbought. With the MACD, you're interested in looking at extreme levels of the histogram as compared to recent past performance. If you observe that the histogram suddenly rises significantly higher than it has at any other time in your chart range, then that tells you that the MACD line is rapidly accelerating past the signal line. The interpretation is that the price is too strong relative to its own past performance and, therefore, should correct to the downside.

Figure 13.2 shows a stock that is trading in a sideways range with a slightly bearish bias. Part of our assessment of the bearish bias comes from the fact that the down legs in the price movement are much shorter in

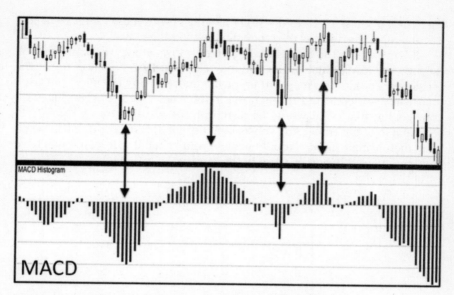

FIGURE 13.2 MACD with a Neutral to Slightly Bearish Stock

duration than the up legs. Using the MACD histogram as an overbought and oversold indicator, notice how the peaks (positive and negative) often correlate to the highs and lows in the stock's trading range. In this example, the MACD histogram serves as a confirmation indicator of short-term reversals within the continuation of the trading range. It helps you determine the points at which the stock is likely to reverse course within the range. Notice also the last negative peak at the far right side of the chart. You can see how the relative size of that peak is greater than the others observed up to that point. That extreme low in the histogram corresponded with the price breaking down to new lows.

The diagonal bear spread would be a good choice for this type of chart pattern. The first trade would be a buy to open to build the long leg. A put option with plenty of time to expiration is what you want. How much time you buy is up to you, based on how long you expect to hold the position. When in doubt, a good rule of thumb is to err on the side of buying too much time rather than not enough. Your strike price for the long leg should be at or above the price highs shown on the chart.

The second leg is your short leg and would consist of a sell to open order for a near-term put. Based on the cycle length observed in the chart pattern, it would be ideal if you could time the short leg to sell each new leg as close to the range lows as possible. Then you could either let each short leg expire or close them as the stock hits highs within the range, replacing it with a new short leg as the stock dips to the range lows.

If you observe the stock breaking to new lows along with confirmation through the MACD histogram, you may elect to close the short leg at the breakdown point. You may end up paying more to buy the short put back than what you collected through the initial sale. That's all right, because your goal at that point would be to morph the position into a bearish directional long put trade. Any subsequent drop in the stock price will result in an increasingly greater profit because your remaining long put will have higher delta as it becomes more in-the-money.

CHAPTER 14

Index Options

How do professional traders get the liquidity, pricing, and execution they need when they're moving millions of dollars in a single trade? It's certainly not by buying and selling mining company penny stocks. Many times the professional traders don't trade stocks; they trade markets. You think we are just referring to using ETFs as a proxy to a market, right? Actually, that's not the case. We're talking about trading markets like the S&P 500, Nasdaq 100, Dow Jones Industrial Average, S&P MidCap 400, and Russell 2000 through the use of index options.

As you'll see, trading an index is one of the purest forms of trading. After all, the forces that influence an individual stock's movements are quite random compared to the forces that can affect an entire index. For example, a stock's price can change dramatically based on comments from a talking head on a financial channel, an analyst upgrade or downgrade, a product announcement, or even the illness of a key executive. Factors like this have far less of an influence on an index simply due to its size. The impact of a significant event for one company is tempered by the fact that that company represents a minor part of the overall index.

When we teach a live class we often illustrate this point by likening a stock to a kayak and an index to a cruise ship. The kayak can move forward and backward and maneuver via the action of one person with a single paddle. That same person isn't going to change the direction or speed of a cruise ship one bit. It would require thousands of paddlers all paddling in the same direction to begin to change the direction or speed of a cruise ship. Likewise, we are often able to define trends and movements better with an index over a single stock because it moves with the movement of

197

the group. We can further add speed and direction to the underlying index through the use of index options. Because options afford you considerable leverage, you can trade a cruise ship-sized product with the maneuverability of a kayak.

GETTING TO KNOW THE STRATEGY

Although there are hundreds of indexes available to trade, the most common trader indexes are the S&P 500, Dow Jones Industrial Average, Nasdaq 100, Russell 2000, and S&P MidCap 400. Through the use of these option contracts, institutional traders are able to speculate and hedge billions of dollars each day. Without these index options, trading the S&P 500 index would literally require 500 separate single-stock transactions to fully establish a large-cap index position.

Trading index options comes with advantages, disadvantages, and unique characteristics as compared to equity and ETF options. Therefore, it's critical that you understand the differences and how they may affect your strategy decisions. We'll describe common characteristics of the majority of the index options, but note that there are sometimes exceptions to the rule. For absolute certainty when considering trading any index option, you should refer to the product-specific page on the underwriter's Web site or request written information. Your broker may also help you with understanding product-specific characteristics. For example, novice traders might assume that the only difference between trading the SPY (ETF) contracts and trading the SPX (index; sometimes referred to as $SPX, where the $ sign denotes an index) contracts is that the SPY is one-tenth the size of the index. The differences are much more than that, and the unique characteristics of index options form the basis for several of the strategies you have at your disposal.

Contract Size

Like most equity options, index options typically use a multiplier of 100. Unlike most equity options, however, the value of many indexes is often as high as a few thousand points. This is an important consideration when deciding on the number of contracts appropriate for your portfolio. The Nasdaq 100 index ($NDX) was trading around 2,300 at the time of this writing. One contract of an at-the-money 2,300 strike price option controls an index value of $230,000 (2,300 multiplied by 100). Even traders who are accustomed to trading 10, 20, or 30 contracts per position will have to scale the number of contracts for their position when the trade involves an index.

To further illustrate the point, let's look at the relationship of the $SPX to the S&P 500 ETF (SPY). The valuation of SPY is approximately one-tenth that of the $SPX. If you are accustomed to buying 1,000 shares of SPY or trading 10 contracts of the SPY option, an equivalent trade would be just one $SPX contract. This may help to lower your commissions and fees. If your broker charges a ticket fee of $9.99 and $0.75 per contract, a one contract purchase of an $SPX index option would be $10.74, whereas the same-sized transaction using the SPY would be the $9.99 ticket plus $7.50 in contract fees, or $17.49. If your account doesn't have sufficient equity, even one contract of the $SPX might be too large and you would need to trade the SPY ETF to stay within your position risk limits. You could also consider the CBOE XSP, which is an index option that matches the dollar level of SPY options.

Cash Settlement versus Physical Delivery

One of the common refrains we hear from nontraders is that options are too risky. Somewhere along the way they heard that most people end up losing money because the majority of options expire worthless. If the option expires worthless, then they're sure the trader lost money—it would seem to make sense on the surface. Here, the investing public has grossly misinterpreted a simple fact. The truth is that most options expire unexercised. According to the Options Clearing Corporation, in 2010 only 7.9 percent of options were exercised. To the option-illiterate, an unexercised option means a worthless option and, therefore, 90 percent of option traders lose money. For starters, if 90 percent of option traders lose money than there must be 10 percent who are swimming in profits and that's all the more reason for you to sharpen your option trading skills. But the simple fact is most options are not exercised because very few option traders are interested in dealing with the physical delivery of the underlying shares.

Let's look at a simple example. An investor has 100 shares of ABC he purchased for $380 per share. ABC is currently at $390. He decides to write a covered call against his position by selling the $400 strike because he thinks the price will remain below that level for the next 22 days until expiration.

Another option trader buys the $400 call with the expectation that ABC will break above $400. The call buyer pays $5 per share so the covered call writer collects $500 for one contract. The open interest on the ABC $400 has been increased by one (1 contract) as a result of this transaction. Twenty-one days later, the day prior to expiration, ABC is trading at $408 and the $400 call is bid at $8.05. The buyer of the $400 call knows that if she doesn't close the position to realize her profit, she will be auto-exercised the next day. Her account will purchase 100 shares of ABC at $400 and $40,000 will be withdrawn. If she doesn't have the money or want the shares, then the logical decision is to close the position by selling to close the call at the bid price of $8.05 per share. She does just that, profiting $305 less fees.

The call seller also recognizes that if he doesn't take action on his short contract, he will be auto-assigned over the weekend and his account will be debited 100 shares and credited $40,000. Because he doesn't want to sell his shares of ABC, he must close his obligation by buying to close the $400 call option at the ask price of $8.10 per share. He enters the order to close the position at a cost of $810, resulting in a $310 loss to his account.

In this example, one contract reached expiration unexercised. The buyer closed one contract for a profit and the writer (seller) closed one contract for a loss. No physical shares of ABC ever changed hands. Think of the markets as having their own version of the First Law of Thermodynamics—energy is neither created nor destroyed, it simply changes form. Money in the markets is neither created nor destroyed, it simply changes hands. Most options never reach expiration. Instead, they are unassigned because the buyers and sellers of these instruments close them prior to expiration to realize profits or losses rather than taking or making physical delivery.

An important characteristic of index options is that they are cash settled. Equity options are physically settled through the buying and selling of shares of the underlying stock. Cash settlement means that no physical shares are exchanged at expiration; the trade is settled with cash. Cash is either deposited or withdrawn from the accounts based on the intrinsic value of the option strike price relative to the underlying index.

Options Style

Another important option characteristic to understand is the difference between American-style options versus European-style options. Most index options are European-style. First of all, these two terms have nothing to do with the geographic location of contracts, exchanges, or the traders themselves. The difference relates to the terms for exercising and assigning the contracts. Most equity (stocks and ETFs) options trade American-style contracts. American-style simply means that the holder of the contract has the right to exercise his right at any time during the life of the contract. Most index and currency options are European-style, meaning they may be exercised only upon expiration. Therefore, there are no early assignments with European-style option contracts. You should not confuse the right to exercise with the ability to close a position in the open market. Both American-style and European-style options may be bought or sold to close an option position at any time the options are trading on the open market. Understanding the difference between the two will be important for index option traders.

Nasdaq 100 INDEX OPTION

Oct 7 '11w	Oct 22 '11	Nov 19 '11	Dec 17 '11	Mar 17 '12	Jun 16 '12	Sep 22 '12	Dec 22 '12	Dec 21 '13	All Months		
	Calls >				Dec 17 '11				< Puts		
Open Interest	Tot. Volume	Deliverables	Option Style	Last Trade	Strike Price	Last Trade	Option Style	Deliverables	Tot. Volume	Open Interest	
16	0	Cash Settled	E	281.77		95.40	E	Cash Settled	0	11	
663	0	Cash Settled	E	271.06		100.67	E	Cash Settled	0	3331	
89	0	Cash Settled	E	244.23		107.70	E	Cash Settled	0	110	
4	21	Cash Settled	E	152.80		145.00	E	Cash Settled	10	38	
23	4	Cash Settled	E	142.99		132.71	E	Cash Settled	0	48	
690	2	Cash Settled	E	130.13		102.60	E	Cash Settled	0	1998	
85	6	Cash Settled	E	116.65		145.00	E	Cash Settled	0	286	

Nasdaq 100 ETF OPTION

Oct 7 '11w	Oct 22 '11	Nov 19 '11	Dec 17 '11	Jan 21 '12	Mar 17 '12	Jun 16 '12	Jan 19 '13	All Months			
	Calls >				Dec 17 '11				< Puts		
Open Interest	Tot. Volume	Deliverables	Option Style	Last Trade	Strike Price	Last Trade	Option Style	Deliverables	Tot. Volume	Open Interest	
2900	0	100 QQQ	A	5.79		2.69	A	100 QQQ	8	23437	
6961	220	100 QQQ	A	4.72		3.09	A	100 QQQ	26	7221	
6525	0	100 QQQ	A	4.46		3.48	A	100 QQQ	69	52086	
7781	250	100 QQQ	A	3.45		3.94	A	100 QQQ	70	33337	
19420	45	100 QQQ	A	2.89		4.42	A	100 QQQ	162	44621	
29239	24	100 QQQ	A	2.43		4.92	A	100 QQQ	80	34640	
22500	7	100 QQQ	A	2.00		5.54	A	100 QQQ	95	30684	

FIGURE 14.1 Comparison of Nasdaq 100 Index versus ETF Options

Figure 14.1 shows two actual option chains for the Nasdaq 100. The chain at the top is for the Nasdaq 100 index. Notice that the column labeled "Deliverables" indicates "Cash Settled" and the column labeled "Option Style" indicates "E" for European. Contrast that with the second chain for the Nasdaq 100 ETF. You'll see that the deliverable is 100 shares of the underlying ETF (QQQ) and they are labeled "A" for American-style.

Expiration

Most index options will ordinarily cease trading on the business day (usually Thursday) preceding the day on which the exercise-settlement value is calculated (usually Friday). The fact that Thursday is typically the last trading day does not change the fact that most index options expire on Saturday, as do most equity options. The expiration date has little direct relevance and you should be more concerned about where the underlying value is as the end of the last day to trade the option. An important distinction to be made here between an index option and an equity option is this: An equity option's closing value is set by the closing price of the underlying equity on the last trading day prior to expiration (usually Friday's close). This is not the case with most index options. Thursday is generally the last day to trade an index option, but the actual value of the index is most often established by the opening prices of the stocks that make up the index the following morning (Friday). This process is called final settlement.

Final Settlement   Following is the description of final settlement from the Chicago Board Option Exchange's web site telling when and how the settlement price of the SPX options is determined.

> *The exercise-settlement value, SET, is calculated using the opening sales price in the primary market of each component security on the last business day (usually a Friday) before the expiration date. The exercise-settlement amount is equal to the difference between the exercise-settlement value and the exercise price of the option, multiplied by $100.*

Because the final settlement is determined by each component, there is the strong possibility that many of the stocks within the population of 500 that make up the index will open higher or lower than their closing values from Thursday. Therefore, you should not assume that your trade will be settled using the closing level of the index from Thursday. Although there is some associated gap risk, a large index like the S&P is less subject to gap risk than a narrower-based index like the Dow Jones Industrial Average (comprised of 30 stocks). In order to avoid any potential gap risk, you would want to close your position on the last trading day prior to the closing bell if your position is near or at-the-money.

Trading Hours

Most index options go through a process called the opening rotation, at the same time the general market opens (9:30 A.M. Eastern). However, unlike most equity options, index options trade 15 minutes beyond the general market's close. This additional 15 minutes gives you the advantage of a few extra quiet minutes to work your order. Prices often will drop slightly due to the loss of volatility and an anticipation of overnight time decay.

Advantages

Although there are differences in the way index options trade that can add to their complexity as compared to equity options, some advantages are the following:

- **Liquidity**—Because large institutions and professional traders frequently trade index options, they often enjoy massive liquidity. Daily volume in the hundreds and thousands is typical in SPX contracts and open interest can be in the tens of thousands. Because one contract can represent a significant dollar amount, the retail trader is often but a flea on the back of an elephant.

- **No fundamentals**—For a technical trader, the opportunity to trade a product based strictly on the price movement is the purest form of trading. A technical trader assumes that all known fundamental data is already factored into the price. He can therefore react to price alone versus news or other nontechnical variables.
- **Reduced gap risk**—Many indexes are made up of dozens, hundreds, or even thousands of individual stocks. As a result, no single stock's move can influence the overall index price by a great deal. Although an index can experience gaps, they are usually fewer and smaller than with individual stocks.
- **Emotional detachment**—It's tough to get emotionally attached to an index. However, if you do find yourself emotionally attached to an index, we'd suggest an extended break from trading. Unlike a stock, which has a product, a brand, a CEO, a reputation, and a history, an index is little more than a number on your trading screen. Emotions are a trader's worst enemy and trading a vehicle like an index is a good way to keep emotions out of the mix.

Disadvantages

As with any choice of product or strategy, there are disadvantages that need to be weighed with the advantages. Some disadvantages to index options are the following:

- **Contract size and cost**—Trading index options is often done by professional traders and advanced option traders, not due to complexity but often due to contract size. The $SPX contract is trading over 1,200 at the time of this writing and has ranged from 1,000 to 1,400 in the past 12 months. Because each contract uses a 100 multiplier, the dollar equivalent of just one 1,200 strike call option is $120,000. This is extreme leverage and often the cost and size of a contract are beyond the account capabilities of many smaller novice traders.
- **Strike intervals**—Due to the price level of many index options, the strike intervals are often far apart in absolute value (although not in percentage). The SPX, for example, has $5 intervals in strike prices whereas the NDX has $25 intervals. The larger strike intervals can pose a problem for proper position sizing and risk management. Fortunately, the index ETFs (SPY and QQQ) have $1 intervals and allow you to position more precisely. Remember, though, they are not index options and should not be considered an equal replacement for trading index options.

STRATEGY IN ACTION

Frank had observed strong price movement and increasing volume in the Nasdaq 100 index. He explored deeper into the top-10 holding that made up the NDX and found primarily high-profile technology stocks. Although the index was comprised of the 100 largest Nasdaq stocks, the top 10 stocks accounted for over half of the valuation of the index. Frank paid special attention to the charts for those 10 because they were carrying the majority of the weight. Based on those charts, he felt more confident about the index being pushed higher by aggressive institutional investors. Volume supported his opinion.

Frank wanted a pure option play on the index, so he decided to buy in-the-money calls on the NDX. At that time the NDX was trading at 2,221. Frank elected to buy the December 2,050 call with a delta of 0.7 and 78 days remaining until expiration. The calls were quoted at 253.30 bid and 257.50 ask. Because the multiplier was $100, the ask price for one contract was $25,750 and the bid/ask spread was $420.

STRATEGY EXECUTION

With index options you can often execute a buy or sell at the midpoint between the bid/ask spread. You simply calculate the midpoint and then place a limit order at that level. As you now appreciate, one contract can be a significant transaction, so it is unlikely that most retail investors will be trading size in these options. This is an advantage when it comes to your execution strategy.

The prices being displayed at the bid/ask on your broker's trading screen are typically good for up to 10 contracts, referred to as a "ten-up" market. The electronic trade systems will execute up to 10 contracts instantaneously if a buy order comes in at the ask price or if a sell order comes in at the bid price. If you enter a buy or sell order at the midpoint, the exchange is obligated to display or reflect that order to the trading public. Otherwise, they must execute the trade if they choose to not display the order.

Suppose that Frank entered his buy to open 1 NDX 2,050 call at a price just above the midpoint, $255.50. The market maker had three choices: (1) reflect Frank's bid to buy at $255.50, (2) fill his order at the limit price, or (3) step in front of Frank. If the market maker decided to reflect Frank's order, then the bid would change to $255.50 and the ask would remain at $257.50. Although Frank's order tightened the market, there was no transaction. The bid/ask is usually good for up to 10 contracts but Frank's buy order is for only one contract, leaving the market maker on the hook for the nine-contract balance at the price Frank established. Frank's offer to buy a single contract would be displayed and may or may not get filled.

Ideally, the market maker wouldn't want to mess with Frank's annoyingly small order (and penny pinching) and would simply fill his one contract without changing the bid/ask. We represent this as a market maker decision but the fact is, those "decisions" are all done electronically. Understanding how the system operates can help you save a few dollars with the right execution strategy.

Remember, you're not going to buy on the bid and sell on the ask; that's the market maker's strategy and you won't beat him at his own game. Splitting the bid/ask spread to get a more favorable execution is reasonable and usually realistic. Adjusting your limit order slightly to the left or right of the midpoint (higher if buying, lower if selling) will also increase the odds of getting a price-improved execution.

In Frank's case, the order filled immediately at his limit of $255.50 for a position debit of $25,550 plus commissions. As always, Frank had conditional orders in place to manage the downside risk and automate his closing transaction. If the NDX were to trade down through support, then Frank had a conditional order to buy to close the position. However, because this order was automated, there would be no opportunity for Frank to attempt to split the bid/ask spread like he did with the opening transaction. Frank's order would be delivered to the exchange as a sell to close at market and would execute at the bid price. This is an unfortunate consequence of using automated orders and stop orders, but there is simply no way around this fact. It's better to lose a hundred dollars on a less-than-perfect execution than thousands of dollars trying to save a few bucks.

For this example, Frank didn't need a conditional order because the NDX went on a bullish tear over the next two months. On the Friday before the option expired but one day after the last trade, Frank still had his one call option of the 2,050 strike. The Nasdaq announced the settlement value for the NDX (symbol NDS) on Friday morning. With the NDX settlement at 2,600, Frank's contract was 550 points in-the-money. Frank did a quick calculation in his head: 550 points in-the-money and a $100 cash-settled multiplier means that he would receive $55,000 into his account on Saturday. Subtracting the $25,550 Frank paid for his contract would net him $29,450—a return on his investment in excess of 100 percent. Index options are one of the purest ways to play an index and are ideal for butterfly spreads and iron condors.

CHAPTER 15

Butterfly Spreads

Your collection of option strategies has a lot in common with your toolbox. If there's a job to be done, there's probably a tool created specifically for that job. Most people can get by with a set of basic tools: hammer, saw, screwdriver, drill, pliers, duct tape, and so on. With these tools, most homeowners can complete the majority of jobs without needing more specialized tools.

Suppose a 175-foot eucalyptus tree falls across your road in a rainstorm. How would a hammer or screwdriver help with this 20-ton behemoth? In that situation, you'd need a tool that's above and beyond what most workshops hold. A Stihl 24-inch chainsaw with carbide-tipped saw blades would be about perfect for clearing the road and turning that tree into firewood. It's the right tool for the task at hand.

Occasionally, special jobs require special tools that you rarely pull out of the toolbox. If you've ever had to replace a screen, you know that there's a special roller tool that will help you quickly install the spline that holds the screen in place. Once you've attempted to install a screen spline with a screwdriver or other makeshift tool, you realize just how valuable the specialized tool can be. You don't need it often, but when you do need it, you're mighty glad it's there.

The same holds true for option strategies. Most traders in the majority of markets do just fine with the standard option strategies: long calls, long puts, debit spreads, credit spreads, and calendar spreads. They will use each of these strategies with minor adjustments for direction and probability based on what the markets are doing.

Now, let's say a market has been quite volatile. It may have been due to an expected earnings announcement, a Federal Reserve statement, or an upcoming general election. Although the markets started with volatility, as the news begins to subside, you expect the markets to settle down and trade within a very narrow range. Which of the aforementioned strategies is the right one in a directionless market with decreasing volatility? None is quite right for the job.

Here's where a specialized strategy like the butterfly spread comes into the picture. Butterfly spreads belong in a category known as combination spreads. A butterfly spread consists of a combination of a debit spread and a credit spread on the same underlying stock, ETF, or index. Although it is a combination in its construction, it is executed as a net debit. In many ways it is the polar opposite to a straddle or strangle. Recall from Chapter 8 that straddles and strangles are used for markets in which you expect a significant directional move with increasing volatility. With a butterfly spread, you are expecting the underlying price to stay in a very narrow range along with rapidly falling volatility.

GETTING TO KNOW THE STRATEGY

The butterfly spread is constructed of three separate legs (also known as the wings and body of the butterfly spread). These legs may be created with all calls or all puts. For this example, we will discuss a butterfly spread that uses calls. We will also use an index option of the S&P 500 index, SPX.

The first leg involves buying an in-the-money (ITM) call with a high delta and low theta. This leg will act as one of the wings of the butterfly. The second (or middle) leg involves selling twice the number of contracts as the first leg. You would sell at-the-money (ATM) calls that have a lower delta and higher theta. The second leg represents the body of the butterfly. Remember, at-the-money options always have the highest Theta. Because the butterfly spread involves selling twice the number of at-the-money contracts, it should be clear that the strategy benefits from time decay. The third leg involves buying an out-the-money (OTM) call. The third leg should be the same number of contracts as the first leg. The third leg represents the other wing of the butterfly. This last leg will have low delta and low theta and will serve as a safety net against the short at-the-money calls. Figure 15.1 shows a price chart of SPX, highlighting the price levels for each leg. Notice how the top two legs combine to form a credit spread and the lower two legs combine to form a debit spread. The fact that the middle leg has twice the number of contracts as the wings is what allows for a balanced spread on both sides.

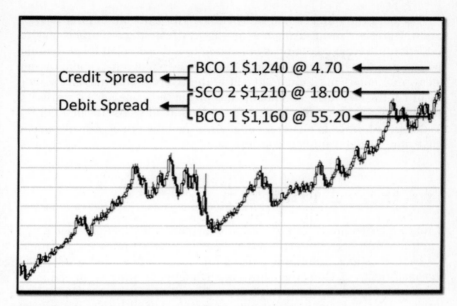

FIGURE 15.1   SPX Chart with Butterfly Spread Strike Prices

Now that we've built the butterfly spread, let's look at each leg to understand how these two spreads work together to complement the trade. The upper leg's sole purpose is to protect the position. It's the insurance policy in the event the underlying moves to a higher level than anticipated. If we didn't purchase the out-the-money long leg, then the short call would be naked and the losses would theoretically be unlimited. Ideally, the trade won't need this protection, and if all goes as planned, it will approach expiration money and expire worthless.

The lower leg is a bullish position. We anticipate it will remain in-the-money at expiration and maintain all the intrinsic value that we initially purchased. The middle leg is our short leg that we anticipate will remain at the same level through to expiration. If the trade drifts sideways as expected, then the ATM calls that were sold for the middle leg would still be at-the-money at expiration. These short calls will lose virtually all of their value due to time decay. At expiration, we expect these contracts will likely be either slightly in-the-money or slightly out-the-money.

The butterfly spread will earn the maximum profit when the SPX closes right at the strike price of the body of the butterfly spread. When this happens, the trade reaches the maximum gain on both the credit spread and the debit spread simultaneously. The profit is made at expiration when all four legs are settled in cash, providing credits and debits to the account.

The butterfly spread could also be closed for a net credit prior to expiration. The credit results from the time decay of the short contracts and the reduction of actual volatility as compared to implied volatility at the time the position was opened. In order to receive the maximum amount of time decay, the underlying should have little to no directional movement over the life of the contracts, essentially finishing at the same level it started. If the underlying does move higher, the debit spread gains in value but the credit spread drops in value. A move lower and the credit spread gains in value, but the debit spread drops in value.

STRATEGY IN ACTION

It was a quarter characterized by dramatic market fluctuations fueled by a handful of surprise earnings announcements, product releases, and political teeth gnashing. Frank was looking forward to a few months of trading "normal" markets. However, Frank was stumped on where to position his next few trades, given the lack of corporate and economic news in the near future. With the recent volatility making the price of both calls and puts expensive and no clear direction in the markets, Frank wasn't sure how to position his next trade. It was then that he recalled that butterfly spread and how they are well suited for that type of market scenario.

Because he knew the strategy is most profitable when a stock, ETF, or index stays at the same level for the life of the spread, he decided to trade contracts on the largest index, the SPX. With the SPX at $1,130, Frank decided to build the butterfly spread using wings at $1,110 and $1,160. He decided to buy one SPX $1,110 call, sell two SPX $1,130 calls, and buy one SPX $1,160 call. All three legs had the same expiration. Here's what Frank's trade looked like:

Action	Number of Contracts	Strike	Days to Expiration	Price
Buy Calls to Open	1	$1,100	48	$79.30
Sell Calls to Open	2	$1,130	48	$60.75
Buy Calls to Open	1	$1,160	48	$44.40

Pay attention to the fact that Frank was a buyer and seller of calls. The buy to open legs will cost him a total of $12,370. When he sells the two $1,130 call contracts, he will receive $12,150. Frank executed the butterfly spread as a net debit of $220 plus commissions and fees. Keep in mind that Frank wanted the SPX to stay as close to $1,130 as possible all the way through to expiration in 48 days. His risk was that SPX would move either up or down and approach expiration significantly above or below the $1,130 price level.

To understand how the butterfly spread is affected at expiration, let's look at how Frank's trade would work out at three price levels: $1,130, $1,180, and $1,080. An important characteristic about index options is that these options are settled in cash. In all three scenarios, upon expiration, Frank would need to take no action at all because each of the four contracts would be cash settled based on their intrinsic value alone.

SPX $1,130 at Expiration

Frank's trade was textbook perfect with the SPX trending sideways for 48 days and reaching expiration trading at $1,130. The $1,160 strike call that he purchased as a hedge would expire worthless. Because the $1,160 leg cost Frank $4,440, he would be out all that money. The body of the butterfly spread, the $1,130 calls, would also expire worthless. Because Frank sold the body, he received $12,150 for the two $1,130 strike calls. The third leg, the $1,100 call that was in-the-money by $30, would have lost all its time value but kept the intrinsic value. Frank paid $7,930 for the $110 strike calls, and because they're cash settled, Frank's account would be credited $3,000 for the remaining intrinsic value. As shown by the following breakdown, Frank's net profit for the trade would be $2,780 less fees:

- Leg 1: ($4,440)
- Leg 2: $12,150
- Leg 3: ($7,930) + $3,000

SPX $1,180 at Expiration

Obviously, the trade did not go as Frank had planned. SPX did not settle into a range but instead moved higher, closing at $1,180. That left all four of the call options to expire in-the-money. The $1,160 call contract would be $20 in-the-money and worth $2,000. The $1,100 call contract would be $80 in-the-money and worth $8,000. Frank's long calls would have a cash-settled intrinsic value of $10,000. This amount would be deposited into his account.

What about those two $1,130 call options that Frank was short? Those options would both be $50 in-the-money. Their combined intrinsic value would be $10,000 and that amount would be withdrawn from Frank's account. With $10,000 being deposited and $10,000 being withdrawn, the net to Frank would be zero. Don't forget that Frank paid $220 for the butterfly spread when he entered the position. He had a losing trade on his hands. Upon final settlement, Frank's net loss would be $220 plus commissions and fees.

SPX $1,080 at Expiration

Once again, with this scenario, the trade did not go Frank's way. SPX had fallen to $1,080 rather than staying flat. With the SPX at $1,080, all four legs of the butterfly spread would reach expiration out-the-money. Therefore, all four legs expire worthless. Because Frank paid $220 plus commissions and fees to put the butterfly spread on initially, that amount became Frank's loss.

STRATEGY MANAGEMENT

Butterfly spreads are often done using a European-style index option because they cannot be exercised or assigned early. All three of the legs will settle at expiration in cash versus shares. If a butterfly spread were created using an equity option, an early assignment could create problems for the overall position. The butterfly spread is designed to capitalize on time decay better than any other strategy. The overall position, although delta neutral, is theta positive. To determine the net theta on the position, you would total the theta of all three legs. You would total the individual legs to arrive at the overall position delta. Frank's butterfly spread in this example started with a delta of zero. The position was market neutral at $1,130 but as the price of the underlying moves up or down, the position may end up being delta positive or delta negative throughout the life of the trade.

Seven Steps to the Butterfly Spread

1. Determine if the market is trending, range bound, or flat. Butterfly spreads are not for trending markets.
2. If range bound or flat, look for a broad-based European-style index option like the SPX.
3. Because the butterfly spread is market neutral, you can build the spread with calls or puts, whichever produce the better values.
4. Select an expiration with four to seven weeks remaining. Because the butterfly spread takes advantage of time decay, you want to use

contracts that are experiencing the most time decay. Options with four to seven weeks have the most time decay per day compared to options with a longer life.

5. Enter the butterfly spread (using calls, for example) in the following order:
   a. Choose the OTM leg. From a technical analysis perspective, this is best done slightly above a point of resistance. Buy one call contract to open.
   b. Choose the ITM leg. From a technical analysis perspective, this is best done by buying a call that is slightly below support. Buy one call contract to open.
   c. Choose the ATM leg. This should be done using the strike price that is pegged at the current price or immediately above the current price.

6. Monitor the position daily. Keep a close eye on the overall market and the selected index itself. Remember, butterfly spreads are a neutral market strategy. If the markets appear to be gaining steam in either direction or if they move through key support or resistance points, consider closing the spread. Watch for news that could potentially move the index. Economic, political, and other significant news could spark a new trend in a sideways market. Earnings season always has the ability to break a flat market into a new direction.

7. Close the spread as appropriate:
   a. Upon expiration, if you take no action your broker will exercise and assign the ITM contracts, debiting or crediting your account the cash delivery values.
   b. If the spread comes under a threat prior to expiration, consider closing the spread by buying back the short legs first and then selling the long legs immediately afterward.
   c. Exit the trade when a profit target has been achieved or a loss threshold has been triggered.

STRATEGY APPLICATION

The butterfly spread is best applied in flat markets with low and falling volatility. The trade benefits from both time decay and realized volatility that is lower than implied volatility. As such, the trend score should be as close to zero as possible. You also want to see a low volatility score or evidence of falling volatility. Figure 15.2 illustrates the scoring region best suited for the butterfly spread.

Market Score Trade

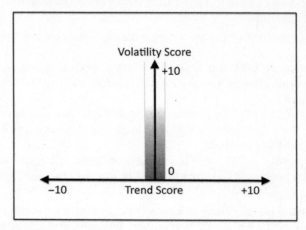

FIGURE 15.2   Market Score Application

Tightening Bollinger Bands

One measure of falling volatility would be a tightening of the Bollinger Bands (Chapter 8). Whereas a straddle or strangle is built on the expectation of an expansion of volatility, the butterfly spread looks for contraction of volatility. You recall from the earlier discussion of the Bollinger Band that a tightening of the bands is the direct result of a lowering of the value of the price standard deviation. Because both trend and volatility are factored into a Bollinger Band that is calculated around a moving average, tightening bands indicate that both dimensions are falling (Figure 15.3).

Keep in mind that Bollinger Bands are used as relative indicators; you want to compare the distance between the bands against previous band distances to gauge whether the bands are close or far apart. That's a subjective call. Because you're looking at price history to make that determination, you want to choose a time frame and then stick with it. If you switch time frames, your relative perspective will change and it may lead you to a different conclusion. That's not data fitting; that's recognizing that stocks have various trends in play at any given time and you need to decide in which time frame you're going to trade.

Note that with the Bollinger Band squeeze setup that we introduced in Chapter 8, we advised against any time frame above daily. Weekly and monthly charts are simply too slow to signal the trade. The reason is that the breakout from a Bollinger Band squeeze tends to run its course very quickly—often in just a few days. For this trade setup, we're anticipating

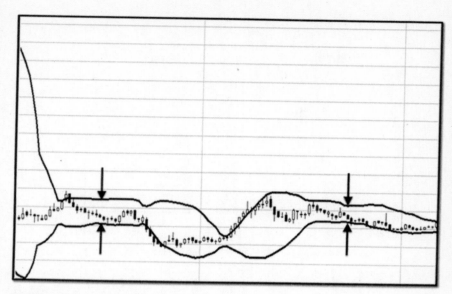

FIGURE 15.3 Tightening Bollinger Bands

that the stock will move into a low-volatility, flat direction for an extended time. For that reason, it's perfectly acceptable to apply the Bollinger Bands over longer time frames. Daily and weekly are best; monthly or intraday would be the second choice.

The butterfly spread trade presents itself when you have been observing a period of relatively high volatility along with some degree of trending as evidenced by the Bollinger Bands being far apart. The bands will almost certainly vary in the distance between them, but you wouldn't expect them to squeeze together as long as there is both direction and volatility. Once you observe the squeeze, you should prepare to build your butterfly spread. Consider building your wings with strikes that are just beyond the values of the Bollinger Bands. An expansion in volatility shown on the charts as a widening of the distance between bands may be useful in determining when to exit the position.

CHAPTER 16

Iron Condors

I magine for a moment you were asked for your opinion about the future price of a gallon of gasoline. That would be a tough request. First, you would have to make a guess about the direction of the price. Second, you would need to know how far out in the future you were expected to predict. Like weather forecasting, tomorrow's weather might not be tough but six months away is nothing more than a guess. It's likely that you would end up missing the mark. The real question is by how much?

The fact is, if you did get the price right, it was probably more a result of luck than knowledge. Now let's change the scenario just a bit. You are again asked to predict the price of gasoline but instead of an exact price, you are asked to choose a range for the price of a gallon of gasoline in the next three months. If you saw local gas at $3.75 and in the past year it had ranged from $2.89 to $4.45, you might be inclined to build your range around the observed price behavior. With that information, you might choose a range from $3.25 to $4.25. People are more comfortable with predicting a range, because a range is adjustable and allows for some lack of precision. If you were more conservative, you would typically increase the range of your estimate; perhaps between $3.00 and $4.50. If you were more confident, then you might feel comfortable with a tighter range and guess $3.65 to $3.85. This is the general idea behind one of the favorite strategies of many traders, the iron condor.

GETTING TO KNOW THE STRATEGY

An iron condor is a market-neutral strategy using two credit spreads placed away from the current price of an index. With an iron condor strategy, you expect the price of the index to stay bounded between the two credit spreads. If you're not confident with a trade that is dependent on direction (long calls or long puts) or comfortable with a trade dependent on a lack of market movement (butterfly spread), you can utilize an iron condor and select a range. By selecting a trading range, you can create a trade that will be profitable if the markets move slightly higher or lower or stay the same. Provided the index stays within the range of the iron condor up to expiration, you will reach maximum profit on each of the credit spreads. Your loss occurs if the trade breaks out above or below the range established. Because the spreads are placed at key support and resistance levels, you are usually afforded ample warning and time to close the spreads.

STRATEGY IN ACTION

Our model trader, Frank, was reading some of the week's headlines when he came across an interesting story with this tag line:

Wild Market Ride Is Driving People out of Stocks

Surge in volatility leaves investors wary; S&P 500 made 20 swings of 2 percent plus this year.

According to the story, more than $2 trillion of paper gains and losses were made and lost over a two-week period. One wealth adviser described the market as "an elevator with only two buttons: 'surge' and 'plunge'." The average investor trading a market that is wildly swinging higher and lower usually ends up at the same place he started with his portfolio but with a lot more stress in his life. He is dazed and confused, not knowing if he should be buying or selling when the market drops. Couple that with the never-ending news reports that accompany each market swing and it's no wonder many investors sit on the sidelines.

Frank recognized that market condition as playing well for the iron condor strategy. It had all the components: a clear resistance point that stocks surge toward before failing and a clear support point that stocks plunge to before rallying. The increase in volatility meant that both calls and puts would be priced high. Because the options premiums were inflated, Frank did not want to be a net buyer of option premium. Instead, he

FIGURE 16.1 Range-Bound Index Chart with Support and Resistance

wanted to be a net seller of premium, and because the iron condor uses a credit call spread and a credit put spread, Frank was ready to put his education, skill, and discipline to work. Figure 16.1 shows the index chart that Frank analyzed for his position.

When determining the location for the upper and lower spreads for the iron condor, it is important to determine where significant levels of support and resistance exist on the chart. In Frank's trade, he identified resistance around 1,360 and support around 1,260. Because the index was trading at 1,320, Frank's support was 60 points below the trading price. Frank placed his first credit spread right at support so he created a 4.5 percent downside cushion before he would experience any losses upon expiration. With resistance at 1,360 and the index at 1,320, he had just 40 points (about 3 percent) of upside movement before the call credit spread would begin to experience a loss upon expiration.

Notice that these losses are indicated upon expiration. As with all option trades, many factors affect how options are priced: An increase or decrease in price, time remaining, volatility, and interest rates prior to expiration may all contribute to changes in the profit and loss calculation. Because none of these variables can be predicted, we cannot determine with any certainty when a loss will occur prior to expiration. Calculating break-even points at expiration nullifies all other variables and distills the calculation down to the only factor that matters: price of the underlying relative to strike price. Ideally, the price of the underlying during the life of the spread will be contained within the range and reach expiration somewhere in between the two spreads.

Unlike most of the strategies we've presented where the position risk is to one side or the other, the iron condor has both upside risk and downside risk. For this example, Frank's main concern was upside versus downside risk because resistance was much closer to the trading price level than was support. In order for the strategy to achieve maximum profit, both credit spreads would need to expire worthless upon expiration. That will happen only if the index stays and closes somewhere in between the two short legs of the iron condor at expiration.

Because Frank's strategy was basically two credit spreads on the same index with the same expiration, he could start with either side of the condor. Some brokers allow the iron condor to be built as one four-legged position for a net credit, other brokers require it be built as two separate spreads, and yet others force you to do four separate orders for each leg of the condor. Although Frank's broker allows him to build an iron condor as a four-legged unit, Frank sometimes will build one side of the spread on one day in anticipation of a reversal. Then shortly afterward he'll add the other side of the iron condor. The risk with this timed approach is that Frank might end up with just one side of the iron condor, leaving him with a vertical credit spread.

To build the two credit spreads, Frank used the predetermined levels of support and resistance as his guide. For the lower level put spread, Frank utilized the 1,260 and 1,255 strikes. For the upper call spread, he used the 1,360 and 1,365 strikes. In this example, Frank would receive a net credit of $2 per share ($200 per contract) on the call spread and $1.50 per share ($150 per contract) on the put spread, for a total net credit of $350 for the iron condor.

Even though the iron condor is nothing more than a bear call spread and a bull put spread, the risks of an iron condor utilizing European cash-settled option contracts are different from the risk of two credit spreads using equity options. The risk of a credit spread is calculated by taking the width of the spread ($5 in our example) minus the credit received ($1.50 in the case of the put spread), which would give the put spread a risk of $350 per contract. The call spread by itself would have $300 of risk. If these were two equity spreads, the total risk would be $650.

However, in Frank's iron condor the risk is just $150. Here's why: Because a European-style option cannot be exercised prior to expiration (and at expiration the price of an index can only be at one place at a time), it is impossible for Frank to lose on both spreads. If it were an equity option using American-style options, a stock could theoretically touch the maximum loss point on both spreads during the life of the contracts and Frank could be assigned on the short legs of each spread. That would be a worst-case scenario and you must always calculate your maximum loss based on the worst-case scenario. After all, this is how your broker will calculate your capital requirements for each strategy you employ. Your worst-case scenario with an iron condor is that you would lose on only one of the spreads. If you were to lose on one of the spreads, your loss would be partially offset by your gain on the other spread.

Although it's impossible for you to lose on both spreads, it is possible for you to win (profit) on both spreads. Because the index can only be at one place at expiration, you want the price to remain between the two spreads throughout the remaining time and ultimately expire between the two spreads. When that happens, you would reach the maximum profit and retain all of the credit received when you opened the trade. In our example, Frank would keep the entire $350. If at expiration the index were trading above the long leg of the call spread or below the long leg of the put spread, Frank would reach the maximum loss of $150 ($500 width of one spread minus the $350 combined credit of both spreads). If the price of the index is between the short leg and the long leg of either spread, Frank may be somewhat profitable or somewhat of a loser depending on exactly where the price is within this zone.

STRATEGY MANAGEMENT

We often prefer market-neutral strategies, credit spreads, index options, and cash settlement. The iron condor combines all these into an income-producing strategy that is relatively easy to manage. However, we don't find too many opportunities to use this strategy. The proper market for an iron condor is a range-bound market in which there is both a clear support level and a clear resistance level. The timing is best when the index is trading spot in the middle between support and resistance.

Because these opportunities are few and far between, we used an example in which there was a skew to the upside but there could just as easily be a skew to the downside. In Frank's trade, the call spread produced a $200 credit but the index was 3 percent from the short leg. The put spread was 4.5 percent away and produced a $150 credit. Novice traders tend to ignore what the chart is saying and they build their spreads based on what they want out of the trade versus what the trade will give them.

In Frank's example, the maximum profit was $350 and the maximum loss was $150. That's an impressive 233 percent return on risk. However, we've executed iron condors that were just the opposite, setting up a trade with a maximum loss of $350 and a maximum gain of $150. That's a 42.8 percent return on risk. Although it might seem that the 233 percent is a better trade, remember that with a movement of just a few percentage points up or down, Frank becomes a loser.

In the less-impressive trade we just mentioned, the wings of our condor (where the spreads are placed) may be 10 percent or more away from the current price. By placing the spreads further away from the current price you give yourself more price cushion. You also buy yourself more time to see a price pattern develop and close the trade well before losses can escalate. Although these types of trades have lower returns, they also have a higher probability of success. When placing any trade in which the risk exceeds the return, it becomes even more important to manage the risk and close a position when a threatening move in the chart emerges. It's imperative that you fully understand the maximum loss on any trade. You should rarely suffer a maximum loss in your account when you properly apply technical analysis and a strict exit discipline.

Six Steps to the Iron Condor

Iron Condors are not as intimidating as some traders may think, but it's still good to have a checklist as you prepare to employ this strategy.

1. Iron condors are best suited to range-bound markets that have formed a clear upper and lower trading range. Condors are not well suited for trending markets.
2. Determine a clear level of support and resistance. These are often marked by the upper channel and the lower channel.
3. Execute a credit call spread at or above resistance.
4. Execute a credit put spread at or below support.
5. Monitor the position daily. Keep a close eye on the overall market and the index itself. Remember, iron condors allow you movement within the range but if the index appears to be gaining momentum toward one spread or the other, it may be time to protect the position and close at least the spread being threatened.
6. Close the iron condor as appropriate:
    a. Ideally, upon expiration, the index will be between the two short legs of the spreads and both with expire worthless. This is ideal because it involves no action to achieve maximum profit.
    b. If either side of the iron condor comes under a threat prior to expiration, consider closing that side of the spread by buying back the

short leg first and then selling the long leg. Alternatively, you could close the entire iron condor.

c. Exit the trade when a profit target has been achieved or a loss threshold has been violated.

Calculations

Max profit	As with any credit spread or combination of credit spreads, the maximum profit is the total amount of the credit received when the spread was opened. For an iron condor, maximum profit will be achieved upon expiration when the price of the underlying is between the short legs of the two spreads. All options will expire worthless and the trader keeps the full credit of both spreads.
Max loss	An iron condor is a defined-risk trade, so losses are finite. It's important to note that iron condors typically use European-style index options that can only be exercise or assigned upon expiration. The index can expire at only one price level and the maximum loss will occur when the index has moved beyond the long leg of one of the spreads. Maximum loss per share is the difference between the width of the widest spread minus the credit per share received.
Break-even	To determine the break-even point for an iron condor, subtract the total credits received from the short put strike to get the downside break-even point. To calculate the break-even point if the upside spread were violated, add the total credits to the short call strike of the call spread.
Capital required	The capital requirements of the iron condor are equal to the maximum loss of the entire position. Because only one side of the iron condor can lose at expiration, you are not required to add the maximum loss of the two spreads together, only the larger maximum loss of the two spreads.

STRATEGY APPLICATION

The iron condor is suited for markets with flat or nearly flat trends and low volatility. Higher volatility will add to the premium collected through the credit spreads but may also increase the probability of the underlying moving into and past one of the wings. More conservative traders should look for trend scores close to zero and volatility scores around 3 or lower. More aggressive and experienced traders should look for trend scores close to zero with volatility scores reaching to 5 or higher. Figure 16.2 illustrates the appropriate scoring graph for the iron condor.

Market Score Trade

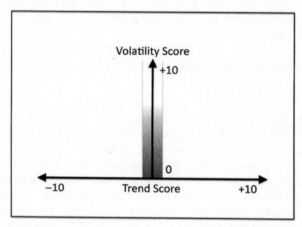

FIGURE 16.2 Market Score Application

Adjusting for S2/R2

One of the great challenges for novice and advanced traders alike is correctly identifying support and resistance levels. This is especially difficult in sideways markets—the very markets you're looking for when considering the iron condor strategy. Your success with the strategy depends on picking the price levels at which the buyers will fail on a rally and the sellers will fail on a drop. Oftentimes, a channeling stock or index will exhibit multiple support and resistance levels. Choose levels that are too tight to the trading price of the underlying and you risk losing to the trend. Choose levels that are too far apart and you collect much less premium through your credit spreads.

There are many ways you can approach the identification of support and resistance levels. Our top three are (not in any order) moving averages, gaps, and subjective trend lines. The latter is simply connecting key inflection points in a channel price. Those points may be all lows (support),

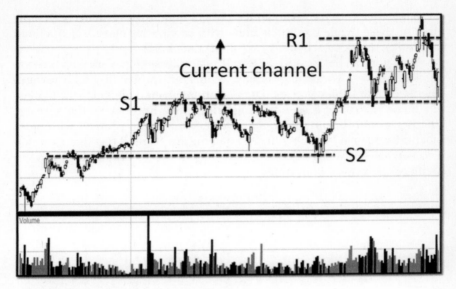

FIGURE 16.3 Multiple Support and Resistance

all highs (resistance) or a combination of the two (role reversal). Notice in Figure 16.3 how both S1 and S2 are defined by a role reversal that is composed of support and resistance points along the same price level.

S1, S2, and such are designations for first level support, second level support, and so forth. Traders often make the mistake of simply identifying support and resistance without acknowledging that there are multiple levels of each. Each level has various degrees of strength depending on such factors as how old the inflection points are (was the most recent point last week or last year?), how many points confirm the level, volume at the points, and candle patterns that develop at the points.

As an aside, a great drill for sharpening your skills in identifying S (support) and R (resistance) levels is to practice on a 15-minute, 10-day, intraday chart. Pick a few stocks with which you have no familiarity; you want to be entirely free of an opinion. When the market is closed for the day, take a look at your intraday chart and identify S1, S2, R1, and R2 for the next day. Use all of the tools at your disposal: gaps, role reversals, candle patterns, price patterns, and so on. After the market closes the following day, review your S and R levels to see how well you did. If you chose the levels accurately, that will serve to affirm your approach. If you missed the boat, understand what you could have done differently to get closer to the right levels. This drill is like the practice putting green for a golfer.

As experienced as you may be, it's always good to stay sharp with your chart analysis. While the drill is done with an intraday chart (for the rapid feedback), the skills transfer to any chart time horizon.

Now you can put your S1, S2, R1, R2 identification to work with the iron condor. As we mentioned, you have to balance probability with reward. Choose S1 and R1 and you get the most premium credit but also the highest likelihood of having the underlying price move into one of the spreads. Choose S2 and R2 and lower your credit, but provide yourself with more of a buffer against loss. Or you can combine any S and R together to create a somewhat skewed iron condor based on where you think the strongest boundaries exist for your trade.

Strategy Profit and Loss Diagrams

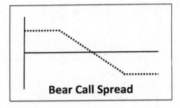

Bear Call Spread

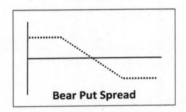

Bear Put Spread

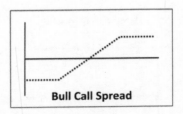

Bull Call Spread

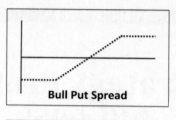

Bull Put Spread

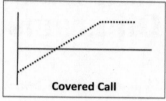

Covered Call

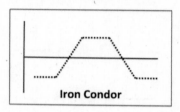

Iron Condor

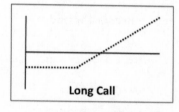

Long Call

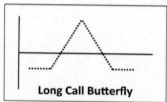

Long Call Butterfly

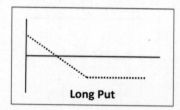

Long Put

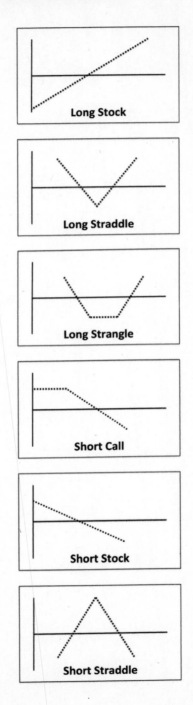

Long Stock

Long Straddle

Long Strangle

Short Call

Short Stock

Short Straddle

About the Authors

Rick Swope

As a veteran in the industry and primary education provider for E*TRADE, Rick has presented in hundreds of seminars across the United States and around the world. His expertise includes technical analysis, market strategy, and risk management.

Rick was the co-owner and managing partner of a trading firm that was one of the pioneers in online trading. He provided technical analysis, trading strategy, and software training to the firm's traders. Rick also traded a partnership account during that time, executing up to 300 trades per day. Rick worked closely with some of the early creators of the small order execution system (SOES), trading the so-called SOES bandits.

Rick has presented with some of the top financial exchanges, including the Chicago Board Options Exchange (CBOE), the New York Stock Exchange (NYSE), and the Nasdaq OMX. Rick created the first market technical analysis consulting team for a financial firm with $1 trillion in client assets. He has extensive media experience, including a regional PBS weekly show, a national PBS pledge program, and numerous radio and television appearances. He is the principal author of the Amazon bestseller, *Five Points for Trading Success* (John Wiley & Sons, 2007). In addition to his market expertise, he has extensive teaching experience, from corporate training to serving as an adjunct instructor in the disciplines of engineering, mathematics, operations research, and statistics. He is married with two children and resides in Atlanta, Georgia.

W. Shawn Howell

Shawn Howell is an accomplished speaker, trader, author, and educator, having presented to hundreds of audiences around the world. Over the past two decades, he has held executive positions with some of the financial industry's leading brokerage and training firms.

Shawn specializes in technical trading and complex derivative strategies. His clients include institutional investors and traders, high net worth individuals, and private traders. He is the managing partner and cofounder of a successful investment consulting firm specializing in retail and corporate investment education. Shawn pioneered and managed a highly successful consulting team dedicated to serving active stock and option traders.

Shawn is a CBOE Master Instructor and serves as the primary educator for E*TRADE. He regularly presents with the CBOE, NYSE, Nasdaq OMX, the Options Industry Council, and many other industry icons. Shawn has lived internationally and traveled extensively. He is an avid outdoorsman and enjoys a multitude of water sports. Shawn lives with his wife and two children on their family ranch on the central coast of California.

Index